a little boring until chapter 12

FIVE YEARS IN HEAVEN

THE UNLIKELY FRIENDSHIP THAT ANSWERED

LIFE'S GREATEST QUESTIONS

JOHN SCHLIMM

157 - Hell on Earth — living in past misery —

I

IMAGE

NEW YORK

Copyright © 2015, 2016 by John Evangelist Schlimm II

Published in the United States by Image, an imprint of the
Crown Publishing Group, a division of Penguin Random House LLC,
New York.
crownpublishing.com

IMAGE is a registered trademark and the "I" colophon is a trademark of
Penguin Random House LLC.

Originally published in hardcover in the United States by Image,
an imprint of the Crown Publishing Group, a division of
Penguin Random House LLC, New York, in 2015.

Library of Congress Cataloging-in-Publication Data is available
upon request.

ISBN 978-0-553-44660-9
eBook ISBN 978-0-553-44659-3

Printed in the United States of America

Book design by Lauren Dong
Cover design by Jessie Bright

10 9 8 7 6 5 4 3 2 1

First Paperback Edition

To
my dad and mom,
Jack and Barb Schlimm

CONTENTS

Finding Heaven on Earth

What if you had the chance to learn the answers to life's greatest questions? And what if you realized you only had a limited time to embrace a divine intervention that would help you discover who you really are and your true purpose in this world?

At age thirty-one, lost and disoriented at a crucial crossroads in my life, I found Heaven on earth. It was a humble, colorful place—long forgotten and tucked away on the manicured grounds of a 150-year-old convent in my small hometown. It was filled with beauty, light, laughter, peace, healing, blessings, and answers. I never knew it was there, practically under my nose for my entire life, but I found it when I most needed it.

There to greet me was eighty-seven-year-old Sister Augustine in full traditional habit. Standing barely over five feet tall and slightly hunched, she welcomed me with a warm smile and twinkle in her eyes that all but said, *I've been waiting for you.* She had started the convent's ceramic shop in the 1960s, but by now she had mostly receded from public view. Still, six days a week, she was content to work alone in her studio, quietly painting and creating while the frenzied world outside passed her by. Until I walked in one late winter's afternoon.

Over the next five years, I visited Sister Augustine just about every week. Her cloistered world became my refuge and my most important classroom. From the beginning, we were teacher and student in ever-changing roles, traversing the ultimate once-in-a-lifetime pilgrimage. Two unlikely friends brought together at the last minute, coasting along on what I came to think of as a gift of borrowed time.

Within those walls, I could ask any question, confide any secret, vent any frustration, and float any brainstorm. No topic was off-limits—from forgiveness, death, and even the existence of God, to love, success, creativity, sin, and my own lifelong struggles with personal demons. Throughout our hundreds of visits, I always knew Sister would have the divinely guided words and lessons I needed at each step along the way. Her advice was as wise and straightforward as her colorful clayware pieces were precious and rare.

During our time together, I was able to return the favor by showing my friend—a gifted artist long hidden away—that her life still had one very important last chapter left to go. And how even in the most remote corners of our existence, second acts are always possible.

Five Years in Heaven is my portrait of the most memorable and life-changing visits I shared with Sister Augustine, who once described herself as "only a messenger." Within these pages, I invite you to pull up a chair and glimpse Heaven on earth as I once did in that sacred place as Sister and I discussed the timeless and universal questions we all have about living a full, purposeful life at any age. May you then find your own inspiration, peace of mind, and meaning in the answers that are revealed.

Where there is darkness, light.

—THE PRAYER OF SAINT FRANCIS

PRELUDE

On the Seventh Day

ON THAT EARLY SPRING DAY, THE SUN HAD STARTED ITS DEscent when I pulled into the convent's back entrance. On one side lay the sisters' pond and tiny cemetery—rows of names and dates on simple weathered headstones. On the other side, St. Joseph Monastery's stone walls soared into the blue sky. When the sun reflected off the windows, the building seemed made of gold.

This is the time of day when everything is either bathed in a brilliant, hopeful light or plunged into sharp shadow. This is when you can either bask in the glow, as if eye to eye with God Himself, or cower in darkness.

Sister Margoretta waited just inside, next to the gift shop she had managed for years. She had closed a few minutes early in expectation of my arrival. Tall, dressed in a traditional habit from head to toe, she always reminded me of Ingrid Bergman in *The Bells of St. Mary's*. Her timeless beauty remained in her wide smile and eyes, framed by black and white. Sister Dolores, petite and blind, stood next to her. She had joined the Benedictine order and moved to St. Joseph's after a life on the outside that included a husband and son. With her gracious poise, I always wondered what she could see that the rest of us couldn't.

"I made it," I said.

They both smiled, and Sister Margoretta told me to follow them.

Sister Dolores took hold of her friend's arm and they proceeded down a steep staircase. I followed them into an inner maze of darkened hallways in which I had never stepped foot before. Large paintings and statues of the Blessed Virgin, Christ, Saint Benedict, various other saints, and biblical scenes lined the corridors. Once inside those walls, even for a few minutes, it was easy to forget that a world outside existed.

I imagined that if peace had a scent, it would be the sacred perfume culled from decades of scrubbing, polishing, candles, prayers, incense, communal meals, and a certain waft of sweetness that I couldn't quite identify, but was inhaling as deeply as possible. Like at Christmas Eve mass, when for those few moments I can close my eyes, inhale the church's warm aroma, and allow myself to believe all is okay in the world. I wanted to fill myself with as much of that rare oxygen as I could. It was like a gift you can only hold on to for a few moments before it must be let go.

I lost all track of time. It could have been minutes, hours, days. Time as we know it doesn't have much use in a place where the aim is eternity. Part of me wanted to walk those halls forever.

We emerged into a long corridor where all the doors were closed, except one. Midway down, sunlight poured out of the open bedroom door, flooding the hallway.

Sister Margoretta and Sister Dolores stopped. "She's in there," Sister Margoretta said, smiling and nodding toward the pool of light.

My eyes widened and I hesitated, just as anyone would before doing something they sensed would change their life forever.

Then I heard her voice, so familiar. "I've been waiting for

you," Sister Augustine called out from inside the room. "I want to hear all about your trip!"

I flashed a huge grin at Sister Margoretta and Sister Dolores. "Business as usual," I said.

"We'll wait for you out here," Sister Margoretta told me, smiling back.

"Okay," I whispered, as if sharing a secret. I was grateful for these women, who, like two guardian angels, had led me to one of those pivotal moments that makes life so special.

I then turned and walked toward the light.

PART ONE

1

IN THE BEGINNING

FIVE YEARS EARLIER.

On a late winter's afternoon, I sat frozen in front of my computer screen, staring at my resume. It was a glorified travelogue from the ten-year journey I had recently brought to an end. The relentless black cursor at the top of the page taunted me with its incessant flashing. As if demanding to know, *Where to next?* Problem was, I wasn't so sure anymore.

The sky outside gray and heavy, gusts of wind pounded against the window next to my desk. My mind spun wildly like a broken compass while a chill coiled around each of my senses, threatening to squeeze the life right out of me.

The past year had been marked by several career disappointments. I had spent the last few years secretly working on recipes for my first national cookbook, which I had hoped would now be picked up by a major publisher, but none had bitten yet. I had also just completed my master's degree in education at Harvard, yet found myself in the thankless role of substitute teacher at my high school alma mater. I was frustrated, confused, and more than a little lost. I was thirty-one; I was at a crossroads.

My best friend Steven stopped by and encouraged me to forfeit my showdown with the unforgiving cursor and get out of the house. But I wasn't sure I wanted to. *What would we even do?*

I wondered, gazing out the window. The world seemed stuck in a permanent whiteout all around me.

I was born and raised in the small town of St. Marys, which is nestled in the rural mountains of western Pennsylvania. Home to me and thirteen thousand other people, it didn't offer a lot of options for fun. Especially on those frigid days that would make even the most cold-hardened, contented Inuit consider relocating.

Steven suggested we explore the local convent's ceramic shop, which he remembered visiting as a young child.

"You mean the gift shop," I corrected. Though I had passed the place a thousand times, I never knew our local convent had a ceramic shop.

"No, the ceramic shop!" Steven insisted. "My great-grandma used to take me there when I was little."

"What do they do there?" I asked, still not convinced that my friend knew what he was talking about.

"Make ceramics, I guess, I don't know," Steven huffed. "I just remember it being a fun little place. I haven't been there since I was a kid."

How didn't I know that one of the most historic sites in our small town had a ceramic shop? I had only ever been to the convent's gift shop, Trifles and Treasures, which was run by Sister Margoretta. That was usually when I tagged along with my mom whenever she needed a special religious medal or rosary, or a First Communion or Baptism gift. It was the only religious store in town.

The idea of an assembly line of cute little nuns painting and singing their days away spoke to the sentimental artist in me, and even made me feel a little hopeful. At the least, this little adventure would be a welcome distraction.

"Sure, let's go!" I said.

Home to the Benedictine Sisters of Elk County, St. Joseph Monastery was a short drive across town from my house. About a mile and a half—head down Brusselles Street, turn right at the light onto South Michael, go over the railroad tracks past Erie Avenue and through the light by the movie theater onto North Michael, then take a left at the light onto Maurus, and the convent will be on your right-hand side after the next intersection. Five minutes tops, three if you hit all green lights and no traffic.

I grew up on these streets and avenues, which by our founders' design radiate out like spokes on a wagon wheel, or rays of sunlight, from a patch of green grass known as the Diamond and a veteran's memorial in the middle of town. From my house, I could see my family's Straub Brewery, which was founded by my great-great-grandfather in the 1870s, as well as many of the carbon and powdered metal factories that were our town's bread and butter. I could still name every one of my neighbors who lived in the houses trailing away from my own in every direction. This was down-home, blue-collar America.

While Steven drove, I looked out the partially frosted window, thinking of the many other roads, all starting from this epicenter, that I had traveled since first leaving home for college more than a decade earlier. I had majored in public relations to score fun and rewarding jobs, and minored in studio arts to further hone my skills as a visual artist.

My career in PR officially started at 1600 Pennsylvania Avenue. During my senior year in college, I pulled double duty, going to class while also serving full-time as the assistant to the Second Lady's communications director at the White House. Soon after, I wrote my first book, *Corresponding with History,* which was published by a small academic press with little fanfare. Once the publishing bug bit, and since I came from one of the country's oldest brewing families *and* loved to eat, the seeds for writing the world's largest beer cookbook were squarely planted. But I decided to keep that endeavor a secret from family and friends until the day I could triumphantly announce I had found a publisher.

I later left our nation's capital, heading out on Interstate 66 with U-Haul in tow to Nashville, where I took my career in public relations to a new level as a celebrity publicist. Whereas D.C. had exposed me to the highest echelons of power and ceremony, Music City USA granted me an all-access pass to the backstages and sprawling dirt-road kingdoms of country music's royalty. Both cities were worlds beyond my wildest imagination.

While Washington, D.C., and Nashville claimed significant parts of my heart during my twenties, this small-town kid eventually grew disenchanted with the dizzying whir of public relations. I started to lose myself in the smoke and mirrors I was paid to create as a handler for some of entertainment's biggest superstars. The boundaries of right and wrong, reality and fantasy became blurred, and soon my own sense of direction and purpose did as well.

The yearning for something simpler and more genuine was pulling me back to my roots, circling me back around to a desire I had had since elementary school to be an English teacher, before life detoured me in other directions. I felt called to inspire and educate new generations, not just about the mechanics of grammar and great literature, but about the world I had experienced firsthand where anything was possible. This latter mission was something I thought small-town students especially needed to know. I also hoped that along the way I would learn a little more about what makes me—*the real me*—tick. A classroom of my own and the cookbook manuscript that beckoned louder than ever to finally be completed both promised something in the way of a new starting line.

So I took a giant leap, leaving job security, friends, and the big-city lights behind. I followed my heart home to St. Marys.

As Steven and I drove through the last intersection on Maurus Street, the convent came into view while giant snowflakes skipped across the windshield. I shook my head with the realization that I had just completed one very long round-trip back to the beginning. Little did I know then where those old familiar roads were about to lead me to next.

We pulled into the main parking lot at the convent's front entrance with a soft snow falling and coating everything with an immaculate glaze. On the western end of town, St. Joseph Monastery, along with St. Mary's Church, a Catholic elementary and middle school, and Elk County Catholic High School, occupied a significant parcel of land. The sacred compound dominates an entire street corner and stretches uphill along tree-lined Church Street in one direction, and along a flat Maurus Street, which leads out of town in the other direction.

"Where's the ceramic shop?" I asked, looking in amazement at the enormous structure in front of us as if seeing it for the first time.

"It's around the side," Steven answered.

It's interesting how you can pass by a place countless times, and even spend several of your most formative years next-door in school, yet never really see it or know what goes on inside. St. Joseph Monastery was the first Benedictine convent in the United States when it was founded in 1852. My own family roots in town reach back to at least the early 1860s.

From the large parking lot and front door on Maurus Street, the convent rose several stories to various cross-topped peaks and continued all the way up the Church Street hill, eventually turning to the right in a towering structure that connected it to St. Mary's Church. Colossal stained-glass windows adorned the church's alabaster wall, each one a multicolored arrowhead pointing upward. It's the type of place about which, independent of its actual purpose, one could let his imagination spin fantastic tales, inventing a mythical provenance for those cloistered, unseen spaces behind such mysterious walls.

Steven and I left two sets of footprints that disappeared in the falling snow as we followed the paved driveway around the side of the convent, first passing the nuns' chapel to our right and then a long wall with stacked rows of identical windows. To our left was the carport, which shielded the few cars and one pickup truck the sisters had at their disposal; the field where the sisters had once maintained a large garden, greenhouse, and chicken coop; and a garage where a few sisters currently ran a recycling operation for extra money. Beyond that, in the distance, was the high school that Steven and I had both attended, and where I was currently working as a substitute teacher and hoping for a more permanent position.

"The ceramic shop is in there," Steven said, pointing toward a long, three-story wooden and stone building. Situated in the center of the convent grounds, it extended outward from the main edifice across a gully to the paved driveway that wrapped around to the exit by the church at the upper end. The nuns' pond and cemetery were also up there. Commonly known as the Guesthouse, which I realized I knew well from when I was in high school, it was connected to the convent's main building by a short, canopied walkway. A covered porch ran the length of the middle floor, which, because the Guesthouse crossed through a bantam valley, was about level with the driveway. "I'm pretty sure it's at the end of that porch, on the right-hand side," my friend said.

I studied the Guesthouse for a moment. "In one of the rooms at the other end of the porch, on the side closest to the road, Sister Mercedes used to tutor me in algebra during freshman year," I said.

For one year, every day after school, I would walk through the gate connecting the high school and convent, trudge onto that wooden porch, and enter a simple, nondescript room with just a table, some chairs, and a portrait of an ever-watchful Jesus. Wide-eyed and smiling, He'd gaze down upon us as Sister Mercedes helped me to make sense of the delicate interplay of x's, y's, and z's so that I could survive my dreaded advanced algebra class for another day.

There was a lot about high school that I was glad was in the past. Which, at that moment, made me only wonder all the more why I had put myself right back into that building as a substitute teacher. Was that really where I wanted to spend the rest of my life?

Considering my history at the Guesthouse, I couldn't believe that I hadn't known back then that only a few doors away there was a ceramic shop. Nor could I have guessed that I would walk into the same building almost two decades later.

Steven and I veered off the road and down the few cement steps onto the slatted wooden porch. The snow was scalloping the porch's edge in undulating patterns, as if Mother Nature were gentling, wielding a wide brush dipped in ivory paint. At the other end, nineteen cement steps led up toward the main building.

When we arrived at the last door on the porch, a yellowing, hand-printed sign about the size of a small note card confirmed that the ceramic shop was indeed still in business and listed the hours: Monday–Saturday, 10:00 to 11:30 a.m. and 2:00 to 4:30 p.m. At the bottom, printed letters neatly rendered in pencil beckoned, "Please come in. Thank you."

"I guess it's open," Steven said, checking his watch. It was about two fifteen.

I nudged him to enter first, since he had been there before, albeit twenty years earlier.

The first thing I noticed upon entering was the calming smell that I associate with anything holy, or at least the scent I've always linked to old, blessed places like cathedrals. From the front door, you could look straight into a brightly lit second room and a doorway at the far back leading to yet another area.

The small front room, naturally lit by two windows that were dressed with white lace curtains, served as the main retail space. There was a built-in display counter to the immediate right along the front wall, three other floor-to-ceiling shelf-lined walls, and an old three-tier red plastic supermarket display case anchored in the middle of the floor like an island.

All of this was mere background, like a primer of gesso on a blank canvas. The foreground, where every surface was completely filled with painted ceramic pieces, was where the enchantment happened.

The anxiety moored in the pit of my chest started to turn into anticipation and excitement. For the first time in weeks, maybe even months, I calmed down and became focused on what was right in front of me, instead of troubles or the unknown. I was able to take a deep, relaxed breath. I knew in a few moments that there was something very special about this place, even beyond all the fantastic curios.

"Hello," I called out. In my mind, I expected to be greeted by a parade of angelic little nuns, paintbrushes in hand and happily humming the afternoon away as they worked. Something along the lines of *The Sound of Music* or, at the very least, *Sister Act*.

But no one responded.

"Hello?"

No response.

Steven and I looked at each other and shrugged our shoulders. The surge of electricity that comes when you sneak into some forbidden place raced through me. Adrenaline liftoff!

My eyes grew wider and wider as I walked around the shop.

The shelves overflowed with hand-painted statues of Mary, angels, animals, clowns, plates, bookends, vases, piggy banks, flowers, birds, plaques, crosses, snowmen, Santas, baskets, wind chimes, and pitchers, as well as a small ebony bust of Queen Nefertiti, a giant ice-cream cone cookie jar, and a honey jar shaped like a beehive. More whimsy and charm than the synapses firing rapidly in my imagination could register. The endorphin rush of colors and images freed all my senses, kicking them into overdrive. The shelves were like my brimming spice racks at home, offering infinite possibilities for exploration.

We kept circling the room in silence, digesting this treasure chest we had happened upon. Finally, I said, "I can't believe this place exists."

There was something so magnificent, so curiously disorienting, yet remarkably innocent about it. The feeling was palpable. The minute we walked through that front door, we became Willy Wonka in his chocolate factory, Alice in her Wonderland, Dorothy in her Oz, Luke Skywalker in his galaxy far, far away. But this place was very real, even though it still felt like we had just been dropped into a secret fantasyland that no one else knew about, which wasn't that far from the truth.

I'm not sure how long Sister was standing in the doorway, amused by our oohing and aahing. I was examining a long, slender statue of Mary, delicately painted in white and light blue with three forget-me-nots trimming the bottom of her robe, when I heard Sister's voice for the first time.

"Welcome!" It was a sweet, throaty tone with a slight quiver that was unforgettable and endearing from the start—a warm, soothing voice as familiar as a grandmother's that lets you know you've found your way to where you belong.

My head swung toward the doorway separating the two rooms.

What I saw there brought on a smile: backlit by the room

behind her, Sister stood just barely over five feet tall, slightly hunched, wearing glasses, and attired in a full, traditional habit of long black veil, white coif, black tunic belted at the center, brown wooden rosary beads dangling from her waist, and sensible black shoes. There was just one deviation: she also wore a blue denim bib apron smeared with paint.

"Hi!" I said back. "I didn't even know your ceramic shop existed until today."

Sister smiled. "It's been here a while." That was the first time I saw the twinkle in her eyes that I instantly knew I'd never forget for as long as I live.

"I'm John, and this is Steven," I told her.

"Nice to meet you both. I'm Sister Augustine."

I felt an instant connection with the old woman. As if we had always known each other. I would soon learn that's one of the beauties of true friendship: the feeling of *always*.

"Your pieces are incredible!" All my words came out in magnified decibels, all of them punctuated by exclamation marks. Poor Steven couldn't get a word in edgewise, so he just gave up and nodded in agreement with what I was saying. I couldn't remember the last time something galvanized me the way this place did, especially being an artist myself. This was the first few seconds after the roller-coaster climbs inch by inch to the zenith, then plummets, leaving your heart dancing in midair.

"Thank you," Sister returned with a soft chuckle.

"How many of you work here?" I looked over her shoulder into the other room.

Sister Augustine grinned and playfully flashed her hands and arms outward. "You're looking at it! Sometimes I have a few volunteers who help out, but it's just me otherwise."

"You do all of this yourself?" I was shaking my head. We were surrounded by hundreds of pieces in all shapes and sizes. Loaves and fishes in a glorious riot of color and joy.

Sister nodded. "There's more in here if you'd like to see it."
She motioned to the brightly lit room behind her.

I picked up a second, gold-glazed statue of Mary that had
caught my eye, and then Steven and I walked into the next
room. We found three more walls of floor-to-ceiling shelves,
filled with figurines, cornucopias, pumpkins, birds and animals,
bowls and pitchers, canister sets, and even dozens of decanters
disguised as firemen, policemen, cowboys, bakers, and fisher-
men. Also, hundreds of Duncan-brand glaze and paint bottles
were neatly organized by color on shelves at the front of the
room.

In the far back left-hand corner was a large sink, above which
two posters with illustrations of butterflies and wildlife hung.
Along the wall to the right below the windows, there was a
checkout and wrapping table in front of a counter that extended
from the front of the room to the back. The counter held a television, some magazines, ceramics catalogs, and plants. Halfway
up the back corner on a shelf, a snow-white statue of the Blessed
Mother watched over the room.

"Look here," Steven whispered, pointing to two small
shelves in front. One was lined with miniature, lifelike turtles
and frogs, and the other with ladybugs. The price of the turtles
and frogs was "Three Hail Marys" and the ladybugs were a bargain at "One Hail Mary," according to the small sign rendered
in Sister's handwriting.

Priceless, especially considering that I couldn't have recited
a "Hail Mary" to save my life had I been asked just then. The
thought of saying what was actually a favorite prayer of mine
in front of a nun made my nerves shudder and my mind go
blank. Silly, considering there wasn't anything intimidating
about Sister Augustine. Still, my mind flashed back to me in
fourth grade at Queen of the World Parish elementary school.
Dressed in my navy blue uniform like a cadet. Reciting the Ten

Commandments to Sister Jane Francis. I got to number eight and blanked. Total brain freeze! Sister Jane Francis looked at me lovingly for several moments while my memory went to mush, then told me to sit down. I had managed to get to murder and adultery, but couldn't make the leap to stealing. I did, however, have a better idea of what an eternity felt like after that. Yes, I'd have to pass on the turtles, frogs, and ladybugs for now.

In this middle room of Sister Augustine's operation, three long, blond-colored tables, like those I remembered being in the library at school, were arranged in a squared-off horseshoe, which opened toward the front of the room. They were covered with ceramic pieces in various states of completion. The table to the left held several rows of identical, unpainted Nativity figures frozen in an elaborate procession. On the table to the right, a stable's worth of animals and other familiar faces already had a base coat.

"Is this your studio where you paint everything?" My piqued curiosity was a spinning wheel of fireworks.

"Yes, I suppose you could call it that," Sister said, still watching us from the doorway. I assumed from her reaction that I was the first person to ever refer to this space as her "studio." "That's where I sit and work mostly, either between the tables or back there." She pointed first to a mint-green spindle chair inside the horseshoe and then to an oak chair at the back right-hand corner. Nearby, a glossy black pedestal cup with a bouquet of paintbrushes served as the centerpiece. I realized that from either vantage point, she could see and anticipate everyone who entered. Except today. I never did ask where she was when we first got there.

"What's in there?" I pointed to the door behind her chair at the back, the one leading into an unlit room.

"That's where I mix the clay and pour the molds," Sister

Augustine replied. "And where I store all the bisqueware." She didn't offer to take us in there.

"We should probably get going," Steven said, nudging me.

"I'd like to buy these two statues of the Blessed Mother," I told Sister. "Can you please sign them?"

The curious look on her face was precious. As if I had asked if she had ever been to the moon.

"I write 'SJC' for Saint Joseph's Ceramics on the bottom of each," she replied.

"You should also sign your name."

I got another befuddled look. "But they belong to the convent, not me."

"But you're the artist!"

From the amused look now on her face, I assumed she hadn't been called an "artist" in a long time, either, if ever, or ever asked to autograph her own artwork.

"That's not necessary. No one needs my name on them. It's God's work, you know."

"Will you please sign mine anyway? I don't think God will mind," I insisted. "Unless, of course, you can arrange for *His* autograph."

Sister laughed and shook her head. "I guess you'll just have to settle for mine then." She walked to the inside of the horseshoe and sat down in her chair, where she was arm's length from the parade of Nativity figures she'd soon bring to life.

"I think I have a pen around here somewhere," she said, searching among the pieces awaiting her attention. "Ah, here it is."

"Be sure to write the date, too, please," I added. "It's . . ." I scanned the room for a calendar. Since lately one day bled into another without much difference, I had lost track of what the specific date was.

"February twenty-first," Sister Augustine said. She glanced up with a smile. While Sister signed and dated the bottom of the statues, I surveyed the other clayware pieces on the table. Several camels, cows, and a few sheep, along with Mary, Joseph, the Wise Men, a shepherd boy, and even Baby Jesus, all stared back at me.

"Sister, how did you do that one?"

I pointed to a tiny cup, about four inches tall, which curved in at the middle and then flared out again on top. It was painted in a cool fusion of turquoise, deep green, and white—the exact colors you might see when looking down through clear water to the bottom of a tropical sea.

Sister paused in mid-signature to attend to my question. "Oh, that," she said with a giggle. "I don't like to waste paint, so when I'm working, I always clean my brushes off on a little piece like that one. When it's covered, I put it in the kiln and see what happens for the fun of it. I never know what's going to come out."

"It's gorgeous! Is it for sale?" I picked it up for a closer look. "It's like a piece of the ocean. I can see the water, seaweed, white foam . . ."

"Oh my!" Her eyes widened. "I never thought of it like that, but you're right."

"I don't see a price tag. How much is it?" In fact, I hadn't seen a price tag on the statues, either, but I was willing to pay whatever the price might be. A divine hand had created these pieces, of that I was sure. And this entire experience had lifted my spirits. You couldn't put a price tag too big on that.

"Let's see," Sister responded, calculating in her head. "This larger statue is five dollars, this gold one is four, and the little vase is . . . how about two dollars? Does that sound okay?"

Eleven dollars for everything? "Sister, you need to charge more!"

Sister Augustine shook her head. "I think that's already too high. I want people to be able to afford them."

I laughed to myself. Maybe forty years ago, but a total steal today. I felt guilty pulling the few bills from my wallet.

After signing the three pieces, Sister took them over to her checkout station, where she carefully wrapped each of them separately in long sheets of white paper, which had been cut identically sometime earlier from a tall roll on the floor. Then she pulled a neatly folded plastic bag from a nearby container holding recycled bags of all kinds. Everything had its place. She put my items in the bag and handed it to me with a smile.

I handed her fifteen dollars. "I don't need change."

"Are you sure?"

"Yes, I'm sure."

"Thank you!" There was that sparkle in her eyes again, this time in gratitude. She placed the two bills in a metal money box and recorded the order on a tablet setting next to it.

"I'll definitely be back," I called over my shoulder as Steven and I headed for the door.

"I'll count on it," I heard Sister Augustine say.

Her jovial tone behind us contrasted with the blast of cold air that welcomed us back to the outside world, which, for a glorious forty-five minutes on a late winter's afternoon, I had completely forgotten was even there.

Looking at the date years later that Sister had inscribed on the statues, I realized how rare it is to know the exact day you met someone who would change your life so profoundly. That date is now circled on my calendar and marked with a little star every year. Like a favorite destination on a map.

2

JOYS AND SORROWS

ONE WEEK AFTER I FIRST MET SISTER AUGUSTINE, I RETURNED to her ceramic shop in midafternoon, this time alone. Steven had gone back to New York by then, but his birthday was coming up in a few weeks and I had an idea for the perfect gift—a special thank-you for taking me to Sister's shop for the first time.

Of course, the gift was just an excuse to return. Something much deeper was leading me back to Sister's studio. I longed for the calm and stability I had felt there amid the otherwise dizzying swirl of my life at the moment: a cookbook that didn't seem to be going anywhere and a teaching career that hinged upon jarring 6 a.m. calls from the high school secretary letting me know I had to fill in for a teacher who was out sick that day. While some centrifugal force seemed to be pushing my goals and dreams further from me, a countervailing force was pulling me into Sister Augustine's isolated world. At the moment, my mind was like a movie projector flapping a continuous loop of anxiety and disappointments in black-and-white. Sister's shop offered the rejuvenating color I needed to add to my life.

This time, I parked in the smaller lot I discovered beside the Guesthouse. The snow crunched like toasted bread crumbs under my feet as I hurried toward the long porch leading to the shop. The convent's main building rose high in front of me like a fortress, a solid wall striped with dozens of windows, leaving me to ponder who might be looking out and watching the visitor who had just arrived. In the distance, I could just barely make out the tip of the steeple and cross of St. Mary's Church peeking up from the other side.

The entire place reminded me of an epic backdrop on a Hollywood set, or one of the storied old manors that you might see on a PBS special, where nobility have dwelled for generations. This place was, at the least, a domicile frozen in some bygone epoch where a more humble gentry fulfilled their sacred calling.

Once home to 125 Benedictine nuns who were active throughout the community they had helped to found, the convent was now home to a dwindling sorority of around twenty sisters, the youngest in her fifties. Perpetually suspended in a more innocent time warp and indifferent to the modern world, this was an uncomplicated place where progress and most modern technology and other corrosive material things were turned away at the front gate.

The essence of this holy dwelling in St. Marys wasn't much different from a certain 101-acre, early 1900s farm sixty-eight miles to the west in the rural Pennsylvania community called Knox, which even today barely tips the scale past a thousand residents. There against a pastoral backdrop—idyllic white farmhouse with a coal stove in the kitchen, pump organ in the living room, welcoming front porch, and nearby water well, large barn and outbuildings, miles of hand-hewed fences, pastures, an apple orchard, cows, horses, chickens, pigs, kittens, and a Saint Bernard named Rex—a young girl named Anna had blossomed and found her divine calling. Eight decades later, our paths would cross.

With an effusive grin stretching pigtail to pigtail and wearing the flowered frock her mother had made, Anna spent her days picking apples and berries and chasing after butterflies, bumblebees, and lightning bugs barefoot, preferring fresh air and tilled soil to indoor chores or going to school. With her brothers and sisters, including Agnes, who would enter St. Joseph Monastery first and take the name Sister Thecla, Anna transformed the farm into her own wonderland. Fueled by her imagination, every new day, every hill and field, every animal and bug, and every found path in the woods offered her a new departure point for adventure. The young girl's curiosity was like a blank sketchbook that she quickly filled.

Anna helped her mother Clara, who was jovial and generous in a white bib apron, can fruits and vegetables grown on the farm, churn butter, and gather fresh eggs that they'd sell in town on Saturdays. She also worked alongside her father, George, a devout and humorous man with a thick mustache, milking the cows, feeding the animals, planting the large vegetable garden, and piling wood on the porch. Every night, the family gathered in the living room after dinner to pray the rosary while a pet piglet named Hank made the rounds nudging each of their toes, which always made Anna giggle.

All of which could easily have been the inspiration for the warmth and hearth conjured in a favorite melody years later— *There's peace and goodwill . . . On Mockin' Bird Hill . . .*

Sister Augustine's Mockin' Bird Hill homestead from eighty years earlier, like St. Joseph Monastery now, seemed immune to the outside world. Divinely inoculated against the forces and challenges that tormented the rest of us. Both, sacred havens for a simpler life grounded in what really matters.

More than ever lately, I could feel the Goliath of that modern world breathing down my neck. But just in the nick of time, some grace had granted me the golden ticket to enter this hallowed space framed by Church and Maurus Streets and where time stood still. It was an escape from publishers' rejection letters, the doldrums of classrooms that weren't my own, and a life dangling on some unknown and vaguely threatening precipice.

Some force inside those walls was calling to me, much as the wide-open spaces of Sister Augustine's girlhood farm had once whispered to her. Not in words, but through a gentle tugging within my heart. Even after only one visit, for me Sister's ceramic shop was a giant magnet, its pull natural and balanced. My own curiosity had turned the page and prodded me toward this mystery.

The air was almost too cold to breathe as I walked toward the Guesthouse. It needled my lungs with every inhalation. My pace quickened as I recalled the warmth inside Sister Augustine's shop from a week earlier.

No hesitation this time. I opened the front door of the shop and strolled in as if I had done it a hundred times before, not just twice. In an instant, the cozy aroma and candied swirl of colors brought me serenity.

This time, I was greeted by a little ball of gold and white calico fur nestled on the counter beneath the front window. My entrance had stirred him from a sound sleep.

"Why hello," I said to the cat, who was as surprised as I was. Like Sister Augustine, I'm sure he wasn't used to seeing many visitors these days in his sanctuary. "And who might you be? You weren't here last time."

The cat's eyes scanned over me quickly and suspiciously, while he remained comfortably perched.

"I see you've met Blitzen," a voice called out from a room to the left. The door to that room had been closed last time. Sister Augustine then peeked out the doorway with a huge grin.

"Yes," I replied, turning to see her holding a small glazed crucifix. "He wasn't here last time, was he?"

"Blitzen usually hides when visitors come. He even gets in between the walls sometimes, and I won't see him for a few days. But he always comes back when he's hungry or looking for attention, *don't you?*" The cat poked his head up when Sister addressed him, but just as quickly lowered it again and closed his eyes. Sister Augustine grinned and shook her head—I caught a glimpse of that young, carefree farm girl from long ago. "That's one of his favorite places, by the window. He can see everything that's going on. When he's awake, that is!"

"Did I catch you at a bad time?" I motioned toward the crucifix in her hands.

"No, I'm just filling the kiln. Come on in. Not many people get to see this."

The kiln room was about the size of a small walk-in closet. It was just big enough to hold a large, octagonal kiln at one end and two tall cabinets of shelves along the side and back walls. The shelves were filled with pieces in dull shades of brown, gray, blue, and pink glaze that would transform into glossy, chromatic sheens once fired.

Above the kiln was a vintage photograph of John F. Kennedy with his most famous quote printed below it: "Ask not what your country can do for you—ask what you can do for your country." Judging from its parched appearance, I assumed the picture of our first and only Catholic president had been hanging there since the shop opened in the 1960s. I imagined the nuns reworking his mantra in their minds, swapping out "your country" for "God."

"Looks like you have a full load today," I observed, referring to the crowded shelves behind Sister.

"Yes, I wait until I have enough to fill the kiln before firing," Sister responded.

She carefully picked up each piece of clayware, and leaning on tiptoe into the kiln, which was almost deeper than she was tall, set it gently down. "None of the pieces can touch," she told me, "or else they'll stick together. We can't have that."

When one level in the kiln was filled, a special stone shelf was inserted and also filled, followed by another and another. A multilayered confetti cake.

"It's like a puzzle, fitting them all in just perfectly, isn't it?" I commented, looking into the kiln. "You're good at that!" I thought how fascinating it would be to watch the pieces be transformed from nondescript to extraordinary inside there via the same choreography of chemistry and magic that turns carbon into diamonds, despair into hope.

"I've been at this a while," Sister said by way of acknowledging my compliment. Her voice was muffled with her head buried inside the kiln. She was arranging the final layer. "Guess that's all we can fit for now. The rest will have to wait."

"How long does the firing take?"

"Several hours. You can't hurry this process, or else it doesn't turn out too well."

Sister paused for a moment, gazing into the full kiln, her lips quietly moving. I could tell she was saying a prayer. She then reached behind her for a bottle of Holy Water that I hadn't previously seen. She lightly sprinkled the clayware with the blessed water, made the Sign of the Cross, and then looked upward. "Francis, please take care of these pieces," she instructed. Then, turning to me, she clarified, "Saint Francis. He's one of my favorites. I always ask him for a little extra help with each kiln load."

"How could he refuse?" I smiled, thrilled to be watching this special routine unfold. I was amused that she called a saint by his first name, as you would a friend. But then, I figured she was one of the few who could get away with that.

Sister Augustine slowly lowered the heavy lid and fastened it tightly.

"I bet it's exciting to open the kiln and see everything finished," I commented.

"Yes, it can be," Sister responded. "There are joys and sorrows when I open it up."

"Joys and sorrows?"

Sister leaned back against the cabinet and looked me in the eye. "I never know what I'm going to find when I open the kiln. Sometimes, the pieces are exactly as I imagined they'd be, or even better, but other times, some pieces are broken, and beyond repair. Either way, it's out of my control. God is boss, you know."

I smiled. "Like life itself, I guess." *Or cooking,* I thought, contemplating this new perspective. It reminded me of when I was working on a new recipe. When I put that first bite in my mouth, I never knew exactly what to expect. It was trial and error, and then *try try try* again until it was right. Likewise, I could see how the classrooms I subbed in were similar to that kiln, where triumph was possible right alongside that same risk of failure. Even as a sub, I had seen uninspired, glassy-eyed teens come to life as they mastered an equation, found their own meaning in a line of poetry, or when I told them about the limitless world waiting for them on the other side of the hills surrounding our town. Just as I had also witnessed students wither at the hands of some tired and apathetic teachers who had mentally checked out a long time ago.

Sister Augustine nodded, apparently privy to the realizations dawning inside my own head. "The important part is to realize that what happens in that kiln is out of my control once I shut the lid. Just like the things that happen in life. We have no control over the joys and sorrows that come to us. There's often no reason why pieces in one load make it out in perfect shape, while others get cracked or even shattered."

"That's the frustrating part!" I interjected, shaking my head and momentarily making eye contact with the hopeful young president, who was frozen in time on the wall. "Not knowing what to expect."

Sister grinned. "When you've been around as long as I have, you see plenty of both joys and sorrows. There are no guarantees in this life. Yet each joy and each sorrow is a gift, John."

"Sorrow—*a gift*?" That was a hard concept for me to wrap my mind around. Sorrow wasn't exactly something I wanted someone to give me. For most of my life, I had suppressed or run away from painful things, not embraced them. And especially now!

"God never gives us more than we can handle. When we see each joy and, yes, each sorrow that comes to us as a gift, and we greet both with gratitude, that's what makes us stronger people. That gratitude is what helps build our faith and gives us purpose while we're here. Otherwise, so much would be unbearable."

"Showing gratitude isn't always easy."

"God never said life would be easy. Gratitude and faith take practice, just like painting. Each step, whether in happiness or in sadness, is a gift. What we do with those gifts is what makes all the difference. That's one of the secrets to building a strong faith. While what comes may be out of our control and beyond our comprehension, God still grants us a choice that is solely ours to make. That's our free will. It's our choice as to which pathway to take. We can choose whether to let that sorrow destroy us or make us stronger, better people."

"What do you do with the broken pieces you find in the kiln?"

"I say, 'Thank you, God!' with each broken piece I pick up. Each piece is a moment that allows me to pause and be grateful," Sister Augustine answered. "Sometimes, there's a lot of gratitude I get to offer when I'm cleaning up a mess in the kiln," she added with a giggle.

I could envision her retrieving each shard of clay, just as I might contemplate each struggle in my career as a teacher and writer. Feeling the rough, jagged edges, while mindfully embracing the piece gently in the warmth of her hand. Art imitating life.

It was at that moment, imagining this old woman cleaning up a failed batch of clayware, that I realized an important teacher had entered my life. Which made perfect sense considering her namesake, Saint Augustine, was one of the greatest spiritual teachers since Jesus Christ. A sinner-turned-saint, Augustine's illuminated words and lessons revitalized early Western Christianity and reverberate to this day. It also wasn't lost on me that the great saint from Hippo was my age at the time of his conversion and rebirth. Likewise, Sister Augustine spoke with a voice that was humble yet transcendent. Relatable and infectious.

I smiled at my new friend. The instinctual pull I had felt to return to this place now made more sense.

I also suddenly remembered my original purpose for the visit.

"I have a favor to ask."

"Ask away," Sister said, widening her eyes in anticipation and motioning for me to follow her through the shop into the second room, which I called her studio.

"You know that pretty little cup you created that I bought last time? The one you said you cleaned your brushes off on."

"Yes, you said it looked like the sea," Sister recalled, glancing over her shoulder at me with a grin.

"Have you ever done that technique on a larger bowl?"

"No, I never thought to do that. I've only ever done small pieces like the one you bought. I never figured anyone would actually want to buy them, so I've always given them away to the other sisters and family members. I just couldn't waste paint by simply washing it down the drain."

"Well, I'm glad you didn't wash it down the drain!" What a loss that would have been. "So, I had a brainstorm."

By now, Sister Augustine was sitting in her oak chair at the back right-hand corner of the horseshoe of worktables. I sat in a nearby spindle chair—painted the same mint green as the shelves—along the outside of the one table, the windows at my back. This was a seat I would sit in many more times in the years to come, as if it had always had my name on it. An identical chair was set on the other side of the table, where Sister told me she often sat to work. My eyes scanned the floor-to-ceiling shelves that framed the room along three of the walls. Gem after gem vied for my attention.

"My friend Steven's birthday is coming up in a few weeks and I thought maybe you could clean your brushes on a big bowl that I could give to him."

Sister Augustine thought for a moment. "I never used a big bowl to clean my brushes on, but I suppose I could do that," she said with a sparkle in her eyes. "There's a first time for everything."

"Do you have a mold for a larger bowl that you can use?"

"How about one of those? Would they work?" Sister suggested, pointing to two rippled, ceramic bowls on the counter against the wall. They held plants and were painted in solid colors. There was a small version and a larger one.

"The large bowl would be great! How long will it take you to do it?"

Sister chortled at my excited tone. "You can't rush these things, but I do have some painting to get done, which means brushes to clean. How about a few weeks?"

"Perfect!"

"Should I call you when it's done?"

"No, I think I'll be back before then and I can check on it in person, if that's all right?"

"Sounds good."

"Hopefully Steven's bowl will be a joy and not a sorrow," I added with a smile as I got up to leave.

"I guess we'll find out, won't we?" Sister Augustine said matter-of-factly.

Blitzen was still sound asleep beneath the front window when I passed by to leave. For a moment, I was envious. He looked so comfy. I could easily have curled up there beside him and let the rest of the day and world pass right on by.

3

PATIENCE

"HELLO, SISTER . . . WHERE ARE YOU?"

Having visited the ceramic shop several afternoons by now, I never knew where I might find Sister Augustine—the kiln room just inside the front door, her studio in the middle, emerging from the back room, or even shoveling the snow from the steps and sidewalk leading to her shop.

I had arrived a couple of times after my first visit to find her swaddled in a knee-length, navy blue parka with the hood pulled up and her face wrapped in a thick, knitted scarf, clearing away winter's final few snowfalls. I always insisted that she give me the shovel and go inside. She would reluctantly hand me the shovel, but then we'd proceed to chat while I added to the piles she had started. When it was time to go in, she'd always remind me, "Turn around. Go in backwards. But be careful you don't trip. That step's gotten me a few times!" A strange habit, yes, but entering in such a manner prevented our glasses from fogging up when we hit the gust of warm air waiting inside. Plus, it allowed me to see the shop and outside from a new perspective. It's interesting what you see when entering a place in reverse. There was something playful about it—an eighty-seven-year-old nun and a thirty-one-year-old guy walking backward into a building—like the giddiness of breaking a rule when no one else is looking. You don't get many silly moments like that in life beyond childhood.

"Sister, are you here?" I called out again. The cold days were behind us now, emphasized by the cozy current of fresh air swirling throughout the rooms.

I walked into the studio and paused by the mint-green spindle chair that I now thought of as my own. This was where most of our afternoon chats took place.

"In here," a voice called out finally from the back room, sounding like an echo reaching the cave's maw.

I had never been in the back room. Never even peeked in. Our visits so far had been confined to anywhere along the stretch from the outside walkway to our matching chairs that faced one another across the table on the right-hand side of the horseshoe.

In those places, and in those quiet, private moments, Sister Augustine and I had begun to talk about everything and anything. From which color she should paint the bow on a small ceramic piggy bank to more serious issues, like navigating the daily challenges that life throws our way and how best to point ourselves in a purpose-driven direction no matter who or where we are. Inside those walls, we were friends, as well as teacher and student in ever-reversing roles. What we may or may not be to the outside world evaporated for a few hours each week. A little old woman in a full-length black and white habit was no more or no less than a young man walking a tightrope toward the next phase of his life. We were in it together.

"Come on back," Sister called out.

She didn't have to tell me twice. The back room was a place that was off-limits to most, giving it a prohibited allure. Something magnificent happened back there, I was certain of it. Now I was about to get a glimpse of what that magnificence was.

The doorway leading into the back was smaller than the

others in the shop, perfectly sized for Sister. I had to duck or else risk banging my head.

"Hi!" I said, walking into the fourth room that completed the suite of Sister's ceramic shop and studio. In fact, this was where it all began.

"Good, you're just in time to help." Sister was wearing a midnight blue bib apron decorated with a pack of baying wolves.

The back room was a long, narrow space, double the width of the first two rooms, but half the length. The earthy scent of clay mingled with the honey-sweet aroma of the old building. Two long stretches of tables divided the room in half widthwise, both covered with a hodgepodge of moist, muddy-gray greenware and a scattering of molds currently in use.

The entire back wall contained floor-to-ceiling shelves filled with a sea of white bisqueware, which is the stage after a piece of greenware has been fired and is ready to be painted or glazed. There was everything imaginable: statues of Mary and Jesus, angels, birds, dogs, cats, flowers, vases, plates, cups, steins, crosses, fruits, lanterns, candlesticks, holiday decorations, and even bases for lamps. Further down toward the far end of the room were stacks of plaster molds that looked like giant sugar cubes.

My mind quickly tabulated that there must be thousands of pieces, including hundreds of molds. I made a mental note to explore the cache of molds on another day with Sister. The entire place was a spectacular trove that seemed to have no end.

"Sister, this is amazing back here!"

A big smile was flashed my way. "All of this has been here a long time," Sister Augustine commented, panning the room. She then lamented, "Not many people want this stuff anymore, though. Maybe a cross or statue every so often, and my Nativities still sell, but that's about it."

"I can't believe that. There are so many cool things here." I walked around the tables to get a closer look at the bisqueware on the shelves. It was like staring into a 3-D coloring book with white shapes and figures all waiting for inspiration to strike. Multiples of each piece filed back from the edges to the wall.

Sister laughed. I imagined *cool* wasn't a word she heard very often in her shop, or in reference to her pieces. "They're all antiques now, like me!" she declared.

I ran my fingers over the bisqueware. They were stark white with the texture of very fine sandpaper. I couldn't imagine them remaining untouched all these years, and unseen except by Sister Augustine and Blitzen.

"People don't seem much interested in ceramics these days," Sister explained. "I still like painting them, though. Animals and birds are my favorite to do." I had noticed on my first visit that the shelves in the shop and studio were like a virtual Noah's Ark, with ceramic puppies, kittens, deer, bears, squirrels, rabbits, turkeys, pheasants, penguins, cardinals, blue jays, owls, ducks, swans, even unicorns, and so much more, not to mention the tiny turtles and frogs for "Three Hail Marys" each and the ladybugs available for "One Hail Mary." Likewise, in the back room, only these creatures looked like they had been sculpted out of snow.

"I think people maybe just need to be reminded you're here. I didn't even know your shop existed until Steven brought me. Which reminds me, before I forget, Steven loved the bowl you made for him for his birthday. He wanted me to be sure to thank you. It's now displayed in his New York apartment."

A week earlier, Sister Augustine had completed the very special bowl I had commissioned her to paint for Steven, using her technique of cleaning off brushes on it while painting other pieces and then firing it. What emerged was a bowl wrapped in a rippling coat of many colors—a deep cobalt rim atop a flowing landscape of red, green, orange, lavender, brown, periwinkle, blush, yellow, and navy.

It was the kind of piece that an artist could never plan to create, or sketch out beforehand, yet one that only a truly gifted hand could create on instinct alone. An abstract spectacle that keeps the viewer endlessly fascinated with ever-new things to discover as his eye wanders up and down its curved exterior.

"That's one part my hand and one part God's hand," Sister had commented when I first saw Steven's finished bowl and gushed over how exquisite the design was. "Sounds like a good collaboration to me," I had told her. I had never seen anything quite like it before. Because I was an artist myself, the piece sparked my creative wick, nudging me forward with my own creations—primitive Americana folk art paintings and sculptures, which I mostly did to give as gifts to family and friends.

"Now I'd like you to please do a bowl for me. The same size," I requested.

"I can't promise it'll turn out the same way, or turn out at all," Sister warned. "I thought that was a one-time deal," she added, raising her brow and laughing.

"I'm sure however it turns out will be fantastic." It occurred to me that I had just asked for lightning to strike twice.

"You think everything is 'fantastic' in here," Sister admonished jokingly. "How can that be?"

"Must have something to do with the artist."

Sister playfully swatted her hand toward me. "I'm just doing God's work."

I checked out the items on the tables that sliced the back room in half. "Hey, here's a large bowl you can use for mine." I started to pick it up, not realizing how fragile the clayware was when it's first removed from its mold. The soft, damp green-ware bowl promptly crumbled in my hand and dropped onto the table with a heartbreaking *thud*.

"I'm so sorry! I didn't mean to . . ."

Sister rushed over to the table. Even Blitzen made his debut, hopping down from an upper shelf with what I thought looked like a *tsk tsk tsk* expression on his face as he sniffed the damaged goods.

"I guess that one's a sorrow right off the bat," Sister Augustine remarked with a giggle.

"I feel terrible!"

"Like I told you, there are joys and sorrows, inside *and* outside the kiln. No worries, I'll clean that up later," Sister said by way of absolution. "Come down here with me, please. I need your help with something."

Leaving the sad little clump behind, I followed Sister Augustine to the far end of the room, where a huge tub was filled with liquid clay.

"The thing about ceramics is that they take patience to create. They start as this thick, muddy clay that is carefully mixed in precise proportions of powder and water," Sister explained, slowly stirring the dark mixture as if it were a vat of chowder. "If it's too thick, it doesn't work, and you need to add more water. Too thin, and it runs all over, making a mess. You need to then add more powder."

As a struggling new teacher and as a writer who was also trying to take that aspect of my career to the next level, I was the first to admit that my patience needed a little polish and shine. For starters.

Sister then moved to the table beside the tub of clay. She maneuvered a large, heavy white mold closer to the vat. The two halves of the mold were held together by thick, black rubber bands and a belt that was fastened tightly around the middle.

"Here, hold on to this mold," she instructed.

The mold was smooth and cool to the touch. I gripped it tightly. This was my act of contrition for the little disaster I had caused on the other end of the room. I didn't want to mess this one up, too.

"What is this a mold for?"

"The Wise Men." Sister picked up a thick hose as if at a gas pump and flipped a switch, igniting a roaring compressor on the floor. She inserted the hose into a small opening at the top of the mold and squeezed the lever, flooding the mold with liquid clay.

It was literally an epiphany in the making. I all but hugged the mold now, waiting for the clay to gush out over the top like a science fair volcano gone haywire, turning us both into living sculptures. But it didn't. After decades of doing this, Sister instinctually loosened her grip on the hose lever a moment later and then let up completely just as the clay gently tapped the inside rim.

"This now has to set overnight so the pieces inside harden enough to be removed. Even then, they're still fragile, as you just found out. It all takes time. There's no rushing it." My friend winked at me.

"Time and patience," I added, still atoning for the wrecked greenware bowl. "Something I'm not always that great at."

"It takes practice, just like anything else, and even then, nothing is guaranteed," Sister Augustine explained. "After these pieces harden into greenware, the kiln will get a hold of them, and one never knows how that will go."

"I'd think that prayer and Holy Water you add before closing the kiln provide a little extra insurance anyway. Not to mention Saint Francis watching over everything."

"God has a mind of His own," Sister said knowingly. "Even after the pieces become bisqueware, they need to be handled with love and care while being painted, and then any glazed pieces go back into the kiln for another firing. If they make it through all that, they go on the shelf, where Blitzen might then find them one night on his little adventures around here, which means I might find them on the floor the next morning."

"Sorrows?"

"Moments of gratitude," Sister Augustine corrected. "This process is a slow one that tests each piece along the way over time. More often than not, they're tougher than you'd think by just looking at them."

Just about every day, I was greeted with a thanks-but-no-thanks form rejection letter from a publisher in my mailbox. Each letter would sting, causing me to question whether I was meant to write my cookbook. But like Sister said, the act of creating and producing is a process, which takes time. I began to understand that each of those rejections was a test with only one question: do I give up and quit, *or* do I get back in the kitchen to create even more recipes and then send out an even bigger, better manuscript to more publishers the next day? Thanks to Sister Augustine, I knew there was only one answer to that question.

Though rejection was painful and was wearing me down, there was also something hopeful starting to stir inside me that began to boost my spirit. Her words echoed in my mind with the sway of a prayer: *Tougher than you'd think.*

Like you, I thought, looking at this little unassuming woman, who had a unique knack for lighting up a room and holding her own.

And, yes, just maybe like me, too.

PART TWO

4

FORGET-ME-NOT

"Is this for a gift?" Sister Augustine asked from across the table one afternoon. Watching her work, I marveled at how agile she was. She had turned eighty-eight some months earlier, in November, just before I turned thirty-two. In one hand, she cradled a bisqueware teacup. In the other, pinched firmly between her forefinger and thumb, was a long, thin brush that had been dipped into a light blue glaze. She was working her way around the rim of the cup, five dots at a time.

"Yes, a gift for myself," I replied, smiling. "I've decided that I need one special cup for my green tea. Every time I open the cupboard, there are a ton of not-so-special ones in there. You know, all those touristy and old Christmas mugs, and the ones with cheesy sayings that people seem to think make clever gifts. I swear they multiply when I'm not looking. It's overwhelming. All junk."

"Funny how that works, isn't it? When we're not looking, all that stuff *magically* accumulates around us."

"I guess I can add magician to my resume now, too," I said like the guilty packrat I was.

Sister giggled.

"At the least, I figured that I should have one teacup that means something to me and get rid of the rest. I like to drink hot green tea. It helps to energize me."

"So you're simplifying," Sister clarified, her eyes focused on the forget-me-nots she was painting. "That's a good thing."

"I guess you could say that. Having only one special cup in the cupboard instead of two dozen makes at least one daily decision a little easier. Plus, your forget-me-nots always bring a smile to my face, ever since I saw them on the robe of the Blessed Mother statue I bought on my first visit here."

I wasn't doing too much smiling these days, so every little bit helped. In addition to cringing every time I opened my mailbox, expecting rejection letters, I also dreaded hearing the phone ring at the crack of dawn, letting me know I was needed as a sub at the high school. I'd wake up around five or five thirty, with a knot already weighing down my stomach, and just lay there, waiting for the phone to torture me. Sometimes the call came, sometimes it didn't. Sometimes, I'd take the phone off the hook and watch the digital numbers on my nightstand flip until I knew the school would no longer call. I'd then replace the receiver, tears often pooling in my eyes as I tried to go back to sleep. I felt like a complete failure. Subbing was a thankless job. For many students, a sub meant a free pass to do whatever they wanted; for me, it was six and a half mind-numbing hours of sitting at someone else's desk as a benchwarmer.

Overall, the student body at Elk County Catholic High School, which numbered only a few hundred, consisted mostly of good kids from hardworking, blue-collar families who had always been the backbone of our small factory town. Those kids were a joy. But a few students especially tested the limits of my patience. I had told Sister how during one recent class in the computer room I was writing instructions on the chalkboard when the small metal ball from a computer mouse hit the board a quarter inch from my head with an earsplitting *CRACK!* I didn't even bother to turn around. I simply murmured, "Someone's a really bad aim," and kept writing. I then hoped they wouldn't try to prove me wrong.

Even worse, at the beginning of the school year, I had been called upon to cover math classes for a teacher who simply left and didn't come back. For several weeks until a certified math teacher was hired, to my horror, I had to relearn algebra and geometry to keep one step ahead of the students. I almost had to call Sister Mercedes to tutor me again! I drew the line when it came to the calculus class I also covered, giving those students a month of study halls.

All of this was definitely not what I had in mind when I left my career in Nashville and went back to school to get my teaching certifications.

On the bright side, I had recently applied for the full-time English position at the school that would start in the fall. I felt fairly confident of my chances for landing it. After all, this was my alma mater, I was their busiest sub, the students for the most part liked me, and I had dual teaching certifications in secondary English and speech communications, and a master's degree from the number-one graduate school of education in the country. Plus a decade of other work experience that was neatly bulleted on my resume.

However, I feared factors beyond my control would trump all that. Even the best qualifications often fall prey to politics and the whims of those in charge. The greatest obstacle to securing the full-time position would likely, and ironically, be what had been my most enjoyable assignment as a sub so far, when I taught the headmaster's Advanced English IV class while he was recovering from surgery.

It had been such a treat to actually *teach* the same subject—and something that was within my expertise—for an extended period of time. For several weeks, the students and I basked in the abstractions and deconstruction of poetry of my choosing. A. E. Housman, Lord Tennyson, William Wordsworth, Pablo Neruda, Elizabeth Barrett Browning, Lord Byron, John Updike, Langston Hughes, Robert Frost, and my favorite, Constantine P. Cavafy—*As you set out toward Ithaca, hope the way is long, full of reversals, full of knowing.*

But apparently the headmaster didn't like the fact that his students preferred me over him, something the teenagers were quick to tell when asked, thinking their compliments were helping my chances of getting hired. I could only hope that my future wasn't teetering on one man's fragile ego. Time would tell. Until then, I'd wait in anguish.

I felt such an innate draw to the classroom, to teach and inspire young people. That's where I belonged. Instead, I was slipping underwater, as if Jaws had clenched my legs, dragging me down. What optimism I had was deserting me.

Was I destined to be a sub forever? The thought spun continuously in my mind.

Sister Augustine finished trimming the teacup with the forget-me-nots and set it on the table. She then picked up the saucer to circumnavigate it as well with her fine-tipped dots.

"So much in nature tends to have a calming effect on us," she said. "Is there anything simpler than a tree, a rainfall, a full moon, or a field of flowers? That's why nature is a perfect retreat."

"Absolutely," I said, nodding. "Any time I get stressed-out, which is a lot lately, there's an old dirt road leading to a large field where I like to go. It's in a place called Bear Run that my family on the brewery side owns outside of town." During an earlier conversation, I had told Sister how I'm a fifth-generation member of the Straub Brewery family in St. Marys, a heritage I greatly cherish. "I figure it's easier for God to see me there in that wide open field. Can't hurt to remind Him I'm still around." I was pretty certain though that if God was up above watching, He would have 20/20 vision no matter where I was.

I told Sister how I liked to find a little patch of soil or grass in the middle of that field and sit there, or sometimes lie on my back. Birds chirping from a nearby branch, bees and flies buzzing overhead, ants and other little bugs silently making their way around me. Scents sweet and spicy. And if I remained very still, occasionally a deer sauntered into the field at dusk to eat. We would connect eyes—both of us vulnerable and at the mercy of the raw earth around us—and the world stopped in an even more glorious way for a few minutes. Walking on that road and hitting the pause button on my life in that field, I imagined hearing God whisper words of comfort to me in the breeze. While there, I better understood why farmers live to a ripe old age. *But what about the rest of us?* I would wonder. We only got to visit occasionally.

After twelve years of Catholic education, deep down I knew God was everywhere and available to me whenever I needed Him, even if the answer to my prayers wasn't exactly what I wanted. But I also knew that sometimes the challenges we face can overwhelm and even cause us to lose sight of that fundamental understanding, like an encroaching tidal wave that blurs the horizon.

"Do you know how the forget-me-not got its name?" my friend asked.

"No, how?" I watched closely as Sister's steady hand applied the five lobes of each flower with equal parts practice and grace. There was no pattern or guide to follow. She didn't measure the space between each dot. She created organically, by instinct. Each forget-me-not: a small circle of *dot dot dot dot dot*.

"German legend has it that when God was naming all the plants and flowers on earth, this little blue wildflower called out, 'Forget me not, Lord!' To which He responded, 'No one ever will again, as that will be your name from now on.' I think that's a nice little prayer for us to remember: *Forget me not, Lord!* Those few words say a lot."

"That's beautiful," I said, my eyes following Sister's brush. More than a few times lately I had wondered if God had indeed forgotten me. It's easy to jump to conclusions when prayers aren't answered as quickly as we hope. I often had to remind myself that those unanswered prayers didn't mean God wasn't listening, but still I wondered. I also thought of how Sister had sat there, quietly working the days away, for decades. Like a tiny wildflower herself. Hidden away from a world that had forgotten her, even if God hadn't. She didn't seem to mind.

"I love how delicate your forget-me-nots are," I then told her.

Sister Augustine glanced up from the saucer. "Look closer and you'll see that what may appear to be delicate is actually very strong and resilient. Much like the actual flower itself, that while small and modest, can grow in some very dark, damp places."

A muddled expression spread across my face.

Sister held the saucer up so it was facing me. Show-and-tell time. With her right forefinger, she tapped next to one particular dot. "Look at this one dot. A dot is the simplest mark we can create. A light dab of the brush. A speck only. At first, it may look unassuming and powerless. Simple. That's the beauty of it. But this simple dot is what punctuates even the most important statements as a period. On a map, this dot can mark the location of a small remote village just as it can the largest city in the world. A dot is what differentiates one dollar from one million dollars as a decimal point. This fleck could be the pupil of an eye or the spark that ignites an inferno. When multiplied and scattered, it becomes a universe of stars and planets for us to gaze upon. And, when one is looking down from those same heavens, this dot, making its way across the earth, is you and me.

This simple dot, which isn't much bigger than a grain of sand or a freckle, is powerful."

I stared at the iota of gray that the kiln would turn blue as a summer's sky. That dot—one petal of a forget-me-not—suddenly looked resolute to me. It mattered. Without it, the forget-me-not would be something else, something less than what it was. As a result, so too would the world.

Sister continued: "The forget-me-not, and each of these dots, is really a symbol for simplicity."

I was reminded of one of my favorite Bible verses, Matthew 6:28–29: "Consider the lilies of the field, how they grow; they toil not, neither do they spin: And yet I say unto you, That even Solomon in all his glory was not arrayed like one of these." The Gospel writer could just have easily been describing one of Sister Augustine's forget-me-nots.

"Even saying the word *simplicity* makes me feel more relaxed," I commented, thinking how uttering those four syllables felt like releasing a long deep breath. "There isn't much simplicity in our complicated and chaotic world anymore. Or in my life at the moment." Isn't that what I had moved back home for? To find a simpler, more genuine path. Where was it? Where was my trail of forget-me-nots to follow?

"That's because simplicity begins with each person. The world is complicated and chaotic because people have made it that way. But that's not how we were given the world."

"What do you mean?"

"Think about the world at the beginning of time. Sure, it may have been wild and untamed. Yet there was a simple order to it. Sunrise, sunset. Birth and death. And beauty. Forests and jungles, and seas, all teeming with a natural order of life. Then when we entered the picture, we brought disruptions, emotions, ambitions, greed, sin. We devoured and polluted that simplicity to suit our own desires and temptations. In the end, though, we only ended up hurting ourselves. Today, it's a free-for-all. We've forgotten what simplicity is, and just how powerful a force it can be."

Sister continued painting the forget-me-nots around the saucer. *Dot dot dot dot dot.* Her own Morse code, signaling simplicity to anyone willing to pay attention. Once fired, the flowers on the two pieces would pop against the clear-glazed background. Like a fine piece of porcelain.

"How can we return to that simplicity?" The first part of the scene Sister Augustine had described was Eden. It was her Mockin' Bird Hill farm from childhood. Then I realized, it was also the old field in Bear Run, surrounded by blue skies and seas of tall green grasses and wildflowers. A cathedral without walls. But still, I couldn't live in that field forever. There had to be more to the answer than momentary escapes from reality.

How can we weave simplicity into everyday life? I needed to know.

Sitting there in Sister's studio, I became aware that at least part of the larger answer to that question was right in front of me. I was surrounded by simplicity. An orbit of shapes and colors. Earth and fire. A slumbering cat under the table. Even the air I breathed there was facile, uncomplicated. At the center of it all was the artist. She embodied the ideal of simplicity. Over our many visits so far, I noticed how Sister Augustine wore the exact same habit—the black cotton cloth thinned and threadbare— almost daily. Reminiscent of the few homemade frocks she had as a young farm girl. No need for fancy wardrobe changes or a closet full of trendy options. She had even told me that the top portion of her coif, which was the stiff white structure rising above her head and giving regal form to her long black veil, had been crafted from a plastic Clorox bottle.

"Regaining a sense of simplicity is up to each one of us," Sister explained. "When you talk about complications and chaos in the world today, those are there because we layer ourselves in them. Each day, we pile on the layers, and never shed them. Even animals shed their coats like clockwork every year, but not us. We are so often our own worst enemy. It's like putting on multiple new layers of clothes day after day and then walking out into a heat wave only to be baked alive beneath all that stuff."

I thought of my small bedroom at home. At last count, I had about forty sweaters, three dozen pairs of jeans and dress pants, just as many shorts, enough T-shirts and button-downs to outfit a small army, about a hundred ties for work, close to twenty pairs of shoes. I pictured myself putting everything on until my closets and drawers were empty. Until I was suffocating and unrecognizable to myself.

"I can totally feel that," I said. "It's uncomfortable. Restrictive. Hard to concentrate."

"Exactly. Eventually you can barely move or even breathe. Sooner or later, you reach a boiling point and then a meltdown."

In other words: my life at the moment. "But that just makes it sound like a point of no return. Like it's a hopeless situation." Was I hopeless? *Heaven help me!* I had doubled down on my dreams, returning home to pursue a life of teaching and writing. While others my age were ten years into their jobs, with spouses and kids, I was a new recipe being assembled from scratch.

"For some it becomes a point of no return, but it doesn't have to be. Not even in the worst cases." Sister finished working on the saucer. She picked up another thin brush and dipped it into a Duncan bottle of glaze labeled Sun Yellow. Studying the teacup for a moment, Sister Augustine then began to add a pinpoint of light to the middle of each forget-me-not. "Those layers of complications and chaos assault us from inside and out, and from every direction. The secret is to remove them one by one. Clean out. Open the windows. Let in the light and fresh air again."

"That's the hard part."

"Is it?"

Is it? My friend had stumped me. I pondered her question while she slowly added more cheerful dots to the world, doing so now around the saucer. Each atom of color was a clue to the answer she had in mind. She was leading me to discover the solution for myself.

I finally ventured, "Maybe it's not hard, but there comes a point when it seems all but impossible, or at least useless, and that can paralyze a person."

"We're dealing with simplicity here, not rocket science," Sister reminded me with a wink. "Simplicity is something you should definitely not overthink. I'll never understand why people think big problems require complicated solutions."

Okay, note to self: lighten up! "How can we peel away those layers then?"

"A simple deep breath a couple of times a day can help to start peeling away those layers. Sitting in a quiet place for even just five minutes each day, *with a hot cup of green tea if you wish,* can help peel away the layers," Sister offered. "You can also start looking around and asking yourself, 'What can I live without: A TV in my bedroom? All the knickknacks, magazines, books, clothes, or whatever else is piling up? Feeling the need to be perfect and impress everyone? Making mistakes and letting them dog me?' You can pick a day once a week, once a month, or whenever and literally clean out the clutter that's all around you. That's a grace you give to yourself."

"Why don't they teach that in school?" I said with a crooked grin. "The world would be such a better place if we all did that."

Sister Augustine smiled. "You've already started peeling away those layers."

"I have?" I half expected Sister to look at me and exclaim, "Duh!" What was I missing here?

"For starters, your field in Bear Run sounds lovely. Try to go there more often, and never forget what it's like to be there even when you're far away. Also, every time you open your cupboard and are met by those shelves of meaningless mugs, you feel overwhelmed, right?"

Yes, I nodded.

"So, like you told me, you decided to simplify that situation by using only one, special teacup. You said it yourself: that makes at least one daily decision easier. After all, you can only drink from one cup at a time, so there's no need to have two dozen. That leaves a lot of clear shelf space. That's a breath of fresh air you're about to welcome into your life every day when you use it, as soon as I get this teacup finished, that is. When we clear away the physical clutter around us, we set our spirit free on the inside as well."

I nodded again. I was starting to understand. "That kind of cleaning out can then be applied to every other aspect of my life," I realized. "Just getting rid of a little junk is a step in the right direction, isn't it?"

Sister nodded this time, adding the last Sun Yellow dot to the saucer. "Yes. The same goes for keeping up appearances, or 'keeping up with the Joneses,' as some call it. I always wonder, *For what reason?* Why do people feel the need to impress others or keep up with anyone? All that effort and anxiety also bury you alive and take you further and further away from the simple path and from who you really are."

"I always wonder, *Who are the Joneses anyway?*" I joked.

Sister and I laughed.

On a more serious note, her point brought to mind a man in town. And how these materialistic layers people create around themselves not only defy simplicity, but, as his case showed, could also be a sign of evil incarnate.

I told Sister Augustine about how the man's determination to keep up appearances had led him to prey on kind, elderly people, especially if they were wealthy. He would ingratiate his way into their lives by running errands, doing lawn work, driving them to appointments, and essentially making their world revolve around him. Pretty much everyone in town was on to his game, except, it seemed, the vulnerable individuals, whom he drained of their independence and money like a parasite. All so he could acquire more, more, and more stuff—layers of clothes, jewelry, decorations, cars, trips—on their dime. In one case, he convinced a dying widow to change her will, bequeathing him even more money than she had generously allotted for him. The woman was so incapacitated from a stroke by that point, she could only sign the codicil he presented to her with an X.

Sister shook her head disapprovingly. "Sounds like he's more a case of someone trying to keep up with the Judases!" she quipped. "And we all know how that ended for Judas."

I shook my head as well, not sure if it was appropriate to laugh, but I wanted to.

Sister's earlier comment about keeping up appearances also stirred memories of my days working with celebrities. "You know, Sister, when I was a publicist in Nashville, it was my job to create and maintain those layers of appearance around the country singers I represented. I didn't fully understand that when I arrived there. My first clue though came one day early on while I was talking to my boss. I was raving about a client's autobiography, which I found so inspiring. My boss laughed and said, 'You'll eventually come to learn what's true and what's not in that book.' That really made me pause and think.

"I guess up until then I was just a naïve kid from a small town. Not that I hadn't experienced some bad things of my own growing up, but I believed what people told me. I expected people to tell me the truth, not lies. That job really opened my eyes. Then I became part of the problem. As a publicist, I helped to create the smoke and mirrors, and the images and mythologies, that were wrapped around my clients, which often had little to do with who they truly were. I saw firsthand what that did to those celebrities behind the scenes. How it changed them. How it complicated their lives to a point where I wondered if they even remembered who they really were anymore. I'll see them on TV even now and I'll think, *That's not really who you are.*"

Sister Augustine listened closely, continuing to shake her head. I was presenting an entirely new worldview she had never experienced before. Showbiz was foreign to her. Nashville might as well have been Timbuktu as far as she was concerned.

I continued: "This one singer I knew was married with a couple of kids. I was constantly telling the media what a great husband and dad he was. Only to find out that he was cheating on his wife when he was out on the road doing concerts, and he did it with the help of his own crew. I was so disappointed when I learned that. But still, day after day, I had to add new layers onto his myth. Layers of lies."

"That's a shame," Sister chimed in. "Not all of the poor souls are in Purgatory."

"Nashville was a great adventure for me. I met so many amazing, good-hearted people and experienced things I'll always cherish. But I also witnessed a really ugly side to the business and to human nature. A complicated side where simplicity was only manufactured for photo ops and press kits."

"You were wise to leave when you did," Sister said. "When people stay in those kinds of environments too long, it corrupts them by association."

I agreed with a weak laugh. "Somewhere along the line, I also allowed my own simplicity to become buried. I regret that."

Sister Augustine was inspecting her quiet rows of wildflowers wrapping around the teacup and saucer. "Regrets are a waste of valuable time. Don't look at it that way," she said. "Instead, always stay focused on the journey ahead. Just as patience or any other virtue is a process with its own learning curve, simplicity is something we also cultivate over time, like a garden."

"Like a garden of forget-me-nots, perhaps?" I could see myself, years ahead, sitting at my writing desk and studying that cup and saucer just as Sister was doing now. By that time, the pieces would be chipped, the glaze crackled, and the inside tea-stained—rendered all the more priceless. My eyes and fingers would slowly trace the trail of forget-me-nots while each sip warmed my entire body. And I would understand the world a little better.

"Yes," Sister said, grinning. "Never underestimate the power of simplicity. It can free your mind and heart, and it can help you to see what you never knew was right there in front of you the whole time."

From her lips to God's ears. Perhaps my search for answers really did come down to the audacity of connecting the dots.

5

Lost and Found

"You sound sad," Sister Augustine said. Her back was to me when I walked in and greeted her on that summer afternoon, the dog-days humidity outside near one hundred percent. Inside the studio, the air was cool and inviting. My friend was standing at the sink in the far left-hand corner of the room, filling Blitzen's water bowl. It was amazing that she could garner my tone from a simple "Hello."

"I didn't get the full-time teaching job over at the high school," I said, while sinking into my mint-green spindle chair. I had moved back to my small hometown in search of my purpose, but this latest rejection had me more confused than ever. *Why? Why? Why? Our Father Who Art in Heaven, Are you even listening to me? Was anyone?* Question marks swam in my head like a school of minnows scattered by a rock thrown into the water. Frenzied, directionless, scared.

"*You didn't?* But you've been subbing there for a long time and the students really like you. I thought you'd be a shoo-in," Sister said in a perplexed tone. She returned to her spindle chair now and observed me from across the table while picking up a half-painted Saint Joseph statue that she had started before lunch. Blitzen leaped onto her lap and quickly dozed off. "You even taught the headmaster's class while he was out sick. That should count for something. Shouldn't it?"

I rolled my eyes. "I'm not sure those qualifications were what mattered in this decision."

"Ah, I see. Politics," Sister said. "I'm well aware of a few people at that school who are less than honorable. I may be tucked away over here, but I still have eyes and ears. I'm always amused at how people can do work in the name of God, yet . . ." Sister Augustine stopped before finishing her thought, then added, "God sees all, so we don't have to be the ones to judge. Luckily, there are also some really good, kind people over there for the students' sake." She capped her observation with a smile, lightening the mood and shifting the burden to where it belonged.

"Yes," I agreed. "You're right." I further explained how the majority of the teachers at the high school and the vice principal, who had been my seventh grade homeroom teacher at the beginning of her own career in education, were all on my side. I had received a flurry of supportive calls and notes from them following this latest setback. They were a reminder that goodness still existed in the world.

As for the unfortunate politics of it all, I was often surprised how well Sister Augustine understood such things in the way she did. I figured that in her cloistered world at St. Joseph's, and especially within the serenity I experienced in her shop and studio, the cat-and-mouse politicking that manipulates so much of our society didn't even register.

To make matters even worse, I told my friend how a gossipy aunt of mine, who was not involved in my life whatsoever, was running around town spreading the rumor that I didn't get the job because she "heard" I had no teaching certifications. She even had the gall to tell my mom that. Salt drizzled into a fresh wound would have been a kinder gesture than her ridiculous hearsay.

Had my aunt bothered to ask me, I could have shown her two teaching certificates and a master's degree, which all hung near my writing desk at home. Plus, a letter to me from one of the seniors in the headmaster's Advanced English IV class, who wrote: "All the students just love having you, especially at this time in our lives. . . . You are truly an asset to Saint Marys and to Elk County Catholic. . . . Your work touches so many different lives and it is so vital to many people." Those heartfelt words meant more to me than any certificate or Ivy League degree. Meanwhile, with a trail of nasty, judgmental words over the years behind her, my aunt as well as some at the high school were a valuable reminder, as Sister told me, that "the Devil is hard at work, too."

"Did you ever consider that you're better off?" Sister Augustine asked.

My mind froze for a moment, the peculiar question dangling in front of me. Finally, I answered, "Not really. I believe one of my purposes in life is to teach. Ever since I was in first grade, I wanted to be a teacher. I just happened to take a few detours to get to this point. Now I just feel completely lost."

Sister resumed painting Saint Joseph's eyes, applying the brown paint with a thin brush and stable hand while several more statues waited their turn in front of her. "There are many ways to be a teacher," she said, eye to eye with Saint Joseph. "Being in the classroom is just one of them."

"I never really thought about it like that." My mood began to thin. I started to feel a little lighter just knowing she was about to share her wisdom with me.

"I think you should be grateful." Suspended in her hand, Saint Joseph gazed across the table at me with one eye done and one to go, as if he were seconding her words with a wink.

"Grateful?"

"Yes, grateful that they didn't give you that job," Sister Augustine reiterated. "Remember all those broken pieces of pottery— those sorrows—I sometimes find when I open the kiln?"

I nodded, the image of her gathering up shattered clayware vivid in my mind.

"Do you remember what I do with each one of them?"

"You use each as a moment to thank God for the many blessings in your life."

"That's right. Each broken piece presents a moment for me to pause in gratitude. I wouldn't otherwise have all those extra moments of gratitude if the original piece emerged untouched from the kiln. It's God's way of slowing me down from time to time to focus on what's truly important."

"But it's really hard to offer gratitude when you feel like you were treated unfairly."

Sister nodded, causing Blitzen to gently stir and then relax back into a deep slumber on her lap. Saint Joseph maintained his wink of support. "That's when gratitude counts the most. It's in those challenging moments when we get a little closer to our true purpose in this life. We need to be thankful for those challenges."

I deeply exhaled, hints of defeat slipping out. I hadn't yet even told her, or anyone else for that matter, about my additional challenges trying to get a cookbook published. That would be for another day. "That makes sense, but still I feel like one of my purposes in life is to be in the classroom. When I was little, I'd race home every day after school to then play school for hours. I even had a desk, textbooks, and a classroom full of imaginary students." I laughed at the memory of me talking to an empty room that only my imagination could see transformed into a bright, welcoming classroom. "I'd fill out the worksheets and tests I created, pretending the students had done them, and then I'd correct and grade them. . . ." I trailed off with another laugh. Even at ages seven, eight, and nine, I took my make-believe classroom to heart.

After earning my dual secondary-education certifications in English and speech communications at the University of Pittsburgh at Bradford, I had turned thirty years old while working on my master's and standing proudly in the middle of Harvard Yard at the stroke of midnight on a chilly December 1. Anything seemed possible at that moment. Now, almost three years later, my own high school alma mater wouldn't even hire me.

I continued: "However, also when I was in first grade, my teacher Sister Josepha told me I would grow up to be a priest. I've always worried that might be my destiny, even though I have no calling or desire to be a priest. Noble as that is, of course. Or maybe *that* was my calling and I just don't know it!"

I could tell Sister was often amused by my rambling, as she was now. Sometimes, it was like I tossed my words into a blender without the lid and flipped the switch on HIGH. It didn't matter in that sacred space. Inside her studio, I could talk, talk, talk and work through my thoughts as much as I needed. Sister would paint on one side of the table or at her station in the back corner of the horseshoe and I would ramble on or ponder life's mysteries on the other side. I had come to count on the fact that no matter the problem, situation, or question, Sister had an answer that made sense.

"I'm only a messenger," Sister Augustine said humbly during one of our very first chats, when I praised the advice she had given me. She only described herself like that one time, as if to put her role in my life into perspective from the start. Or perhaps it was a slip on her end—like a secret that's too good to keep to yourself—accidentally revealing her true purpose on this earth. Either way, I never felt the need to ask for whom she was a messenger. That was a given.

Sister had now returned her attention to finishing Saint Joseph's other eye, while helping me to better understand my current situation. "Just as there are different ways to be a teacher, there are different ways to minister as well. Being a priest or nun is only one of them. If you had the calling to be a priest, you'd know it for certain. So you're off the hook there." She chuckled while dipping the thin brush into the Duncan bottle of paint labeled Walnut.

I responded with a laugh. I was relieved to know I was not likely destined to be a priest, but that maybe there were other ways I was meant to "minister," as Sister called it, or at least spread a positive message. On the primitive folk art pieces I was creating at the time, I often used words like *love, hope, peace, grace, joy, awe,* and *laughter* to further convey inspirational messages. And my cookbook promised something of a tasty and fun, positive message if it ever made it out into the world.

Maybe she's on to something, I thought. Though the specifics were still foggy.

"Perhaps you have a higher purpose. Something else you're meant to do," Sister continued. "God works in mysterious ways. You didn't get that teaching job, even though that's where your heart is right now, because you weren't meant to."

"You really think that could be the case? That I wasn't meant to get that job?" I was looking for reassurance, a lifeline. Otherwise, I'd just feel like a failure, which is a hard feeling to shake. Being lost and not sure where your life is headed is just as nerve-racking. It's so hard to have faith in a greater purpose that you can't see or easily explain. Or to find belief in a world that no longer seems to believe in you.

"That's always the case," Sister Augustine confirmed, finishing Saint Joseph's second eye so that the humble carpenter, descended from the line of King David, now looked across the table at me with a full, knowing gaze. "God has His ways. His reasoning may not seem obvious to us at the time, but someday you'll look back and say, 'That's exactly how my life had to happen, good *and* bad, right down to the second, to get me where I am.'"

That sentiment caused me to glance down to the far end of

the table. Five large and small rippled bowls, each painted in a kaleidoscope as if shredded Rothkos had been collaged around them, stood in a row. More than a year earlier, Sister had created the first such bowl as a birthday gift I gave to my best friend Steven. Then she created one for me. After that, I told her she should make some to sell in the shop.

When I saw the first four she created for the shop, I bought them all as gifts. I also told her she needed to charge more for them than the eight dollars for the large bowls and six dollars for the small bowls she was asking. "In the city these would sell for so much more," I told her. Sister Augustine wouldn't hear of it. "But we're not in the city," she countered. "I want anyone who wants to buy one to be able to afford it. It's God's work, not mine." That was that.

She then created six more bowls, which someone saw as she was removing them from the kiln and bought all six of those on the spot. I had vowed to let these five currently on the table waiting for her neon orange price stickers make it into the shop, even though I would have bought them all as well. To me, each one was a piece of a puzzle. The swirls and splattering, and amalgam of colors woven and threaded, flowing and blended, were like a secret code carrying an important message that I was sure I needed to decipher.

As if reading my mind, Sister said, "Yes, just like those bowls. They each start with one brushstroke, followed by another and another. I never know what they'll look like in the end. But when I open the kiln, I see that each stroke on those bowls had a purpose. Each bowl wouldn't look the way it does if even one of those brushstrokes was missing."

I thought of the new squares of plywood, two feet by two feet, that I would chip away at with a hammer, then smooth with rough sandpaper, to fast-forward and re-create Time's own handiwork in my own studio at home. The boards became the weathered canvases for my primitive folk art paintings, which I would then give away as gifts. Indeed, each chance imperfection and blemish I made, like Sister said, was just as necessary in the end as her brushstrokes. Just as each ingredient in my recipes played its role, great or small.

"Each of your bowls is such a masterpiece!" I declared. "So many of them are great examples of abstract expressionism, like Jackson Pollock is famous for. Or like works by other great artists."

"You never run out of words, do you?" Sister Augustine said, shaking her head while barely hiding a smile that let me know the contemporary art reference was lost on her.

"Not just anyone could create these bowls, Sister," I emphasized. "You have some of the most important gifts an artist can have: a natural instinct for combining colors *and* knowing when a piece is finished. It's remarkable."

Sister softly petted Blitzen, who responded in purring whispers from her lap. "It's God's hand that guides my own," she insisted modestly.

"Have you come up with a name for them yet?" I had suggested that she give the bowls a name, something we could possibly market to the general public. I had started brainstorming ideas as to how we could get more people into the shop. Already, my word-of-mouth campaign had started a trickle of new customers, including the person who bought the six bowls fresh out of the kiln before I even got to see them. This was such a welcome distraction from everything else going on in my life at the moment.

"As a matter of fact, I have."

"What is it?"

Sister smiled, holding me in suspense for a few beats. "I'm going to call them Gussie's Special."

"*Gussie?* Where did you come up with that name? It's so unique."

As if on cue, the front door swung open and Sister John Paul, who in her fifties was one of the youngest nuns at St. Joseph Monastery, hurried in. She was always bubbling with energy and a clear affection for Sister Augustine. "Hey, John!" she greeted me. I waved back. She then turned her attention to Sister Augustine and Blitzen.

"Hey, Gussie, I'm checking to see if you need anything. Sister Jacinta and I are running to the store."

My eyes grew wide and a smile overtook my face as I looked at Sister Augustine.

"No, I'm good," she replied, flashing me a grin.

"Nice bowls," Sister John Paul commented, examining the Gussie's Specials at the end of the table. "Are these the ones you were telling me about?"

"Yes," Sister Augustine answered.

"You never cease to amaze me, Gussie," Sister John Paul said. "I hear you're responsible for this," she added, looking at me.

"I'm going to make Sister Augustine a superstar," I said, only half jokingly.

Sister Augustine swatted her hands at me. "Now stop that!"

Sister John Paul teased, "Just remember us small people when you're famous, Gussie!"

Sister Augustine shook her head and rolled her eyes. "Oh, you two!"

"Gotta go," Sister John Paul said, turning and heading toward the door. "See ya, John! See you at supper, Gussie!"

"You're Gussie!" I exclaimed after Sister John Paul had left.

"That's my nickname around here. So I thought it was a good name for the bowls."

"I think it's a *perfect* name for the bowls!"

Sister Augustine glanced at her watch. "It's time," she said, nudging Blitzen from her lap and rising. Saint Joseph, in full color now, was set on the table amid a village of paint bottles and bisqueware.

"Time for what?"

"Follow me, you'll see."

Sister rounded the tables and led me into the back room. She paused by a middle table filled with square and rectangular white molds.

"This one," she said, pointing to a large cube, its two halves held together by thick black rubber bands and a belt. "What's inside?"

"What do you mean?"

"What's inside this mold?" She rephrased her question, tapping the top for emphasis.

I realized that this was part two of the lesson my friend had started before Sister John Paul walked in.

I was still lost. "Um, I don't know." I wondered what I was missing here.

"Please remove the rubber bands and belt, while I hold the mold together," Sister instructed.

I proceeded to slip each of the eight black bands from around the white plaster block, careful to not snap Sister or myself in the process. I then unhooked the belt that had also been fastened around the middle, while Sister continued to hold the two halves together.

"Now, please help me to turn the mold on its side." Once the heavy block was on its side, Sister Augustine rested her hands on top. "Last chance. Can you tell me what's inside?"

"I don't have a clue," I lamented, feeling like a failure for not grasping the point of this little exercise.

"Grab hold of that side of the top half and I'll get this side," Sister directed me. "Now, let's carefully lift it off."

On an unspoken count of three, Sister and I raised the top of the mold, slowly and steadily.

"It's a bowl!" I announced, as if I had discovered a diamond in the rough rather than a moist piece of greenware. "A Gussie's Special! Or at least it will be one."

Sister smiled. "On the outside, all fastened shut, this mold is a mystery, isn't it? You know its general purpose, but that's it. It's like you knowing you're meant to be a teacher, and whatever else you may dream of, but you're just not sure exactly in what way yet."

Another switch flipped on in my mind.

Sister Augustine continued: "When you free this mold from all its bindings and you open it, *that's* when you see what the real purpose is inside."

"I just need to look a little deeper inside myself, is what you're telling me," I ventured.

"Each time you don't get the job you thought you were supposed to, or each time you exchange anger, fear, and confusion for gratitude, you remove another restraint that's holding you back. You free yourself to step a little closer to finding your larger, true purpose."

"We're all wrapped in lots of these black rubber bands, aren't we?"

"Yes. That's how God puts us here, like a big gift, wrapped in many ribbons. Then life adds a few of its own rubber bands. God already knows the potential inside us. It's already there, just where He put it, waiting to be discovered. But it's up to us to figure that out for ourselves and to unlock our purpose, one binding at a time."

"*I'm really scared,*" I finally confessed, laying it all on the line as raw and bluntly as possible. "I'm scared I'm going to be a failure. I'm scared I've made wrong decisions. I'm scared of taking the wrong direction in life." My fractured soul was laid bare.

"That's perfectly natural," Sister said, her tone soothing my rough edges. "The feeling will pass when you eventually see what God has in store for you."

"Have you ever been scared?" I asked.

"Of course, many times," Sister Augustine replied with a warm grin. "There's a story I've never told anyone else, but I'll tell you."

My eyes widened.

"When I was a little girl, late one afternoon I got lost in the woods near our farm, as I did from time to time. Only this time, it was different. I was chasing after a butterfly—the first one I had seen since before winter. I always loved the adventure of seeing where the bugs I followed would lead me. Before I knew it, I was in the middle of the forest and had no idea which direction was home. It was early spring and the days were still short."

"What did you do?" I could see little Anna's angelic face. Giggling and framed by brown pigtails. In her homemade calico frock, racing after the monarch, not a care in the world. The white farmhouse and barn fading behind her in a swell of fields.

"I started to cry, especially after I lost track of the butterfly. Then I really felt alone, and scared. The deeper into the forest I walked, the darker it seemed to get. I imagined all sorts of horrible things: What if a wild animal got me? What if my family never found me? . . ."

Sister paused, letting the scene of a helpless and frightened child wandering through an ominous land sync in my mind. "But then I heard what I thought was my father's voice calling out ahead of me. He sounded far away at first, but I was so relieved. The faster I walked in the direction of my father's voice, the clearer it became. Only he wasn't saying, 'Anna.' He was yelling, 'Augustine,' which I found strange. I had never heard that name before."

My friend could see I was clinging to her every word. I was right there in those woods with her, surrounded by towering pines, chestnuts, and oaks; hoots, chirps, and howls; the crunch of dried leaves, pine needles, and fallen twigs underfoot. The darkness, menacing and encroaching.

Sister went on: "I then started running toward the voice. The faster I ran, the louder it got until finally the trees opened up into a large field of grass and budding wildflowers where the sun was shining brightly just above the treetops."

I thought of my favorite field in Bear Run, edged by a thick forest. The way the sun engulfed it all day long.

"Was your dad waiting there for you?"

"No. Yet I kept hearing the voice say, 'Augustine, Augustine.' I wondered, *Who's Augustine?* I looked around and no one else was there. I soon realized that it was me the voice was calling to. Then the sun seemed to grow very large. Its white rays came together almost like a blizzard even though winter was over and the air was warm."

"What did you do then?" In my mind, I was now in that illuminated field with her.

"I just stood there," Sister answered. "I wasn't blinded by the light at all. In fact, I was able to look straight into it. The longer I stood there, the less afraid I felt. It was like the light was hugging me. Then the voice said, 'Augustine, you are blessed.'"

"*Wow.*" I exhaled, sensing what that must have felt like. "Then what?"

"That's all the voice said: 'Augustine, you are blessed.' Shortly after that, I heard my father calling from the woods behind me. 'Anna, Anna!' he yelled. I turned to see him running toward me with the biggest smile on his face. I was so happy to see him!"

"But that voice you heard? It had to be . . ."

Sister brought her hands to her chest and said, "I've carried it in my heart ever since. From that moment on, deep down I knew I would dedicate my life to God."

"Why haven't you ever told anyone about your experience that day?" I felt so honored and humbled that she chose to tell me.

Sister Augustine grinned. "Every story has its time to be told, John," she said. "Even if it is more than eighty years later."

All I could do was nod my head where words failed me, and somehow feel a little less scared and lost.

6

TINY CROSSES

I PAUSED ON THE FRONT PORCH, LOOKING INTO THE CERAMIC shop through the screen door while a warm autumn breeze curled around me. At the one long table in her studio, I could see Sister Augustine, in full black and white habit and a flowery bib apron. She was standing over two medium-size balls of clay with a large rolling pin in hand. Even though I had been visiting her almost every week for nearly two years now, each time was a unique experience captured detail for detail as a vignette in the memory book of my mind.

As I watched, she proceeded like a master baker, using the rolling pin to press one of the balls gently down and roll. The wooden rosary beads suspended from her waist swayed with each back-and-forth movement. She repeated this feat for several minutes, exhibiting impressive forearm stamina, until the gray ball was a smooth pancake spread out on the table.

"You could always moonlight in a bakery, if you wanted," I called out through the shop when I finally entered.

Sister turned toward me and laughed. "This dough wouldn't be too tasty, would it?" she deadpanned with a huge smile.

The table she was working on had been cleared of everything else in preparation for the current project.

"What are you making?"

"*Your* crosses." Sister motioned to the small tin cookie cutter that would soon carve disks of clay into miniature crosses about two inches wide and three inches long. I had originally seen a few of the painted and glazed crosses in her shop early on and bought them to give away as small tokens of my appreciation.

About a week earlier, I placed this current order for a special, new batch that I intended to send back to Honduras with my cousin Father Herald, who was a Franciscan missionary there. When I told Sister of my intentions, she reacted with that twinkle in her eyes I had come to cherish since meeting her. The thought of her small crosses making the journey to another country excited her as well.

"Want some help?" As an artist myself, I was drawn to any project where I got to work with my hands and get a little messy, whether it was sanding and hammering a board to get it ready for one of my folk art paintings or hauling large stones and transplanting shrubs to freshen up some little corner of mine in the world.

"How are you at rolling out dough?"

I laughed. I had had my practice while working on several beer bread recipes for my cookbook, but still there was an art and a science to it that seemed forever relegated to the domain of moms and grandmas. "I probably won't be as good as you. But I'll give it a shot!"

"Good, because my arms could use a rest. There's nothing to it, just a little old-fashioned elbow grease."

Right, I thought.

Sister Augustine handed me the old rolling pin, which I suspected had been used at the convent for many years, likely starting out in the kitchen, then finding its way to the ceramic studio to be repurposed for a different kind of art form. Sister sat in her nearby mint-green spindle chair, where she could supervise and guide me.

"The key is to roll back and forth with even pressure, until the clay is flattened to about a quarter inch thick. It might seem like you'll never get there, but you will. Balls of clay like this take time to get them where you want. The crosses don't turn out so well if they're too thick or too thin."

She had made the first pancake, which would likely yield about ten crosses. A second ball was now awaiting my handiwork.

"This will be a good practice in patience," I said with a laugh. I was still working on that virtue.

"Yes," Sister confirmed with a wink.

I was stiff at first, locking my elbows, tightly gripping each end of the rolling pin, and pushing the wooden cylinder down hard into the ball of clay. I could practically hear the *smoosh* as the rolling pin separated the ball into two messy clumps and came to rest on the table, producing a *thud* in my mind.

Sister raised her eyebrows and giggled. "You were a bit ambitious on that try!"

"Guess I won't be getting a job in a bakery anytime soon."

"Just knead the clay back into a ball and begin again," she instructed. "You'll get the hang of it."

I pulled the rolling pin from its mushy clay sandwich and set it aside. I then started to work the lumpy blob with my hands. The clay was cool, moist, and stubborn. Muscles that I never knew I had in my hands and forearms began to protest while I wrestled the tough clay back into a ball.

In that space during our visits, Sister and I were like two lone explorers cloistered on a deserted island. Living off the land with only each other to rely on. Teacher and student. Master and apprentice. But mainly, friend and friend.

Some of our most memorable discussions began with a simple question. For me, each answer was like wisdom fresh off the vine. Rarely in this life do you get to ask someone any question you want and know that there will be an answer *and* it will have a transformative meaning for you. It's also by some uncommon grace for sure when we realize that the messenger herself standing before us is a rare gift we've been given.

As I worked at re-creating the clay ball, I turned to Sister.

"Of everything you've learned in life, what is the most important lesson?" I was well aware that I had pulled no punches with this question and lobbed a biggie in my friend's direction.

"Oh my," Sister Augustine uttered, coaxing Blitzen onto her lap from under the table. He promptly hopped up and awaited her gentle hand on his back. "There isn't just one lesson. I could give you a whole list."

"Then you pick one to start." I continued to squeeze and form the tenacious clay into at least something that resembled Sister's perfect orb.

She looked down at Blitzen, petting his thick calico fur. I could tell my friend was carefully contemplating her choice of topic for the day.

"Forgiveness," Sister finally said, looking up at me without a hint of doubt.

"Forgiveness," I repeated.

"Forgiveness is the crucial turning point for so much of what happens to us in this life. People often see it as an end goal. But it's really a beginning. With it, we move forward. Without it, we are at a standstill."

"It's not easy to forgive," I commented, the scene of a young, skinny boy on a cool fall day long ago coming into focus. His arms being pulled taut by two older kids as if they were playing tug-of-war, his feet being pinned to the ground by a third. He's taunted with cruel, ugly words. A fourth kid, the ringleader, stuffs the young boy's shirt, pants, and mouth with dirt, grass, and dried leaves, like he's a living scarecrow.

"Sometimes, forgiveness seems impossible," I added. The image in my mind was a personal demon rearing its ugly head.

A persistent torment that had rived my childhood innocence much like a butcher tears meat from the bone.

"Nothing is impossible," Sister said. "But, yes, forgiveness is not easy. By design, it's not meant to be easy. If it were, it would have little meaning. Yet, it's one of the greatest gifts in this world that we can give to one another, and to ourselves."

I looked quizzically at my friend, the clump of clay still turning in my hands like one of those rubbery stress balls. It was starting to take form, justifying the dull ache still spreading in my fingers and arms. Perhaps those pangs signaled a release—a long-held toxin finally working its way out of my muscles and pores.

"When someone hurts us, especially in a very deep way, what is our first instinct as human beings?" Sister asked.

"To hurt them back." My eyes fixated on the wad of earth being transformed in my hands. It was amazing how quickly those words flew past my lips with little need for thought. That boy—that younger, doe-eyed version of me—stared helplessly back at me now across two and a half decades. With pleading, desperate eyes. The bullies during those years never looked into my eyes.

"Exactly. But that's the wrong approach, always. That, unfortunately, is the common response most people have when someone hurts them. That approach, though, only mires our heart and soul in quicksand."

"Why do you think our general reaction is to hurt back?"

"These days, people are so caught up in a world that's competitive and full of temptations. Everyone wants something bigger or more than their neighbor has. A bigger house, a bigger job, more money, more clothes, more gadgets, more popularity, more things. Everyone tries to outdo one another. It's rare to hear of someone who wants a bigger heart, a bigger faith, or a bigger sense of gratitude for what they already have. This kind of materialism and attachment makes people greedy and territorial. It's all about *me, me, me* and *mine, mine, mine* for so many people, especially our young people today. So when someone hurts us, the temptation to strike back is often too great to resist. All just to prove we're right and that we know best."

"We have a right to defend ourselves, don't we?" I challenged her. I could feel the bullies tugging on my arms again like they were trying to pull them off and holding my feet tight to the ground. I was paralyzed. Helpless. I could taste the grittiness of the earth and dried leaves forced into my mouth, the scratch and shame as they were pushed by the fistful into my shirt and down my pants.

"Eye for an eye?"

"Something like that. Maybe not *literally!*" *Maybe just a handful of dirt shoved into their mouths,* I thought. *See how they like it.* Even twenty-five years later, wounds still gape and bleed.

"But it is just that, *literally.* Whether it's eyes, feelings, possessions, or life itself. Whatever you do to me, I'm compelled to do right back to you, maybe even worse to really prove the greatness and the dominance I think I have or deserve over you. What does that accomplish?"

I thought for a moment. "You gouge out my eye, I gouge out your eye," I answered. "That just leaves the two of us blind."

"Which only makes the world a little darker for everyone." Sister then nodded toward the ball of clay in my hand. "I think that's ready."

I glanced down to see a smooth sphere in my hands, just like the one Sister Augustine had created to begin with. The tension in my hands and arms was replaced by the calm that comes after a good, long morning stretch. I laughed. "Not too shabby."

"Be more gentle this time with the rolling pin," Sister advised with an impish grin. "Gently and firmly move the pin back and forth from the beginning, instead of pushing straight

down. Remember, it takes time. A steady and consistent motion will eventually transform that ball into the full moon we're
looking for."

Okay, I nodded, and did as she instructed. Slowly, the ball I
had formed began to soften into a thick oblong and then a wider
disk.

"But what about someone who has hurt us badly? How do
we forgive them?" I circled back around to the topic at hand.

"Do you have someone in mind?" Sister inquired. She often
knew exactly what I was thinking.

"Yes, there is someone . . . well many people, who hurt me
very badly a long time ago, and I'm still struggling to forgive
them. Of course, it seems that just about every day someone
hurts us in some way."

"I see," Sister said, slowly nodding her head as she caressed
Blitzen's back. She never pressured me to tell her more than I
was ready to reveal. I wanted to spare her the indelible snapshot
of me splayed and humiliated on that field as a child. "Who do
you think forgiveness is for?"

"Well, we forgive the person or people who hurt us, so them,
I guess."

"Forgiveness is an act of love and compassion. Yes, it is a gift
we give to the person who hurt us, which is often the hardest
part for people to understand. In our minds, that often means
we're letting that person off the hook for whatever they did to
us. But ultimately, when we forgive someone, that act is also a
gift of love and compassion, *and* freedom, that only we can give
to ourselves."

"I never thought of it like that before." I paused, soaking
in her words. My clay discus was halfway to where it needed
to be for the crosses. "It's usually hard to actually tell someone
you forgive them." The little gang of bullies from that fall day
and the others I had encountered at school were now scattered,

raising families and working in various professions. It wasn't like I could go knocking on each of their front doors bearing a basket of forgiveness. They probably wouldn't even remember what they had done to me. Even though I would never forget.

"You don't have to say it out loud," Sister said. "Sure, you can tell someone, 'I forgive you,' or write it in a letter. But more often than not, that isn't feasible."

"So then what?" I had resumed my rolling back and forth, heading into the final stretch. My large gray moon was taking shape.

"You can simply envision that person in your mind and what they did to hurt you, and then say, 'I forgive you.'"

"It's that easy?" I was skeptical.

Sister laughed. "Yes, and no. Was it easy rolling out that clay?"

"No, not really."

I looked down to see a full moon spread out beneath my rolling pin. Sister picked up a nearby wooden ruler—the brunt of many stories and jokes about strict, knuckle-cracking nuns told by my parents' generation—and measured. I chuckled to myself.

"A quarter inch exactly," she said.

"Like you said, it took time," I commented.

"And a steady, consistent hand, which you didn't start out with," my friend added. "You may have to repeat those three words, 'I forgive you,' to yourself a dozen times, a hundred times, or maybe even more whenever the thought of that person pops up in your mind. Eventually, though, that anger and hurt you feel will disappear. You'll finally be able to let it go and find peace. Then, when you think of that person, it can be with love and gratitude for the lesson they taught you."

I was quiet for a moment, thinking. "Our enemies then become our teachers," I realized.

"Now you're catching on! Let those who hurt you become the wings that lift you up and help you to soar."

On a top shelf nearby, the statue of an eagle—the symbol of my namesake Saint John Evangelist—caught my eye for the first time. His concentrated gaze seemed to emphasize Sister's words. Still, I doubted. "But doesn't that still let them off the hook?"

"What do *you* think?" Sister Augustine turned the question back over to me. One of her greatest lessons—the benchmark of a genuine teacher—was showing me how to unlock answers within myself and to further refine my own guiding principles.

While I tossed the question around in my mind, Sister placed Blitzen on the floor, where he scurried away to some certain mischief. She then stood and examined the two large circles of clay side by side in front of us on the table.

"Perfect," she declared. Sister then picked up the old cookie cutter. I assumed the small tin cross had also once been used in the convent's kitchen during a bygone era. Its sturdy construction and sharp edges were now ideal for working with clay.

Starting at the edge of her original circle, Sister Augustine firmly pressed the sharp metal rim of the cookie cutter straight down, then pulled up in reverse. The clean outline of a cross was left cut into the clay. She then repeated the simple motion, leaving a procession of crosses dancing around the circle.

While she did this, I closely studied the gold band on her right ring finger. I knew Sister would have received it upon taking her final vows almost seventy years earlier. The ring's raised design and inscriptions had been worn down to a smooth burnish. Its sheen complemented the eighty-eight-year-old hand it adorned. For me at thirty-two, it was a comforting symbol of time and devotion. Something to aspire toward.

"I agree with you," I finally answered. "Forgiveness is also a gift we give to ourselves; maybe it's even a greater gift to ourselves than to the person who hurt us." Shoving dirt into those bullies' mouths would only have made all of us choke. No good would have come of that.

"Yes," Sister confirmed, pressing another cross into the clay.

The simplicity of her affirmation encouraged me to continue with the realization sprouting in my mind. "The freedom you mentioned that comes to us when we forgive, it doesn't mean that the person who hurts us gets a free pass. It means we get relief from the hurt." I paused. Took a deep breath.

"And we get detachment from the burden of holding a grudge, or clinging to anger and hatred," Sister said, elaborating upon my thought. "As for the person who hurt us, God sees all. He'll know how to take care of them in His own way and in His own time. That need not be our concern."

I could once more see those young bullies on that field. Once more feel my arms outstretched and my feet pinned to the ground by their brute hands and hatred. Once more taste and feel the sting of dirt, grass, and crunchy leaves. I was looking straight into my own eyes as a child, across decades of hurt and embarrassment. I smiled and nodded my reassurance to that young boy, who was me. For the first time, I then turned to each of those bullies circling me on that field like wild animals. Eye to eye, to each one of them I said, "I forgive you." It was a start.

"Your turn," Sister Augustine said, pulling me back to here and now, and handing me the miniature tin cross. Her circle was filled with crosses, which she was starting to gently remove like cookies with a palette knife.

I felt another weight lifted from my shoulders. A fresh, toothsome breeze through the screen door baptized the moment.

I emulated what I had seen Sister do, pressing the cross's edges straight down into my clay moon, then pulling up, again and again.

"How can we understand forgiveness for the most awful

things?" I pushed on, thirsting for more of Sister's refreshing insight. "Like a drunk driver killing another young driver. Someone abusing their spouse. A rapist. Or, how about a terrorist who kills thousands of people? I can't wrap my mind around those kinds of things, let alone even think about how forgiveness comes into play."

"The easiest answer I can give you is literally at your fingertips," Sister replied, nodding toward the table.

I looked down, feeling the perimeter of the tin cross dig into my forefingers and thumbs as I pressed it into the clay. "Father, forgive them, for they know not what they do," I said automatically, as if I were in sixth-grade religion class again at Queen of the World Parish elementary school, standing in front of Sister Joachim reciting my catechism.

"Yes, that's the clearest answer we have in the Lord's own voice to questions of evil and forgiveness," Sister said. "We must never forget that the Devil is hard at work, too, in this world. In so many ways, we've become a world that no longer values life. Born or unborn, human or animal. Even our living planet is being massacred every second somewhere. Instead of being seen as precious, life has become something to be wasted and discarded without much thought. Yet still, there are those glowing examples we see of parents forgiving their child's murderer, a woman forgiving her rapist, a paralyzed man reaching out in forgiveness to the person whose car struck him. Even look at abused animals and how they return lovingly to us human beings, recognizing that we're not all bad."

"What you're saying," I interjected, "is that forgiveness is deeply ingrained within every living being. We each have the capacity to forgive and to let go."

"That was proven by our Lord on the cross as surely as it is by each of these other examples from everyday life," Sister Augustine confirmed.

I paused, my circle halfway filled with crosses. Images of such people, hurt and brutalized yet still forgiving, passed through my mind. Examples of these people filled the news every day for us all to see.

Sister Augustine continued: "Those people, who forgive under the most extreme circumstances, they are messengers. But too often we hear their stories, we look in amazement at their compassion toward their persecutors, and we think, *I could never do that.* Then we move on to the next thing. While they forgive, we, unfortunately, too often forget."

"That we do for sure," I said. My eyes traced the cruciate lines within my circle. Delicate and unassuming. Continuous and powerful. I realized that while the adage "To whom much is given, much is expected" holds true, even more potent is the understanding that from whom much is taken, much is also expected.

"What we fail to realize is that those people are you and me," Sister said. "But for the grace of God, they, and whatever atrocities happened to them, *are* you and me."

I proceeded to fill the remainder of my flat clay moon with crosses, finishing just as Sister removed the last of her clay crosses with the palette knife. She was a step ahead of me. Her circle was now a template of tiny, rood-shaped windows. It looked like it was waiting for stained glass to be inserted so it could then punctuate some vaulted chapel window. Instead, Sister gathered the skeleton of clay in her hand, kneading it into a small ball. Waste not, want not.

"Have you ever had a hard time forgiving someone?" I asked. I was now using the palette knife to remove my crosses while Sister Augustine once more used the wooden rolling pin to transform her new clay ball into a petite pancake.

"Of course," she said without hesitation, her eyes focused on her work. "These black robes don't make me any less human.

The Devil is hard at work everywhere. Which means we must be, too!"

I laughed. *Of course,* I thought. "But I suspect the Devil would meet his match in you."

Sister laughed. "Forgiveness is an everyday practice, even inside these walls."

"Finished," I exclaimed, proudly lifting the last cross from my circle and setting it up above on the table with the others. "We've got quite the lineup there!"

"You're not finished yet," Sister said with a grin. "You can ball up the clay you have left there and roll it out to make a few more crosses, if you'd like." Which meant a few more crosses that could then be fired and painted by Sister Augustine, and sent to Honduras with Father Herald.

I trusted that each cross would deliver its own message to its eventual recipient, whom I'd never likely meet. That person would never know of the conversation about forgiveness that an old nun and a young guy had a world away from them one sunny autumn afternoon. Or, that a redemptive warm breeze was kneaded into the fired clay they held in their hands.

They would find their own meaning in that tiny cross—so fragile, yet resilient—which had found its way to them. I had faith they would happen upon their own answer to a question or an atonement for a hurt they might have. And just maybe, holding that handmade cross, and seeing Sister Augustine's initials, "S.M.A.," which I would insist she write in black Sharpie on the back, they'd realize that someone somewhere in the world loved them, no matter what.

"Yes, a few more crosses," I said, beginning again to work my clay into a perfect little globe.

PART THREE

7

JOYFUL MYSTERIES

WE BEGAN THE AFTERNOON IN THE KILN ROOM, WHERE I handed glazed pieces to Sister Augustine, who then meticulously arranged them for firing. This was followed by her customary prayer, a sprinkling of Holy Water, and the brief invocation to Saint Francis to help ensure that the joys outnumbered the sorrows when the process was complete.

After she closed the lid, I asked, "Sister, do you by any chance have a mold for a snowman?" Even though it was an eighty-five-degree summer day, I was already thinking ahead to Christmas.

"I do," she replied. "Haven't used it in years, but it's in the back room somewhere. Should we go have a look?"

Sister Augustine led me to the far corner in the back room. Hundreds of white plaster molds that looked like exaggerated sugar cubes in all different sizes filled the shelves, as well as claiming significant real estate on the floor.

"Now let's see," Sister said, running her hand along the smooth molds on a middle shelf. "These are mostly the Christmas ones. That snowman should be around here somewhere. Saint Anthony, a little help here would be nice." Many of the molds were labeled with a pencil in Sister Augustine's handwriting. But it didn't matter, she seemed to know them by heart.

"There are so many," I said with wonderment.

"You won't find many of these molds anywhere else. They've all pretty much been with me since the beginning. All antiques now that no one wants anymore."

I doubted that last part was true and I was going to prove it to my friend one way or another. "How long has it been since you've used these molds?"

"Ages," Sister answered with a chuckle. "Here it is," she then said, pulling a small rectangular mold from the shelf. She unfastened the thick black rubber bands holding the two halves together. "Yep, here's your snowman," she confirmed, handing it to me.

I ran my fingers over the scooped-out impressions inside each half. "This looks like a snowman from the fifties or sixties," I said excitedly. I could see him singing and dancing across a snowy black-and-white RCA screen while paper flakes fell all around.

"I wouldn't doubt it. These molds are as old as Methuselah, just like me."

I laughed. "Oh stop!" I pretended to scold. "I have a cousin who collects snowmen. She'll want one of these for sure. Plus, you should do a few to have in the shop for the open house. And one for me, of course."

"I suppose I can do that," Sister Augustine said. "But I don't know how many I can get done with the Nativity orders and the Gussie's Specials you think we also need for the open house." She raised her brow. "Especially since you keep buying just about every bowl I make." It was her turn to scold me, with a smile.

We both knew that up at the Trifles and Treasures Gift Shop, Sister Margoretta was already busy spearheading plans for her annual Christmas Open House, which was still several months away. Held on the first weekend in December, the event served as a kickoff to the holiday season in St. Marys and raised money for the convent. The epicenter for the festive event had always been the gift shop. This year, for the first time, Sister's ceramic shop was also being included in a big way. A few months earlier, I had suggested this possibility to Sister Margoretta, who happily agreed, saying, "The more the merrier!" It really was a no-brainer. I couldn't believe the ceramic shop was never a major part of the open house before, but I suspected my friend's penchant for privacy and modesty had something to do with that. I then asked Sister Augustine if she'd like to be a part of the festivities. She thought for a moment, then replied, "I think that could be fun! There's a first time for everything." Many in the community would now get to discover Sister's unique and beautiful work just as I had two and a half years earlier.

I had an idea as to how Sister could quickly produce enough snowmen for the open house. "All you have to do with these snowmen is paint them white."

"Really? All white? No colors for the eyes, or hat, or scarf? Only clear glaze? I can't imagine anyone would want something so simple."

"People will love them," I assured her. "Trust me. Especially anyone who collects snowmen. You can't find vintage ones like this anymore, and certainly not handmade."

"Okay, that I can do! Sounds easy enough."

"What are those molds for way up above?" I pointed to the top shelf and moved in for a closer look.

"Just some old vases."

"Can I take a look at them?"

"Sure," Sister replied, stepping back. "Have at it."

"Kid in a candy store" would be vastly understating how I felt in that moment. I had been waiting to explore this area since the first time I stepped into the back room. I pulled one large mold from the top shelf and set it on the floor. I unfastened the belt and removed the rubber bands holding the halves together and separated them.

"Sister!" I exclaimed, seeing a carved-out impression the size of a small watermelon. "This vase is so Mid-Century Modern!"

Eighty-nine-year-old Sister Augustine grinned and swatted her hand toward me playfully. "There you go with your words again. You never run out."

"I'm serious, people would pay a lot of money for a vase like this and it wouldn't even be handmade like yours. These kinds of pieces are all the rage now."

I could tell from the befuddled expression on Sister's face that she thought I was crazy.

"Can you make one or two of these for the open house? Maybe do them as Gussie's Specials," I continued.

"Yes, set the mold over here," she replied, being a good sport and pointing to the small, empty patch of floor space next to the tub of wet clay.

I proceeded to work my way methodically through each mold on the shelves, setting off a series of exclamations about the treasures I was discovering, followed by Sister's bemused reactions. I could see all of them being transformed by Sister Augustine's hand into an entire shop full of colorful, classic pieces the likes of which people go to great lengths to find. I explained to Sister how entire television shows and magazines drooled over this kind of stuff, and what they had wasn't brought to life by someone as talented as her.

I opened a long, flat mold. "Sister, what is this plate? It's incredible!"

"That one is for an ashtray, not a plate," Sister corrected with a laugh. By now she was sitting on top of three large rediscovered molds—one for a taller snowman and two others for a Santa and Mrs. Claus, all of which had been added to her open house to-do list. "I made a lot of those ashtrays in the sixties."

"This would make a fun candy dish."

"You think? An ashtray as a candy dish?" The look on her

face registered doubt along with a playful glow that let me know she was game for the ride.

"That's called taking artistic license," I declared. "No one will even realize what it *was* meant to be. Maybe do it in that great turquoise blue you have that I love so much."

"Add it to the pile," Sister deadpanned, nodding her head to the left.

"What are these?" I asked next, opening a series of other molds and lifting them toward Sister. Even Blitzen had come sniffing around by this point to see what all the fuss was about.

"Small ceramic boxes." Sister Augustine leaned forward for a better look. "That one is a heart-shaped box with doves on top. The other is a round box with a lacy pattern. I made a bunch of those once upon a time, too."

"Any chance . . ."

"On the pile they go," Sister said, like it was the refrain to a song she and I were composing. "*Piles* now! Good thing I have a few months."

I covered my mouth, looking around at the mess we—*okay, I*—had created.

Sister Augustine and I were surrounded by a half-built igloo made of plaster molds. Large cubes, small cubes, long blocks, and short ones that hadn't seen the light of day in decades. Each about to be resurrected.

"Doesn't look like God is planning to let me rest anytime soon," Sister remarked with a glint in her eyes. "Guess He knows best."

"Nor am I going to let you rest," I joked.

Sister shook her head. "I'd probably have better luck getting a day off from God!"

Speaking of Whom . . . The topic of God had been weighing heavily on my mind lately. I started to have major doubts as I continued to face personal and professional challenges. I prayed, and pleaded even, for God to help me with so many things, but I feared either He was hard of hearing, since I was still not seeing the results I was hoping and asking for every day, or that no one was on the other end of my long-distance call for help.

I looked around the room, amazed at the stockpile of molds Sister had managed to amass over the years. God clearly gave her many gifts as a nun, artist, and teacher. It got me wondering if she had ever encountered a crossroads, a moment when she had questioned the uncertain road ahead.

"Sister, do you ever doubt God?" I asked, sitting cross-legged on the floor, my back against the wall of plaster blocks. The two halves of the heart box mold rested on my lap, like an open locket.

"No," Sister Augustine answered without hesitation. Blitzen was now situated comfortably on her lap, purring and watching me. "I always know God will lead me in the right direction, whether I want to go or not at the time."

Sister then told me how during the 1970s, God had called her away from St. Joseph Monastery and her ceramic shop. She was sent to Dacada, Wisconsin, where she worked as a teacher and did sacristy work at a parish there. "It was hard to leave my shop that I loved so much," Sister recalled, "but I knew that was what God wanted me to do at that time in my life. It was part of His plan for me. I guess He just wanted me to experience a little bit more of His world and expand my horizons. I trusted that God knew what He was doing, and eventually He brought me right back here. That's what having faith is all about, John, and the knowledge that comes with having outlived just about everyone else." My friend trailed off in a flurry of soft giggles, delivering that last part like the punch line to a joke that may have started with something like "You know you're old when . . ."

Sister's story reminded me of my own journey that had taken

me away from home and then eventually brought me back. Her unwavering devotion and trust in God as the ultimate pilot of her life was inspiring. I wondered if I could ever have that depth of faith. Especially with the doubts and questions I had. At the moment, I was more like those who had wandered the desert on a forty-year journey that should have only taken eleven days.

"Do you think it's a sin to doubt God, or to wonder if He even exists?"

"I think it's perfectly natural to question God. Even Jesus did that," Sister replied. "Doubt and questions are pathways that lead to answers, if you allow them to."

An only child, I was born into a very faith-driven family. Three of my great uncles and a great-great-uncle had been priests, and two cousins on the Brewery side of the family currently were—Father Paul and Father Herald. When I was a kid and my Grandma Schlimm lived with us, she would regularly invite her friend Father Cyril to say Mass in our living room. He gave me my first picture Bible and a book about angels.

Each night, my dad, Jack, a former stock car racer, butcher, and grave digger turned businessman who could play the piano and accordion by ear, knelt beside his bed to pray. My mom, Barb, a former secretary and volunteer teacher's aide who stayed home to raise me, spent an hour every day quietly saying the rosary, followed by a litany of prayers and novenas. She practically had Saint Thérèse on speed dial and sure enough the red roses and answers came. They were even married on the Feast of the Guardian Angels, October 2. My parents came of age in the fifties—high school sweethearts, Class of 1956—a simpler, more innocent time. I thought of them and their friends as the *Grease* Generation. In my mind, Dad and Mom were Danny Zuko and Sandy Olsson all grown up. Meanwhile, instead of going to Mass these days, many Sundays their Gen-Xer son would wander through the woods or drive around for the hour. Weekly pilgrimages, but in search of what? Purpose, direction, acceptance, the Promised Land? All the above?

I pressed on with my questions like a dedicated interviewer who had dropped by the Pearly Gates one afternoon to do a little fact-checking. "Don't you ever wonder why, if God exists, He would allow a tornado, or a flood, or an earthquake that kills and hurts so many people? Or how about a terrorist attack?"

"Or the murder of His own son?" Sister Augustine paused, wide-eyed, letting that one hang in the air for a few heartbeats. "There are some questions that we'll never have the full answers to in this life, such as why evil exists. You always have to re-member, the Devil is hard at work, too," she continued. "But I never blame God when those terrible things happen. However, I do see Him at work during those times."

"How so?"

"Think of how those tragedies bring everyone so close to-gether to help out, and think of the rescuers during those di-sasters, and the miraculous stories of survival that each of those tragedies has. That's all God at work. It's all tangible, something we can see."

"It's hard sometimes to believe in *someone* we can't see, though, you know?"

"What is it you think you should see exactly?" Sister turned the question back on me. I clearly wasn't getting it yet.

I thought for a moment, juggling the possible answers in my mind. "I don't know. Maybe a really old man with a long white beard. Sitting on a throne. Surrounded by lots of angels. Every-thing floating somewhere way up in the sky. It almost seems easier to just believe that what you see is what you get here on earth." I managed a weak, unconvincing smile. Even Blitzen looked unimpressed with my answer.

"Maybe you're looking with the wrong eyes," Sister said. "If the existence of God was as easy as an answer to a yes-or-no question, or someone we could see standing in front of us, there wouldn't be much substance or purpose, now would there?"

"I suppose not," I answered, "but what do you mean by wrong eyes?"

"I mean God is something you have to work at to under-stand. I'm still working on it. It's a lifelong mission. So often these days, people walk around blind when their eyes are wide open. They fail to see what's right in front of them. You can see God with your physical eyes, if you really look. Those rescue workers, the other generous people who pitch in during trage-dies, and the miraculous cases of survival—that's all something you can see, and that's God at work. Even the disappointments in this life, God's in those, too."

"Then I guess He's visiting me a lot lately!" I said sarcasti-cally.

Sister laughed. "All those sorrows and disappointments are also part of His plan for getting you to where you're supposed to be."

Then it clicked. "The road to yes is paved with many nos," I said slowly, purposely sounding out every syllable to grasp the intricacies of this new language I was learning. Maybe there was still hope, then, for finding my dream teaching job or a pub-lisher for my top-secret cookbook project, or simply peace of mind. "What you're saying is that God is found in the yeses *and* the nos in this life."

In theory it made sense, or maybe it was just my inner pub-licist's spin to make something sound better than it really was.

Sister nodded. "Yes, God is everywhere." She then went on, "The sun, trees, flowers, snowflakes, stars—there isn't a human being alive who can re-create any of those things. When you look at them, you see God's creation."

I interjected, "When I look at your Gussie's Specials, at all those colors and patterns, and the thoughts they inspire in my mind, I see something divine there, too." Each rippled bowl was an allegory—clay and paint radiating something much greater than art supplies—a vibrant nod to the "treasure in earthen vessels" that the apostle Paul describes in 2 Corinthians 4:7.

Sister's modesty prevented her from acknowledging, or confirming, my observation with anything other than a smile and a quick wink.

She continued: "When you look into someone else's eyes, whether they're a loved one or a person who has hurt you, you're looking into eyes that have been molded by God. Even when we gaze into an animal's eyes, you see God's handiwork, if you're really looking."

In that case, I laughed to myself, God's handiwork, rendered in calico fur, was staring mischievously at me from Sister's lap. I wondered what Blitzen thought about all this. Maybe his contentment at the moment answered for him.

"But that's just one way of seeing God," Sister said. "Each of your other senses is also an eye with which to see God at work, with your hands, your nose, your ears, your taste buds. No human being can re-create any of those senses, either. God gave you those gifts that only He can create in order to let you see the world and feel Him around you in infinite ways."

"How can someone open all those eyes and really see God?"

"It's getting harder in this modern world, when so many people are attached to material things and quick fixes. Everything is moving so quickly, leaving little time for people to stop and contemplate, and experience, what is right there in front of them. God isn't just *out there* somewhere; He's also all around you wherever you are," Sister said. "By design, God doesn't mean for you to see or understand Him all at once. I imagine that would be rather overwhelming. Instead, He's like a giant jigsaw puzzle you slowly put together moment by moment over years and eventually a picture forms. Or like this mountain of molds here."

I looked around at the fortress of white plaster blocks surrounding us. I felt cozy and protected there on that floor.

Sister Augustine asked, "When we first walked in here today, what did you see in this corner?"

"Lots of ceramic molds." My answer felt so banal.

"Yes. Blocks of many shapes and sizes, each sealed shut with rubber bands and belts."

Her point started to become clearer. "And one by one, I opened each of them," I said.

"And judging from your reaction each time, and the pile of work I now have to keep me busy for the next few months, I'd say you were excited and happy with what you saw."

"Yes, and in my mind, I can see what each one has the potential of becoming."

"Each time we pause to study a blade of grass, savor a fresh, juicy orange, marvel at a firefighter racing into a burning house to save someone, or even when we handle these molds, we allow ourselves to experience God at work in this world. The smell of the wet clay in this room and the sound of the motor that runs the hose I use to fill these molds with that clay, those, too, are opportunities to experience God. We have to see, with our entire bodies and souls, before we can truly understand."

On my lap, my fingers swept around the carved ridges—a Braille for the soul—that would soon become a heart-shaped box. Literally and figuratively, I was surrounded by God's building blocks. The haze in my mind inched upward like a stage curtain, affording me a peek beneath so that I might understand God, and the journey before me, a little more clearly.

8

GOD'S TIME

I SAT FOR TWENTY MINUTES AT THE TABLE WHILE SISTER Augustine slept in her mint-green spindle chair across from me. Just below a tiny, peaceful smile, her head was gently propped in place on the stiff white linen portion of the coif under her chin. Wearing a blue-and-white-checkered bib apron, she was bathed in an aureole of white sunlight pouring in through the window directly behind me.

She held a paintbrush in one hand and in the other she loosely held a flat, egg-shaped plate on her lap. It was partially outlined in the forget-me-not pattern—five sky blue dots for the petals, a Sun Yellow dot in the middle, and a few green wisps for leaves—once reserved only for her cookie-cutter crosses, Easter eggs, and the Blessed Mother's robes. And my special teacup and saucer, which I now used every day. The flowers were like ones Grandma Moses may have scattered across a sunny pasture. Simple punctuations, confirming that the medium was, indeed, the message.

The plate in her hand was one I planned to give to friends as a wedding present in a few weeks. I had already given dozens of Sister's pieces as gifts, and bought many for myself. She had even etched the couple's names and the wedding date, along with her signature, into the bottom during the greenware phase. The

inscription on the piece of bisqueware was as permanent as I
hoped their marriage would be.

Nearby on the table was a Gussie's Special in progress. Sister
now always had one of the large or small rippled bowls at her
side to clean off her brushes, creating the abstract universes that
were my favorite. Sometimes, it took her up to a week to create
just one, but a few times so far she gathered up all her nearly
empty paint bottles and would create several Gussie's Specials at
a time to meet the growing demand.

It amused Sister Augustine how much the bowls excited me
and everyone else who had seen them. "You're just being nice,"
she'd say when I gushed over a new Gussie's Special fresh out
the kiln. Few ever made it into the shop. Either I bought them
for myself or as gifts, or whoever was lucky enough to walk in
and see a new one usually then walked out with it, still warm
from the oven. A joyful exodus of the colorful bowls was in full
swing at St. Joseph Monastery.

I glanced at my watch, then to Sister. She looked comfortable enough, so I didn't think I should wake her. Settled into my
own spindle chair, I wished I could sleep that well, especially
lately, when my mind kept me awake night after night with the
fervor of a twitching nerve, shifting from one worry to another.
Maybe that would change now that some good news had finally
come my way, which was my purpose for the visit. I couldn't
wait to tell my friend!

Blitzen, on the other hand, was anything but the slumbering cat I had seen cozying up in various locations around the
shop and studio. Sister's lap seemed to be his favorite snoozing
nook, but he could also be found on the counter under the front
window in the shop, in his bed beneath the left-hand table of
the horseshoe in the studio, on a top shelf in the kiln room,
or even tucked snugly in among the bisqueware in the back

room. Today, while Sister napped, Blitzen dashed around the studio like a chirpy tour guide, keeping me entertained until our friend woke up. He hopped from shelf to shelf, then from shelf onto the far table, where he maneuvered through an obstacle course of Nativity figures while I held my breath, and then leaped across the shallow ravine onto the table at which Sister and I sat. He was aware of my eyes following his every move while he performed.

Just when I thought he'd send the pair of ceramic fawns or watchful clayware eagle on the top shelf plunging to a violent demise, he'd slip past them or over them with skilled precision and grace. He seemed to take particular pleasure in taunting me as he pounced onto the table and looked me straight in the eye.

I knew this game well by now, but I still fell for it every time. I'd reach out my hand to pet him, only to have it swatted away, then see a flash of calico dash past me. The only thing missing was him teasing, "Ha, ha, ha, betchya can't catch me!" All the same, the message was loud and clear.

Sister still looked so peaceful and I didn't want to disturb her. Plus, I didn't exactly have any other place I had to be. I felt tranquil in her presence, so I sat there and happily indulged Blitzen. He and I reenacted this swat-and-dash scene about a dozen times.

When Sister Augustine awoke, it was with a chuckle, seeing Blitzen and me in mid-stare-off in front of her. "He takes a while to warm up to people, especially guys," she repeated for probably the fiftieth time since I'd first met the cat. "Come now, Blitzen, John just wants to play with you. Be nice."

The cat turned to look at Sister, then quickly returned his uncertain gaze at me. I put out my hand again, fully expecting the dismissive whack I'd become accustomed to.

This time, Blitzen sniffed, but didn't swat and dash like usual. He remained where he was.

"Go on, Blitzen," Sister urged, nudging the cat from behind.

"I'm not going to hurt you," I repeated, also for probably the fiftieth time since I'd first met him. I inched my hand closer.

Blitzen stared at my fingers hesitantly for a moment, sniffed again, and then leaned in with his left cheek, brushing against my skin. I smiled at Sister. "This is progress," I said.

"See, Blitzen, he's not so scary," Sister cooed.

I slowly moved my hand upward and began to massage Blitzen's neck. A few minutes later, I put my hand down on the table again and slid it back toward myself. Blitzen followed in slow motion with one paw forward, then another, once more nuzzling my hand.

"I think you made a new friend," Sister said with an approving nod.

Something coppery and round dangling from Blitzen's collar flickered in the sunlight streaming through the window behind me. "What's that on Blitzen's collar?" I had never noticed it, since he had never been this still at close range before.

Sister smiled. "A Saint Francis medal," she replied. "Since Francis loved animals, I've put him in charge of watching over Blitzen, especially considering what he gets into around here."

"Seems to have worked so far, for Blitzen *and* your ceramic pieces," I said, referring to Sister's custom of saying a quick prayer to the saint before closing the kiln lid.

"Most of the time, anyway. Not even Francis is perfect, though." Sister flashed a quick wink.

I began to caress the calico's neck again, and then I stopped. Each time I did this, he stepped closer, tempted by the free massage. After doing this a few times, Blitzen nuzzled nose-to-nose with me and then found his way onto my lap. A small victory.

"Yes, I think I've found a new friend," I said, rubbing Blitzen's back as he settled in. He purred his approval, then promptly fell sound asleep. It was like we had always been pals.

"He'll be your buddy for life now," Sister declared.

I was contemplating the addition of this new furry little friend into my life when I remembered I had news to share.

"Oh, I have to tell you my good news! I've been hired to teach in the Communication and the Arts department at Pitt-Bradford," I said, referring to the University of Pittsburgh at Bradford. "I start in January for the spring semester."

"That's terrific! Congratulations!" Sister threw her hands up in the air and clapped them together like celebratory cymbals. "I guess that means the high school is about to realize what they passed up by not hiring you. Their loss is the university's gain."

"You were the one who told me I wasn't meant for that job over at the high school," I reminded her. After I didn't get the high school job, Sister's guidance prompted me to cast a wider net with my resume. "And you were right." Like a refracted ray, started in one direction, life then steered me along a different road where I was really meant to go all along. Incidentally, my one-hour commute to the university would start by taking me past both the convent and my high school alma mater as I headed out of town. It was always a great feeling to see Sister's advice become a reality in my life. I told her how it was also poetic that my new place of employment was the same university where I had gone back to school only a few years earlier to earn my dual teaching certifications. Another giant circle back to the beginning. Another new beginning.

I now felt only forgiveness and gratitude toward the headmaster and the few others at the high school who had prevented me from getting that full-time English position. As the years ahead would show, they actually did me a great favor by not hiring me.

"Yes, see, God had other plans for you," Sister said.

It was clear how God had used those people at the high

school and their ulterior motives as navigational instruments, sending me on the right pathway. I could only hope He would have mercy on them for what they had done, but I was no longer looking back.

"It's very exciting!" I said. "The first course I'll be teaching is called Promotional Writing."

"You're where you're meant to be," Sister Augustine said. That was a sentiment packed with layers of important meaning for me.

One piece of the puzzle that was my new life was finally coming into place. Yet the rejection letters from publishers still kept taunting me. I hadn't mentioned my cookbook, or the struggles it had brought into my life, to Sister yet even though we had been friends for a while now. In fact, I had managed to keep it a secret from everyone. I didn't like talking about an important thing like this until something was actually happening with it. I had been holding out for the day I could surprise her, and my family and friends, by announcing that I had landed a publishing deal. Thing is, I wasn't sure anymore if that day would ever come.

But now with one item on the Get-My-Life-Back-on-Track list checked off, I felt like I didn't have a choice. I was hoping my friend could shed some light on this other endeavor and give me the nudge forward I had come to expect from her.

"Not only do I get to teach something I'm actually interested in," I explained, "but I'll also have the time I need to focus on my writing career. I'm working on a new cookbook that I'm hoping will be my first big national book."

"That sounds like fun," Sister Augustine said with wide eyes. "What's it about?"

"Beer!"

"Oh my!" she exclaimed with a smile.

"It'll have hundreds of food and drink recipes that you make with beer as an ingredient. I want it to be the world's largest beer cookbook."

"That's quite the undertaking."

"Yes, especially considering that I'm not a chef. Though I do love to eat, and beer flows through my veins, in a manner of speaking."

I reminded Sister about my family's history, which lent me the street cred to undertake a project of this magnitude. I told her again how we owned the Straub Brewery, which along with St. Joseph Monastery, was one of the most historic sites in our small town. It was founded by my great-great-grandfather, Peter Straub, in the 1870s. At age nineteen, he left his home and family in Germany with nothing more than a strong belief that God would lead him to where he was meant to go, as well as a few gold pieces sewn into his jacket and a recipe for beer. He sailed across uncertain seas and then traveled by horse and buggy to St. Marys to claim his slice of the American Dream.

I explained how the courageous and faith-driven Peter had become a role model for me. I often reflected upon a passage from his obituary, the sentiments of which we might all like to have expressed about our life at its end. But for the living, something of a blueprint also presented itself amid these words, which I held close to my heart:

"Judged from every viewpoint, Mr. Straub was a man par excellent among men. His business principles were founded on the highest plane of honesty and fair dealing. As friend and neighbor, he was a tower of strength in times of stress and need . . . and his home was ever a home of welcome and good cheer to his many friends. Above all he was a Christian gentleman and in this respect his exemplary life will always remain an inspiration to all who came within the sphere of its influence. He no doubt, had his faults too, but they were hidden in the folds of his many manly virtues."

These were roots I was proud to have my feet firmly planted upon.

Peter's arrival was preceded by that of the three Benedictine nuns who had also left Germany, braving tempestuous seas and an uncharted wilderness, to found a convent on the other end of town from where his brewery would one day stand. As further evidence of his indomitable faith and character, a stained-glass window in St. Mary's Church—one of those brilliant arrow-heads pointing Heavenward not far from where Sister and I were sitting—was dedicated to my great-great-grandfather. It depicted Jesus handing the keys of the Church to Saint Peter.

"There certainly aren't too many people like him around anymore, are there?" Sister Augustine said rhetorically. She then told me how her grandfather, also a God-fearing man, who was named Valentine, came from Bavaria. He owned his own whiskey distillery called V. Huefner & Son, which he started in the 1880s in Clarion, Pennsylvania.

We laughed over the similar journeys and interests shared by our two ancestors.

I wondered if her grandfather and my great-great-grandfather had ever crossed paths, both being around the same age and in the same boozy line of work in western Pennsylvania. I liked to think that maybe they had, perhaps sharing a few laughs and a round of boilermakers assembled with their respective creations. Maybe even sharing a hearty toast to the future. If they had met, they would never have known of the special way their families would intersect once more almost a hundred years later.

"Did you know that the oldest brewery in the world was originally a Benedictine monastery in Bavaria?" I asked.

"I've heard that," Sister replied with a grin. "Did *you know* that Saint Augustine is the patron saint of brewers?"

"No, I didn't," I said, hoping I might then have another Heavenly ally on my cookbook project.

"Have you ever had a beer?" I asked next.

My friend muffled a laugh, then scrunched up her face. "Only once, but I didn't much care for it."

"Well, I promise you'll like my recipes, especially the desserts made with beer like Double Chocolate Cake."

"*Mmmmm,* that sounds good!"

"*It will be,* if the book ever gets published," I lamented. "I've been contacting publishers about it for a long time, secretly because I wanted to surprise everyone with it. But all I get is one rejection letter after another." The surprise of rejection had been on me. *Who didn't like beer?* Other than Sister, that is. I thought the book would be a shoo-in from the start.

"God's time is not the same as our time," Sister Augustine said. "You just witnessed that with this new teaching job. One of His days might be a hundred of ours. You just have to hang in there and have faith that when the time is right, it will happen."

"I'm doing my best, but it's not easy," I complained. Yet, what Sister had said helped me to start seeing life as more than something that's lived in hours and days, or rejection letters. "As you know, I'm even named after Saint John Evangelist . . ."

". . . The patron saint of writers," Sister Augustine added, finishing my sentence. "Yes, he's a good one."

For sure, I nodded. Though at times during the last few years I had had those *woe is me* moments like everyone does from time to time when I felt like it would have been more apt for me to be named after Saint Jude, the patron saint of the hopeless and despaired. I suppose that was part genuine and part me being overly dramatic.

Glancing up at the stalwart eagle on the top shelf, I explained, "When my Grandma Schlimm was pregnant with my dad, she was at a loss for names. Then one afternoon, she met a missionary who was visiting here from another country. He told her that if she had a boy, she should name him after Saint John

Evangelist. Then my dad wanted me named after him, too. I suppose I was always destined to be a writer."

"I knew a few Saint Johns growing up," Sister said with a grin.

"You did?"

Sister Augustine laughed. "When I was around eight years old, my mother gave me a book about the lives of the saints. I was so fascinated by their stories that I started naming our farm animals after them."

Now I laughed. I could see young Anna strolling around the farm canonizing the livestock.

"Let's see, there was Saint Sebastian, Saint Agatha, Saint Cecilia, and Saint John the Baptist, who were all cows; Saint Susanna and Saint Walburga were pigs; Saint Jude, Saint Luke, Saint Serafina, and Saint John Evangelist were chickens; there was a horse named after Saint Francis; and Holy Spirit was a cat we had. She and her kittens liked curling up with our dog Rex in the barn when it was cold outside."

I was cracking up at the images jumping around in my head. I pictured each of the animals with halos.

Sister continued: "When my father butchered the animals, I even pretended to have funerals for them. I'd pick an old dandelion, one where the yellow flower had turned into a fuzzy ball, and I'd blow the white seeds high into the air. Watching them float away reminded me of souls going to Heaven. I never told anyone, especially my parents, that I was doing all this, because I didn't think they'd approve. After coming here to Saint Joseph's, I told Sister Thecla about it for the first time during one of the late-night chitchats we'd often have—I was almost twenty years old by then—and she still scolded me, but promised not to tattle. She was always the prim and proper one. Then when my father came to live here at the convent following our mother's death, I finally confessed it all to him. He couldn't stop laughing for days afterward. That's what I did while other little girls my age were playing with dolls and having tea parties."

Tears were streaming down my cheeks I was laughing so hard. "I just hope Saint John Evangelist is as good to me as all the saints have been to you."

"I'm sure Saint John will put in a good word for your cookbook and guide you to the right publisher. In fact, in addition to the eagle, a book is another one of his symbols."

I took comfort and had faith in her words. "This cookbook project has also been a nice way of merging my writing with my family's heritage," I said. "The last place my cousins want me is on the assembly line at the brewery. That would probably turn into the scene from *I Love Lucy* when Lucy and Ethel go to work in the chocolate factory. Total mayhem!"

"You best stick to writing then." Sister then glanced at her watch. "You don't mind if I continue working while we talk, do you?" The half-painted forget-me-not plate was still cradled on her lap. "I've gotten quite a few orders in the last few weeks that I'm trying to get finished. The days have been flying by lately. And especially with the pieces I need to also get finished for the open house."

"No, go right ahead," I replied. "Most of those orders are probably mine anyway," I added with a crooked grin.

"Yes, or people you know. Seems like every other person who comes in now tells me, 'John said I had to stop in to see you, Sister.'"

"Well, I told you I was going to make you famous!"

"Stop that now!" Sister flicked her paintbrush at me. "Though traffic has certainly picked up around here lately."

"When did you know you wanted to be an artist?" I asked, gently stroking Blitzen's back.

"An *artist*. Is that what I am?"

"Absolutely."

"If you say so, John." Sister shook her head and focused on the plate. "For me, this has always just been something I've enjoyed doing."

"Well, that's one way of defining an artist," I said. "How did you learn how to paint?"

While Sister Augustine nimbly dotted blue forget-me-not petals along the plate's edge, she recalled how she started: "Back in the sixties, a woman here in town invited me to a few lessons she was teaching on how to make ceramics and I went. It was fun. The prioress then came to me and said she thought a ceramic shop might be good for the convent. She asked me if I'd be interested in running it. I didn't have any training beyond that one class, but it sounded like something I might enjoy, so I said, 'Yes.' Not that I would have ever told the prioress no."

"Do you remember the first thing you ever painted here in the shop?"

"That was a long time ago. Something simple, I imagine, until I learned how to paint better. I had to mostly teach myself. I started doing Nativity sets early on, which have been my most popular item over the years. I once figured out that there's one in every state in the U.S., and even some in foreign countries."

"Wow, that's impressive! It's something to be really proud of!"

"It's all God's work, and I just do as I'm told." She trailed off with a giggle, now adding the center dots to each flower that the kiln would burn into a trail of tiny suns.

"I took art classes in high school," I revealed, "And then minored in studio arts in college." This was another part of my life I had kept hidden from Sister, preferring instead to focus on her art while I was in that sacred space. Every so often though we would surprise each other by unveiling another piece of ourselves. Today was a twofer.

"So you're also an artist, as well as a writer and teacher. So many gifts!" Sister interjected.

I nodded, thinking how sometimes even gifts came with a hefty price tag. Mostly an emotional cost. It's often a struggle to discover your God-given gifts and then an even bigger trial to flesh out how exactly you're meant to use those talents in this world.

"But now I do primitive Americana folk art like checkerboard and flag paintings, birdhouses, wooden stars, and stuff like that," I explained. "I've purposely tried to *un*learn all the classic techniques I was taught in order to create pieces like the self-taught folk artists I admire, such as Grandma Moses and Howard Finster."

"You'll have to show me your art sometime," Sister said, looking up to emphasize her request.

The mere thought of showing my artwork to Sister Augustine initially unnerved me, which is also why I had never mentioned it to her before. Even though my pieces were inspirational and probably to her liking, I was in such awe of the work she was creating. I guess my apprehension on this was along the same lines as my silly fear of reciting a "Hail Mary" in front of her, or any other holy person for that matter.

"You're a jack of many trades," my friend commented.

"I suppose, but I've taken a roundabout way of getting here," I said.

Sister looked up again, from the leaves she had started adding in single grass-green wisps, three per forget-me-not. "God has certainly given you quite a journey."

"But I still feel like I'm hanging in some limbo, unsure where I'm headed," I said. "The university job will be great, but those rejection letters from publishers are tough to take." Each one was a sucker punch to the gut. *Dear Author: Unfortunately, blah blah blah.*

"God's time," Sister repeated. "Look at the gifts and journey that got you to where you are today."

"It's been such a long journey so far," I bemoaned, rolling my eyes childishly and missing her point about the many blessings I had been given along the way. When wandering in the deserts of our lives, even a few years can feel like they've been multiplied fourfold. Especially if we don't own up to our share of the responsibility for getting lost to begin with, and when we allow our whining and self-pity to turn into roadblocks.

Sister Augustine smiled. "It can take a long time, and a lot of rejections and disappointments along the way, to get from one point to the next, each a new starting line. But eventually you'll come to appreciate the journey itself. When I entered the convent in 1932 at seventeen years old, I never thought, *I'm going to teach school,* but I was once a teacher, too, just like you. Only I taught elementary school. I never thought, *Someday I'll run a ceramic shop and create the pieces myself,* but then that opportunity presented itself. Something called a Gussie's Special never crossed my mind for eighty-seven years. It was God's plan and on His time frame."

Her words were like streetlamps being flipped on one right after another for as far as I could see. I was reminded that even when we do begin to better understand the road ahead of us, falling off the wagon from time to time is to be expected and is an important part of the journey. I suddenly realized that Sister and I had more in common than I thought. Both of us were teachers and artists, in our own ways and of our own times. That's why we understood each other so well. We connected along a common thread. I pondered how perhaps all of our relationships in this life were like that to some degree. You just have to find the intersection you share with another person, be they a stranger or even a great-great-grandfather, and then watch the bond flourish from there.

"Now *you* just need to write a book," I told my friend.

"I'll leave that to you, John Evangelist," she said playfully. "I never thought I'd be around this long, and especially not running my shop at this age. One day became another day, and one year after another passed by, then another and another."

"There certainly aren't many people who are your age and still working full-time," I said. At thirty-three, I knew many people around my age who weren't working nearly as hard as she was.

Sister smiled sweetly and gazed at me for a moment, setting the finished forget-me-not plate on the table. "I'll let you in on a little secret," she said. "I was ready to retire and close this shop, then you walked in."

"I'm glad you didn't close it!" I said. "There's still a lot for you to do." Blitzen agreed by purring from my lap. It would be years later before I fully appreciated what she had just revealed to me.

"Well, I guess I can stick around a little longer. After all, I now have all these orders to fill. And we do have our first open house coming up."

I beamed now. Maybe I wasn't out of my desert yet, but at least there was a brilliant sun guiding me forward as I wandered.

"I have big plans for you, Sister!"

"You know what they say, we make plans and God laughs."

"This is just a beginning for you, too."

"God willing," Sister Augustine said, inspecting the ring of forget-me-nots she had just finished. "I just do as I'm told. He's boss."

9

FOOTSTEPS

A NEW ADDITION HAD BEEN MADE TO THE FRONT PORCH OF Sister Augustine's ceramic shop in early November: a small set of wind chimes hanging from the railing that made music at every breeze. Especially at this time of the year, when chilly winds prompted burnt orange and fiery crimson leaves into a spirited waltz around the weathered wooden slats. It quickly became second nature for me to swipe my hand across the chimes anytime I arrived, letting Sister inside know I was there, and again when I would leave. The chimes had been a gift that I, along with Steven and my cousin Patty, had given to Sister Augustine for her ninetieth birthday.

A few days before Thanksgiving, I swatted the chimes with extra enthusiasm while everything around me glistened with an early morning frost. Patty and I were meeting at Sister's shop to help her get ready for the upcoming Christmas Open House, which was now only a few weeks away. Patty was married to my mother's first cousin Wray. Shortly after I had met Sister Augustine, I took Patty, who was in her early sixties, to the ceramic shop, where, like me, she fell in love with the artist-in-residence. Patty was already a volunteer in the Trifles and Treasures Gift Shop, where she regularly helped Sister Margoretta. She eventually forged her own special bond with Sister Augustine, as did the many others who met her during these years.

I was so excited to soon be able to share my friend with the outside world in a major way. Word of mouth no longer sufficed. I had bigger plans for Sister, and this was just step one. I even resumed my role as publicist when I called several local reporters and invited them to interview Sister Augustine at her shop the next day.

Looking around inside, I knew that once Patty arrived, we would have our work cut out for us. This meant cleaning the entire place, rearranging the items in the shop to include the new holiday pieces and Gussie's Specials that Sister was working on, and preparing her for the reporters who would be descending upon the shop the following day for a press conference, which had never happened before. The open house would be the first time most of the people from St. Marys and the surrounding areas would visit the shop and meet Sister Augustine. I couldn't wait to throw open the front door and let everyone in.

"Sister, I'm here!" The sound of the chimes was usually enough now to ensure a smile was waiting for me when I'd walk in.

Since Patty hadn't arrived yet, I went in search of Sister.

"Back here!" she finally called out.

When I reached the small doorway leading into the back room, there she was, up on a ladder reaching for something on the top shelf against the back wall.

"What are you doing?" Judging from the creaking sounds, I feared the ancient wooden ladder wasn't the sturdiest.

"Getting down the convent's Nativity set, so Sister Jacinta and Sister John Paul can set it up outside in front of the chapel."

I hurried around the table and wrapped my hands around the one side of the ladder to steady it. I didn't dare fuss too much over the dangers of a nonagenarian balancing five feet in the air. Sister was very independent. Still, I nonchalantly gripped the rickety ladder to anchor it and was determined to catch her if need be.

"Here," she said, "this is the Blessed Mother." She handed me a large bundle, forcing me to let go of the ladder. "Just set her on the table behind you where I've cleared a space." The figure was wrapped snugly in layers of fabric.

"Did you make this Nativity set?"

"No, someone else did years ago, but I love it just the same as if I had painted it," she replied. "I touch up the figures when needed and keep them safe in here throughout the year." I could tell that this Nativity set was very dear to her.

Once Mary was situated, my white knuckles were back on the ladder. But not for long. Saint Joseph followed, then the Magi, a shepherd boy, cow, donkey, and finally Baby Jesus. "Last but not least," Sister said with a twinkle in her eyes as she handed me the smallest bundle of joy.

"Be careful getting down from there," I cautioned.

"Yes, yes," Sister Augustine said, swiftly stepping down and brushing her hands against her denim bib apron, while my heart skipped a few more beats.

"Do we need to take these pieces somewhere?"

"No, Sister Jacinta and Sister John Paul will stop in sometime this week and get them when they're ready to set up the Nativity."

We heard the front door open just then.

"That must be Patty," I said.

"Oh good," Sister said, flushed and happy.

Patty greeted us as Sister and I emerged from the back room.

"We were just getting the large Nativity set out for Sister Jacinta and Sister John Paul to set up later this week," I informed her.

"Fantastic," Patty said. She had arrived with two bucketfuls of rags and cleaning supplies.

"Before you two start, I have a surprise for you," Sister announced.

"What is it?" Patty and I both asked excitedly.

"Come over here with me," Sister Augustine said, leading us to the far side of the squared-off horseshoe of worktables in her studio. Rushing in when I arrived, I hadn't noticed that the table over there was completely covered with a large, floral bedsheet. Whatever was underneath created a hilly landscape of wildflowers on top.

"Is this an unveiling?" I asked dramatically. Drums rolled in my mind.

Sister smiled. "John, please grab the corner of the sheet on the other side of the table and help me pull it off."

Patty and I looked at each other with wide eyes.

"I purposely didn't show you any of this before, so I could surprise you today," Sister explained as she and I began to peel back the sheet.

"*Sister!*" I exclaimed, as the treasures beneath were divulged one by one. Suddenly, it was Christmas morning. I felt the same surge of excitement I once did as a little kid rounding the corner into our living room to see an illuminated Christmas tree and all the toys that Santa had left rippling out from beneath it. Camera in hand, my mom always captured the look of pure awe on my face. The same look I had now.

The table was teeming with snowmen and Santas, sleighs, trees, ornaments, animals and birds, poinsettia plates, small heart boxes, mid-century vases, and an Advent wreath. Even the Caribbean Blue ashtray-turned-candy dish was there. And sixteen large and small Gussie's Specials, each one a sublime treasure.

"These pieces are out of this world!" Patty gushed.

"I hope everyone at the open house thinks so, too," Sister Augustine added with a chuckle. "You two get excited about everything."

"Because everything is spectacular," I said, walking back

and forth, and around the table, trying to take it all in. "And this . . ."

"I was waiting to see if you'd notice that," Sister said with a wink.

It was a large piece depicting the Holy Family's flight into Egypt from Bethlehem. Mary on a donkey, holding Baby Jesus, while Joseph walked alongside, brave and determined. A portrait of strength and courage. The mission ahead clear.

"I never saw the mold for this one," I said, studying the details Sister Augustine had captured in living color on the sculpture. Within the brushstrokes, I could vividly feel the movement and emotions the historical piece evoked. The drama of a Remington in the Sistine hues of a Michelangelo.

"I know you didn't see it. I still have a few surprises up my sleeve," Sister quipped.

"You signed it, I hope," I said. "And everything else, too?"

"Yes, just as you told me to," Sister replied. "I even wrote 'Gussie's Special' on the bottom of the bowls next to my name."

"Perfect!" I began picking up the pieces to check out the inscriptions. On some Sister had engraved her name, along with the year and "SJC" for St. Joseph's Ceramics, during the greenware phase, creating the most permanent inscriptions once fired. On others she had used a black or silver Sharpie to ink her name. "Gussie's Special" was inscribed in cursive on the bowls.

"We certainly have our work cut out for us today, setting all of this up in the shop," I declared.

"We better get busy," Patty chimed in, eyeing the clock.

"What can I do to help?" Sister asked.

"I think you've done enough," I said, waving my hand over the table.

"I do have a few Nativity orders to finish up at the next table," Sister said. I glanced over. The main worktable was laden with Duncan paint bottles and a congregation of stable animals in progress. "I put those on hold while I finished all of these pieces, so you'd have them to work with when you came today, and now time is catching up with me." Sister rounded the table and sat in her mint-green spindle chair, where the pyramids of paint bottles towered over her and the clayware cows, donkeys, sheep, and camels.

Patty and I went to work in the rest of the shop. We started by clearing all the shelves and scrubbing them with soap and hot water. It's not every day you get covered in holy dust. Bucket after bucket of blackened water, I laughed to myself. Each shelf became a meditation.

Before we knew it, it was lunchtime and we hadn't even started filling the shelves again.

"Sister, you can go if you need to," Patty said. The sisters always gathered for prayers in the chapel before lunch.

"I've been excused from prayers today," Sister Augustine told us. "But I insist you both join me for lunch. It's the least I can do."

Holy dust and all, Patty and I followed Sister up the outside steps and into the convent's main building, where she led us to the dining room. I had never been in there before.

The first thing I noticed when we arrived in the large open room filled with tables was that each of the chairs had bright green tennis balls on the bottom of their legs. "Those are to prevent the chairs from scuffing the floor and making too much noise," Sister Augustine informed me. "Silence is golden, you know." She laughed softly.

When we walked in, several of the twenty or so nuns looked in our direction, some clearly wondering who the two new visitors were. Many warmly welcomed us and expressed their anticipation of the open house. I saw my sixth-grade catechism teacher, Sister Joachim; my high school theology teacher, Sister Kathleen; and my advanced algebra tutor, Sister Mercedes. I spoke for a moment to Sister Margoretta, who was assisting blind Sister Dolores, to get an update on how open house preparations were going on her end.

Over by the refrigerator, I waved to Sisters Helen and Mary James, who taught music and art lessons in rooms up near the Trifles and Treasures Gift Shop. The convent's historian, Sister Evangelist, hunched over and even smaller than Sister Augustine, smiled as she passed by. Sisters Jacinta and John Paul, just in from working outside, greeted us by the buffet line.

Sister Augustine leaned in and whispered the names of the remaining sisters scattered at tables throughout the room: Victoria, Raphael, Mary Bernard, Gemma, Monica, Laura, Pancratria, Jean Marie, Roberta, Julia, and Mary David. For a brief, shining moment, I was embedded in my own real-life *Sister Act*.

I quickly realized that we were with one of the popular kids there. The respect and admiration the other sisters had for the one they had nicknamed "Gussie" was obvious.

Sister Augustine normally sat with a few other nuns, but today she, Patty, and I were a clique at our own table against the back wall. Saint Benedict, rendered in an elaborate oil painting and hung in an ornate, gilded frame, watched down over us. We enjoyed a full course with all the trimmings, as this was the nuns' main meal for the day. My favorite part was the dessert buffet, filled with cakes and pies that were prepared fresh that morning by the convent's incarnation of cafeteria ladies. I tucked a thought away in the back of my mind: at some point I wanted to explore the idea of doing a cookbook with the convent.

After lunch, Sister took us on a detour to show us St. Joseph Monastery's most legendary work of art: a centuries-old, hand-carved and painted wooden statue of the Blessed Virgin Mary alighted on a crescent moon and holding the Infant Jesus.

She explained, "Three sisters originally came from Bavaria in 1852 to start our convent: Mother Benedicta, Sister Maura, and Sister Walburga. On the ship ride over, they encountered a deadly storm at sea. The captain told them everything without exception, including this statue which they greatly cherished, had to be thrown overboard. . . ."

Patty and I stood entranced before the sculpture.

"The sisters started praying the rosary aloud alongside the statue. But the sailors finally came and insisted that she be thrown overboard with everything else. However, out of respect for the sisters' devotion, the sailors tied a rope around the statue in an attempt to save her in the water alongside the ship. The very minute the statue entered the water, the terrible storm stopped—just like that—and no lives were lost. The statue was pulled back on board and the journey proceeded without any more problems. Had that ship never made it, we wouldn't be standing here today."

I smiled. Miracles rendered through art had a precedent at St. Joseph's.

When we returned to the shop a little after one, it was spick-and-span, as if Mr. Clean himself were determined to convince us once and for all that cleanliness was, indeed, next to Godliness. The renewed shelves beckoned. Patty and I started to restock, while Sister resumed working on her Nativity animals. Playing curator, we moved many of the non-Christmas pieces from the shop onto the mint-green shelves in the studio. That left plenty of space in the front room for all the new yuletide pieces Sister had recently completed.

The shelves along the shop's walls were soon filled with Santa and Mrs. Claus, snowmen, angels, light-up Christmas trees, and *The Flight into Egypt.* The shelves on the wall next to the kiln room were dedicated to baby- and children-themed items: clay-ware clowns, teddy bears, booties, piggy banks, and bookends featuring a young boy and girl kneeling in prayer on each side. Several small, low reliefs of the Last Supper—white and detailed in gold like pieces salvaged from an ancient frieze—filled the wall next to the front door. We also wove strings of multicolored lights throughout all the shelves to really make them pop.

Next, we wrapped a four-foot, artificial tree in small multicolored lights to display Sister's ornaments, which were mostly created using old tin and red plastic cookie cutters. Soon the tree was populated with hand-painted bells, angels, stars, snowmen, Santas, churches, candles, hearts, gingerbread people and houses, poinsettias, and little animals. We set the tree in the corner next to the front window under which Blitzen liked to hang out. Today, however, Blitzen was a no-show, apparently deciding to avoid the commotion that housecleaning and holiday decorating bring.

The sixteen new Gussie's Specials were our grand centerpiece. The pièce de résistance. Patty and I arranged them on the three-level island—a recycled red grocery store display counter—in the middle of the shop. We set a small cardboard box in the middle to create a raised focal point and then covered the entire surface with a frayed square of gold metallic fabric.

A particularly splashy and large Gussie's Special, streaked in a glossy fusion of reds, oranges, and yellows like a burning bush, was set on the makeshift pedestal. Another—in blues, grays, and whites—foamy and choppy like a Winslow Homer sea, was placed on one side. A more minimalist bowl, stark white with apple red chips suspended quietly like a Calder across the rippled surface, went beside it. A large one—grass green dribbled with sapphire—and a smaller version slathered in the yummy tones of my homemade veggie-beer chili flanked the other side. The remaining bowls were arranged on the shelves below. This installation, rising like a shimmering pantheon, would welcome the open house visitors.

"These aren't going to last long," I whispered to Patty. "I wish she could have made a hundred of them!" I made sure Sister didn't hear me from the other room or she would have playfully scolded me.

"I know!" Patty sighed. "But that just makes these few even more special."

"She can always take orders for more," I added, also in a hush. Meanwhile, I was practicing restraint, trying my hardest not to buy any of the bowls I was setting out for others to peruse. They were like scrumptious tapas that practically call your name from the bar top. I relished the thought that I was about to let the rest of the world in on my best-kept secret.

After a few final touches at the end of the afternoon, we called to Sister to come have a look. She had watched us race around since early morning; now she would get to see the fruits of our labor.

Our friend paused in the doorway, wiping her hands on her smudged apron. Backlit by the studio lights, she was exactly as I remembered from the first day Steven and I had walked in almost three years earlier.

Sister Augustine's mouth fell open as she scanned the room, experiencing her oeuvre through new eyes. "It's magnificent," she proclaimed. "This is the most beautiful it's ever been in here."

"That's because of all your artwork," I said.

"And you two knowing what to do with it," she added. "You haven't stopped all day!"

"It's our pleasure," Patty said. "I love doing this."

"Me, too," I said.

"I just can't believe it," Sister kept repeating as she stepped into the room for a closer look at everything. "You two must have walked a million miles today doing all this."

Patty and I both laughed. *Probably,* I thought, as I noticed for the first time the painful revolt starting at the arches of my feet and invading my legs.

"I wish I could pay you somehow for doing all this," Sister lamented, looking now at the Christmas tree in the corner.

"Just getting to do this is payment enough," I said. "This is what friends do for each other. We're as excited as you are about it."

"That's right," Patty said.

Sister Augustine turned around to face us. "God knows exactly how many footsteps you both took today in this shop for me, and He'll reward you for every one of them."

Sister's words reminded me of the familiar saying, Do unto others as you would have them do unto you. Or any number of biblical passages touting the rewards bestowed upon those who perform good works. However you phrase it, what it boils down to is people helping each other.

Rather than expecting a reward for my footsteps that day, or in the years to come, on those old, hallowed floors, I felt that each helpful step I took there was instead my way of paying off a priceless gift I had been given the first day I walked into that shop. My tithing for the gift of a new friend and borrowed time.

Our work for the day completed, Patty left with her buckets, damp rags, and near-empty bottles of cleaning supplies. I stayed a few minutes longer to brief Sister about the reporters who would be interviewing her the following day about the open house.

"Remind me again why I have to do this," Sister Augustine said, sitting across the table from me with a nearly finished Nativity cow in hand. A rainbow of Duncan paint bottles with names like Nordic Light, Country Rose, Galaxy Blue, Peacock, Larkspur, Mocha Spice, Harvest, Light Kiwi, and Indian Summer separated us. I almost had to stand to see her on the other side.

From the first time weeks earlier when I had brought up the prospect of calling reporters to do stories about her, Sister had protested and said no. Heresy, by most PR standards. I had worked with some of the biggest names in entertainment as a publicist and each of them would have cried foul over Sister's reluctance. Those superstars would have surely craved even a sliver of the media's euphoria that I had encountered when I called local reporters to pitch the story about Sister Augustine and the open house. Rarely had the reporters ever been invited into the convent. During Sister's early years at St. Joseph Monastery, the nuns weren't even allowed to read newspapers let alone appear in them, and there were no radios or TVs, either, in the convent back then.

My PR strategy for this event was pretty standard: local print articles and public service announcements on the radio. This was a few years before Facebook, Twitter, Instagram, Pinterest, and all the other social media outlets that would revolutionize how word of events like this can be blasted out to the masses with the push of a single button. Even the release of the first iPhone was still almost two years away. Had those outlets been available to me then, I would no doubt have had a rip-roaring good time introducing my friend to things like posts, tweets, and selfies. *Oh the selfies I would have insisted Sister Augustine and I take together!*

Sister Margoretta was going to make sure a blurb about the open house was placed in each of the church bulletins and various community event calendars throughout the area. I took it upon myself to make sure the story, especially of Sister Augustine and her artwork, headlined newspapers and was planted front and center in the minds of readers.

"If people don't know about the open house, they won't know to come," I said.

"Can't Sister Margoretta just do the interviews?" Sister Augustine asked. "I have nothing to say."

I knew that wasn't true. "Sister Margoretta will be interviewed after you, up in the gift shop. She'll give all the who, what, where, when, why, and how details about the open house," I explained. "But it's *you* the reporters are most excited about!"

"Why me?"

Her question gave me pause. My friend still didn't understand the rare gift she possessed. How each of her brushstrokes was luminous, a glimpse of God's handiwork. Her unyielding humility unsettled me at times. An enigma, wrapped in a riddle, surrounded by the familiar mystery of a black and white habit. I fought off pangs of guilt that somehow I was dragging an old woman out into the public square against her will. I just couldn't wait to share her with the world.

But I also understood that there had never been a fuss like this made over her, especially at Christmastime. Christmases at the convent were largely private observances among the sisters, except for the open house, which Sister Margoretta had always headlined in the past. Long before that, holidays at her childhood farmstead, which I came to think of as Mockin' Bird Hill, were about family and the Birth of Christ. The only gifts were handmade stockings filled with a piece of fruit and maybe a chocolate candy, and wrapped packages containing a new frock for the girls and a new shirt for the boys, each lovingly sewn by Sister Augustine's mother, Clara.

"I think the reporters are fascinated by the story of a ninety-year-old nun in a convent who creates incredible pieces of art," I explained. This was a total no-brainer. To me and everyone else anyway.

"You're the one who's got the gift for words. I'm just doing

God's work," Sister said. "These pieces aren't mine. They belong to the community here at Saint Joseph's."

. That's when I realized how tough it is to argue against true modesty and humility. So I took a new approach.

"Think of your doing the interviews this way: the attention you'll be getting will benefit the entire convent. Those news stories are what will bring people to the open house, which will help raise money for Saint Joseph's." It was a logical circle, and the truth.

Sister thought for a moment. She trusted me. "Well, that makes a little more sense. But I'm only really doing this because *you* want me to. I just hope I can think of something to say!"

"I have no doubt you will, Sister," I assured her with a smile, thinking, *Gussie, you are special, indeed.* "And I'll be right here by your side, in case you need me."

Sister Augustine shook her head and grinned, before returning her attention to the Nativity cow in her hand.

❧

THE NEXT MORNING, I arrived thirty minutes before the reporters. I found Sister patiently waiting in her spindle chair in the studio. She had donned a cheery yellow and brown bib apron.

"Are you ready?" I asked, while setting two more chairs facing her next to the spindle chair I had come to think of as mine. Three reporters would be visiting. I'd stand in the corner, only stepping in if Sister needed me—her self-appointed publicist.

"I guess I don't have a choice," she deadpanned with a smile. I laughed. *Nope.* "These reporters are all very nice. You shouldn't get any questions you can't answer. They just want to hear your story."

"If you say so, John."

Three knocks on the front door signaled that the reporters had arrived, and demonstrated their own hesitancy to enter this largely uncharted territory for the first time. I was counting on them to help change that. I did a quick sweep of the room, moving another small, bright Gussie's Special to the top of the island, before opening the door.

I introduced Sister to the journalists. There was one young man and two young women, all with notepads in hand, and a photographer for one of the newspapers. Each of the reporters settled into the seats I had arranged. The photographer stood nearby. The *click, click, click* of her camera became the main sound effect for Sister's first press conference.

"Okay, fire away," I told the reporters, which garnered me a sharp look from Sister Augustine.

The male reporter asked the first question. "Why a ceramic shop, Sister? What inspired you to open it?"

My friend glanced over at me once more, only this time with vulnerability, hesitancy. This was all new to her. I smiled and nodded my head to assure her that I had her back.

Then she began. "I first started out as a schoolteacher, teaching third and fourth graders, and then I moved on to teaching fifth grade. I did that for seventeen years. But the truth was, I loved the children, not the teaching. My favorite class was recess!" Sister answered with a chuckle.

The reporters, and I, all laughed. They were hooked. She was a natural at this. A star was born.

Sister continued: "Then I was invited to a few ceramic lessons that a lady here in town was teaching, and I enjoyed them. The prioress at the time thought it would be a good idea to have a ceramic shop here at Saint Joseph's and she told me to go for it. That was 1964. The rest is history—a very, very long history. I guess this is where I'm supposed to be. God has His hand in it."

"What was in here before your ceramic studio?" one of the female reporters asked.

"The convent's carpentry shop," Sister replied. I hadn't

known that. *How appropriate*, I thought, as the image of Saint Joseph, both the real-life builder and Sister's countless ceramic renderings of him, ran through my mind. This was hallowed space in many, many ways.

Sister Augustine then proceeded to answer a series of questions about her early life. One of twelve children in the Huefner family, some of whom died in infancy, she had grown up on a farm in another Pennsylvania town called Knox. If you were to pinpoint 41°14'7"N, 79°32'10"W on a map, you would literally find a needle in a haystack—small-town America at its best. Her father worked as a farmer. Her mother sold the butter, milk, eggs, and canned goods produced on the farm. Her older sister, Sister Thecla, a prim and proper academic, was the first of the family to come to St. Joseph Monastery. "I followed her here," Sister quipped. I was sorry I never got to meet Sister Thecla, who had passed away a few years earlier.

As for hobbies, Sister Augustine told the reporters how she liked working outside, especially tending her flower gardens in front of the ceramic shop. The session on her biography was punctuated with a resounding, "I'm ninety years old now," to flabbergasted looks on each reporter's face.

Click, click, click. The photographer's camera was also smitten with her.

Next, one of the female reporters asked, "What was the first thing you ever painted?"

Sister looked over at me. "John asked me that a while ago and I finally remembered after thinking about it," she recalled, returning her attention to the reporters. "I painted candle ornaments that I gave to each of the sisters that first Christmas I had the shop. There were one hundred and twenty five of us back then."

I moved, positioning myself by the doorway. From there I

had a better view of the reporters' facial expressions, which were precious, to say the least. Sister just kept reeling them in. I had once stood guard like this in other rooms hundreds of miles from where we currently were, with the country music superstars I promoted and the national media, which couldn't get enough of them. As a publicist, I would always be just off camera, like a director or, more aptly, a lifeline if my clients needed one.

"What's your favorite thing to paint?" the other female reporter asked.

"Birds and animals." One little, perky animal, however, was apparently more camera-shy than Sister. Blitzen had bailed on the interview, just like on the housecleaning the day before. *What a little diva,* I thought. "But I do a lot of Nativity sets, too," Sister added.

I quickly interjected, "There's at least one of Sister's Nativity sets in every state in the U.S., as well as in Japan, England, and Germany. Plus, one will be raffled off at the open house. It contains twenty-one pieces. And her other clayware pieces have gone to Central America, Africa, and even Russia!" The reporters duly noted my addendums for their stories while Sister sent a quick wink my way.

"Does anyone help you?" the male reported inquired, his eyes scanning the room. "There's obviously a lot of work to do here."

"I have a few volunteers who come in every now and then," Sister said, "but it's pretty much just me. I do everything from start to finish. I'm the only one I can depend on."

Click, click, click.

I was amused by the glances Sister Augustine was sending in the persistent photographer's direction by this point. My read was: *Enough already!*

The one female reporter pointed to a shelf at the front of the studio. "Sister, I see you have ladybugs that cost one 'Hail Mary' each and turtles and frogs for three 'Hail Marys.' What's the story behind those?"

"One of my friends who also did ceramics a long time ago passed away. Her husband donated her paints and ceramic molds to my shop, including those molds. I figure my friend appreciates the 'Hail Marys.'"

I was learning a lot today.

"What do you like to do for fun?" the male reporter asked.

Sister pointed behind her to a photograph hanging in the back corner by the sink. "Fish," she answered. "Every summer I go away for a week and fish for walleye, or whatever will take the bait." The photograph showed Sister with her catch of the day on a previous trip to Pymatuning Lake, which straddles the border of Pennsylvania and Ohio.

I could see Sister was starting to get tired, or so I thought. I stepped in. "How about I take you all on a tour of the studio and shop now?"

We started in the back room and worked our way to the kiln room and shop in front. I thought Sister would take the time to rest up, but she tagged along behind. I was beginning to think she might just be enjoying this a little bit. I explained her process of making ceramics and then pointed out the various pieces I wanted the reporters to focus on, especially the Gussie's Specials and their unique story.

I figured I'd relieve Sister of having to tell a lot of the more technical details of her work, but the reporters insisted on turning to her throughout our tour to capture everything in her words. I was relieved when Sister obliged, right down to the "joys and sorrows" that awaited her each time she lifted the kiln lid.

Click, click, click.

The two reporters sans a photographer had also started taking pictures of Sister Augustine and her pieces. Sister was a good sport. Each *click* was graced with a smile. I diverted my eyes to keep from laughing. I knew exactly what she was thinking.

In the shop, gathered around the island filled with Gussie's Specials, Sister Augustine explained, "I use whatever paint is on my brush at the time to paint these. It's my way of conserving the paint and getting the most out of it." Her hands were resting on top of a Gussie's Special that she'd painted in a cadence of orange, scarlet, burnt sienna, orchid, cadmium yellow, amber, and slivers of blue. A postcard sunset that I had moved up from a lower shelf earlier.

"Why do you call them Gussie's Special?" the male reporter asked.

Because that's her nickname here, the voice in my head answered.

"That's my own private story," Sister said. "I have to keep some secrets." She flashed them an impish grin accompanied by that glint in her eyes.

That was one of the best parts of the story, the history behind the bowl's name. But for now, that would remain a mystery for the reporters. It would keep them coming back for more, I mused. She was handling them like a pro.

"How about one final question?" I said, bringing Sister Augustine's first press conference to a close.

One of the female reporters jumped at the chance to claim the last quote. "Sister, at ninety years old, what keeps you working here in the ceramic shop?"

"It keeps me off the streets," she quipped with a huge smile.

I burst out laughing as the reporters quickly scrawled her final words onto their notepads. Sister Augustine had just perfected the art of the sound bite, proving once again that there was more to her than meets the eye.

What Sister also hadn't told the reporters during the hour they had been there was how when she entered the convent in

1932 at age seventeen, her teary-eyed father told her, "I've never been more proud of you," and her mother gave her a new hand-made calico bib apron. Or, how in her early years at St. Joseph's, during chapel prayers, which were all in Latin back then, she'd often get the giggles. "I figured God had a sense of humor, too, so it wasn't a sin, even if the prioress didn't always see it that way," she had told me once with a wink. Nor did Sister Augustine tell the reporters how on various occasions as young nuns she and Sister Thecla would sneak out of their rooms after curfew to chitchat in some quiet corner or stargaze from a top-floor window, just like they had once done back home on the farm while everyone else was asleep. Those, and other anecdotes, would be our little secrets for the time being.

After seeing the reporters and photographer out the door, sending them up to the gift shop for their interview with Sister Margoretta, I turned to Sister Augustine. She was still standing at the island filled with her Gussie's Specials.

"You were so amazing!"

"Just promise me I never have to do that again," she said with a crooked grin.

I shook my head and responded with a grin of my own. "Cat's out of the bag now. This is only the beginning."

Standing there looking at my friend, I had no doubt that God was also keeping track of every footstep, and brushstroke, Sister Augustine made.

10

THE FIRST NOËL

I ARRIVED AT 7:30 A.M. ON THE FIRST SATURDAY IN DECEMber, the day of St. Joseph Monastery's Christmas Open House, which fell two days after my thirty-fourth birthday. I found Sister Augustine, bundled up in her knee-length, navy blue parka, shoveling the snow off the cement steps and sidewalk leading to her shop. For every shovelful she scooped and tossed to the side, another powdery dusting painted the area in broad, sweeping strokes. We were in a brandished snow globe.

"Sister, give me that shovel."

"I'm fine, I can do this," she declared. "I've been at it for about a half hour now, but I'm afraid God is winning this one."

I laughed. "You should go inside and get ready. I'm sure people are going to start showing up earlier than nine o'clock."

"You really think so?"

"After all the great news articles we got, I'd bet on it."

The headlines from Sister's interviews couldn't have been any better had I written them myself. Our three main local newspapers heralded her just as I had hoped:

ST. MARYS NUN'S CERAMIC ART KNOWN WORLDWIDE

SISTER CRAFTS HER OWN NICHE

90-YEAR-OLD NUN CREATES ART FROM CLAY

With the help of those articles, Sister Augustine and her artwork, both secluded for years, were now front-page news in

St. Marys and throughout the surrounding areas. She was still uncertain what it all meant or if she was even ready for a comeback. She shook her head in awe at each glowing review. "If this is what God wants," she'd say, "so be it."

"Give me the shovel," I now insisted. "I'll be in shortly."

Sister handed over the shovel, but like usual, she stayed to chat. "Are you sure people will be able to find us down here?" she wondered. "They might have to dig their way to us." The epicenter of the open house had always been the Trifles and Treasures Gift Shop, which was located a short walk up the hill from the ceramic shop at the back end of the convent's main building, by the nuns' cemetery and pond. That was a more familiar destination for most people. Sister Margoretta had an army of volunteers who helped her decorate and tend to the five rooms flowing throughout the religious store for the open house, as well as a room across the hall called the Sweet Shop, where a popular bake sale was held.

"Yes, I had signs with arrows put up, directing people our way," I assured her. I had left no stone unturned, making sure visitors would know that Sister Augustine and her ceramic shop were a headlining addition to this year's festivities.

"You worked so hard on this, I hope you're not disappointed at the end," Sister said, always thinking of someone else.

"No chance of that. Besides, you had a little something to do with this, too." I gave her a quick wink.

"I'm just doing God's work. He's boss."

"Well, hopefully He'll turn this snow off for a while so we can pack this place with customers."

"We prayed in the chapel this morning for a successful event."

"If that doesn't do it, not much else will," I said with a laugh. "Okay, I think this is as good as we're going to get it." Shoveling was a losing battle.

"If nothing else, people can slide down over the hill to get to us," Sister joked.

I followed Sister Augustine into the shop. Both of us backward to prevent our glasses from steaming up, swiping my hand across the wind chimes on the porch like I always did. My friend chuckled.

The day before, Sister and I had covered the tables in her studio with red tablecloths and set out paper plates, napkins, and coffee cups, all of which a local company had kindly donated. She also organized the checkout counter in the studio, preparing a notebook to record each transaction for her records and tax purposes, cutting pieces of paper from a large roll to use for wrapping the items, and folding bags for the items to be placed in.

My mom, Barb, and her cousin, Phyllis, as well as Steven's mom, Denise, agreed to help out in the ceramic shop for the day. Patty, who had helped me to clean and decorate the ceramic shop, was assisting Sister Margoretta up at the gift shop.

My mom would handle the money and record the transactions. She had also made fudge to serve and to sell to help raise more money. "I was born here at the convent," Mom told Sister Augustine upon meeting her that morning. Each time I hear her start to tell this story, it makes me laugh, for all the obvious reasons. "In 1938, after the hospital burned, they used the academy part where the gift shop is now for the makeshift hospital," Mom explained. "I remember that," Sister reminisced. "I had arrived here only a few years before that." Mom also told her, "Sister Thecla was my first-grade teacher at Sacred Heart. That year, she chose me and my two friends, Georgia and Janie, to be part of the May Crowning at the church."

Hearing them talk reminded me how so many people in St. Marys had unique and personal connections to the convent and the sisters. The nuns had populated the town as nurses and teachers, and in many other capacities, at one time. Sadly, most of their work was now only encapsulated in the memories of my parents' and grandparents' generations. I knew the open house would be a chance for people to reconnect to this sacred and historic place, and to the women who lived there.

Mom positioned herself at the checkout station next to Phyllis, who was in charge of wrapping and bagging the items for customers. Denise would make sure the cookie tray, which Patty had delivered from the Sweet Shop, was kept filled, and she was also in charge of the coffeepot.

My role for the day: Salesman. Cheerleader. Johnny-on-the-spot.

"What can I do?" Sister Augustine asked. By now she was seated in the middle of the squared-off horseshoe of worktables. From that vantage point, she could see straight through to the front room. She was literally the center of the event.

"You stay just where you are," I answered. "We have everything taken care of. Besides, people are going to want to talk with you."

Sister swatted both of her hands toward me with a grin, as if to say, *Yeah right.*

"Where's Blitzen?" I asked.

"Probably hiding somewhere in the back," Sister Augustine said. "Where I should be!"

Now it was my turn to swat the air toward her and flash a big smile.

Thirty minutes to show time. Since everything was ready in the studio, I headed into the shop to plug in the strings of multi-colored lights that were woven throughout the clayware pieces on the shelves and around the small tree. When I walked into the front room, I was greeted by dozens of eyes staring excitedly in through the front window and glass panes of the locked door. I hurried around to each of the plugs, quickly illuminating the room, and made one final inspection to make sure everything was in place.

"There's a line outside!" I exclaimed, rushing back into the studio.

Sister Augustine's eyes widened. "Are you sure?"

"Yep! Look," I said, directing her attention to the front door and window. The people outside waved when they saw her look in their direction. *Gussie-mania,* I thought, laughing to myself. Though I didn't think Sister would be so amused by that appellation.

"I can't believe this," she said, waving back to them.

"You're a star," I teased her.

"Oh, you! Stop that!"

"I'm going to open the door," I announced. "Are you ready?"

"As ready as I'll ever be."

"Then here we go."

I swung open the door. "Welcome!" I peeked outside to see a line extending the length of the porch to my right and up the staircase to my left. "We're opening early just for all of you. It's nice and warm in here!" It was 8:45 a.m.

"Are those the Gussie's Specials I read about?" the first woman hurrying into the shop asked, darting for the island.

"The one and only," I answered.

She chose two from the bottom shelf—a large one that looked like an ultimate pack of Crayola's best and brightest had melted all over it, and a smaller, more subtle bowl rendered in an earthy Wyeth palette.

"The Gussie's Specials?" the next woman to enter also inquired.

I backed against the closed door of the kiln room and pointed again to the island. The woman snatched the sunset bowl that could easily have had "Greetings from Paradise!" scrawled across it.

People now poured en masse through the door in a rapid procession. Not even Moses himself could have parted this sea.

I kept pointing and repeating, "Welcome! The Gussie's Specials are on the island in the middle."

Soon the ceramic shop was packed and the crowd overflowed into the studio to greet Sister Augustine and peruse the clayware pieces on the shelves in there.

A woman called out to me over several ducking heads, "Are there any more Gussie's Specials anywhere?"

I maneuvered my way to the island, which was now deserted. The Gussie's Specials were sold out. We were only fifteen minutes into the open house. Somewhere, Warhol swooned.

I smiled.

"If you'd like one, you can order it," I suggested.

"That would be great!" she said.

"Me, too," another woman added.

"I want one also," a nearby man clamored.

"Am I too late? Are they all gone?" A lady frowned from across the island.

"Yes, but hold on a second," I said. I scanned the shop, quickly grabbing other items to restock the island. Once I had rearranged a few pieces, I said to the women and man, "Please follow me."

We proceeded into the studio and over to where Sister Augustine sat. A line had formed to talk to her.

"Sister!" I yelled from the other side of the table. "The Gussie's Specials are all gone!"

Her face lit up.

"Can we start a list of orders for them? These people would all like one."

The woman who had been talking to Sister when I walked in turned to her and asked, "Are those the bowls I read about where you clean off your brushes?"

Sister nodded.

"I'd like to order one, too," she told me.

"Can we start a list?" I asked Sister Augustine again.

"Yes," she replied. "Just be sure they tell you if they want a large or small one."

"How much are they?" one of the women asked her.

I had unsuccessfully tried to convince Sister to raise her prices. "Eight dollars for the large and six dollars for the small, and I can't guarantee what colors they'll be," she answered.

The woman exclaimed, "What a bargain! I want three large ones for my kids, who all live out of town now. What a great memento of home for each of them to have."

I then turned toward the checkout counter and asked my mom to start a list of names and phone numbers. The small group who had followed me into the shop promptly went over to Mom to place their orders.

I returned to the shop. The pieces were selling themselves. I merely reminded the customers of their significance in a series of standard lines I would repeat dozens of times:

"Sister makes everything by hand, from pouring the clay into the molds to firing the pieces and then painting them. Some take days to complete."

"Most of Sister's molds have been here since the beginning. It would be hard to find many of these pieces anywhere else, especially painted by a nun."

"The shop was started by Sister Augustine more than forty years ago, in 1964."

"Yes, she's ninety years old and she works six days a week. Can you imagine?!"

"The forget-me-not pattern is another one of her trademarks. She can put it on anything you'd like."

"Each time before she closes the kiln lid, Sister Augustine says a prayer, sprinkles in some Holy Water, and, you'll love this, she asks

Saint Francis, whom she simply calls 'Francis,' to also watch over the pieces."

"When she opens the kiln lid, Sister says there's 'joys and sorrows.' "

"Sister Augustine is a modern-day Grandma Moses meets Berta Hummel."

"If you don't see something you want, chances are Sister has a mold for it. You can place your order with my mom, Barb, at the checkout counter."

And so it would go for the next eight hours. Racing back and forth between the shop and studio, I'd often look over and catch Sister's eye as she was talking to a new admirer. I'd wink and she'd softly chuckle, neither of us breaking our respective rhythms.

In midafternoon, I paused. I once more backed up against the kiln room door in the shop. Just for a moment, to absorb what was happening right in front of me, which Sister Augustine often encouraged me to do. Panning the rooms, I was reminded, as I had also been in the lead-up to the open house, why I had gone into public relations in the first place. It wasn't all smoke and mirrors and mucky layers of spin. This—*this, right there in front of me, happening right now*—was fun, this was electric! And I saw how my work with Sister Augustine was making people happy. *This* was what PR is all about. Faith restored, I was now more excited than ever to share this feeling with my new students in January.

I was also reminded of how PR at its core is retail politics. Hand-to-hand schmoozing and selling. Give the customers what they want, and they will come. Sister and I had agreed that the back room would be off-limits, but several times throughout the day, she gave me permission to take people back to find a particular bisqueware piece or mold for something they wanted her to paint. "You're getting to see something rare. Sister Augustine doesn't allow many people back here," I told each of the customers whom I led there like a safari guide. A chorus of *oohs* and *aahs* followed every time. By then, my mom had started a separate order list for other items in addition to the wait list for Gussie's Specials.

While Denise poured countless pots of coffee into paper cups, Mom and Phyllis were in perpetual motion as a constant stream of Sister's pieces flowed through the checkout line— Santas, snowmen, ornaments, miniature trees, large light-up trees, plates and pitchers trimmed with forget-me-nots, piggy banks, tiny crosses, angels, wind chimes, Last Suppers, animals, birds, baby items, clowns, the Caribbean Blue ashtray-turned-candy dish, *The Flight into Egypt.*

"My piece isn't signed," one man informed me, flipping a decanter in the shape of a rosy-cheeked fireman upside down to show me. Only "SJC" and a neon orange price sticker were on the bottom.

"That's an older piece by Sister, which is why it isn't signed with her name. But she can sign it now," I told him, pointing in her direction.

Sister Augustine was still greeting a line of well-wishers, but managed to overhear me. "Don't keep telling people that," she scolded. "No one wants my signature."

"Yes we do," several people around her chimed in. "We want your autograph!"

I flashed her a playful *Told you so!* grin.

Sister shook her head at me and returned her attention to the person in front of her, who was saying what marvelous articles the newspapers had printed about her.

"I left a new Sharpie by your chair to use for signing!" I yelled over my shoulder before plunging back into the bustling shop.

By 5 p.m., the last few customers had trickled out and I locked the door. My Mom, Phyllis, and Denise helped clean up what they could and then left as well, each exhausted.

I unplugged the strings of colored lights, which snaked their lonesome way now over mostly bare shelves and encircled an empty tree. I decided any further rearranging or restocking could wait until the following week.

I walked back into the studio. Remarkably, Sister Augustine had not moved from her seat the entire day.

"So, what did you think?" I asked my friend.

"I never would have believed it in a million years."

Blitzen poked his head out from the back room. Confirming the coast was clear, he pounced his way over to Sister and onto her lap. "Where have you been all day?" she asked her bashful pal, who purred his response. "You missed all the excitement."

The studio and shop were completely quiet again. Through the windows, we could see a curtain of snow lighting up the darkening sky. If not for the bare shelves and stuffed money box, it might have been hard for us to convince even ourselves that hundreds of revelers had just trotted across those floors. And not a single ceramic piece had gotten broken, which was a miracle in and of itself.

I sat in my chair opposite Sister Augustine and examined the wait lists my mom had compiled throughout the day. "Sister, you have orders for fifty-four more Gussie's Specials and about three dozen other items, not including the seven Nativity sets people ordered today."

Sister looked up from petting Blitzen. "You're to blame for that," she teased with a hearty chortle.

"Guilty as charged!"

I glanced through the list of sales next. Holy *cha-ching*! "Mom didn't get to add up all the sales, but you had to have brought in thousands of dollars."

"Oh boy!" Sister Augustine exclaimed, clapping her hands together. "That's a lot for the convent."

"I imagine they did well up in the gift shop, too. And next year we can make the open house even bigger now that you're involved!"

"You're never going to let me rest, are you?"

"You made a lot of people happy today."

"Then it was a success," Sister remarked, focusing on what was most important.

"It was a perfect way to kick off the season," I added. "You reminded all those people today, and me, of the true meaning of Christmas, just by giving them a reason to visit the convent. Each of your pieces is filled with such love and joy."

"Don't be giving me an ego now!" she retorted.

"No, seriously," I said emphatically. "I think each of your pieces is meant for whoever ends up with it."

Sister smiled. "Well, some of those older pieces that people bought today have been sitting around here keeping me company for many years."

"Waiting for those people to come in and buy them," I added.

"We eventually find what we're looking for if we keep at it in this world, or it finds us," Sister said, reminding me of my own personal journey and challenges. "Even if it's a ceramic snowman."

I waved around the order sheets. "Be sure to get your rest tomorrow, because come Monday, you have a lot of work to do."

"Guess I'll be sticking around a little longer," Sister Augustine said, speaking more to Blitzen than me.

I sure hoped so. My smile grew even wider. I had come to think of every day there with Sister Augustine as Christmas.

PART FOUR

11

NEW YEAR'S RESOLUTIONS

A FEW WEEKS INTO THE NEW YEAR, I RETURNED TO THE CE-
ramic shop. I had last seen Sister Augustine right before Christmas and then I was swept up in a glorious rush of holiday parties
and family obligations.

I had also been busy over the holidays preparing to teach
my first course, Public Relations 1304: Promotional Writing,
at Pitt-Bradford. I meticulously labored over every detail of the
course syllabus, switching around assignments and adding new
material right up until the last minute before I had to send it off
to the administrative assistant in the Communication and the
Arts Division to be copied. I knew this experience was going
to be a fresh starting line in my life, so I wanted to really savor
every aspect and make it as perfect as possible.

Then, on a snowy afternoon in early January, I finally got
to walk into a classroom that was all mine. Before entering, I
paused near the open door, which was at the end of a long corridor in Swarts Hall. I peeked inside and saw about a dozen students, all seniors, who were starting the final semester of their
college careers. Suddenly it struck me: I was about to have the
privilege of traveling this last leg of their journey with them in
the moment right before they would begin again. Just as they
would be traversing my new beginning as a teacher with me. I
took a long, deep breath and walked into my classroom, smiling.

There was a renewed spring in my step these days. In addition to my teaching gig, I was still coasting on the success we had enjoyed with the open house. I was excited to now get back to what I considered to be my home away from home at the convent and see my friend again. I had missed her.

The wind chimes I set in motion on the front porch of the Guesthouse kept tolling after I entered, a reminder of the frigid wind that I was happy to leave behind outside. Through steamy glasses, I saw Sister Augustine sitting in her mint-green spindle chair at the worktable. She was wearing her denim bib apron with its years of paint smudges—a few strokes more and it could have been framed itself.

"Happy New Year!" I called out.

"Hello!" Sister was already looking in my direction, having heard the chimes.

"It's freezing out there. Luckily it's nice and toasty in here." The golden light that engulfed the studio was in stark contrast to the gray-tweed landscape I had just trudged through.

"I see you're a bit fogged up." Sister Augustine chuckled, pointing to my glasses.

"I was in such a hurry to get out of the cold that I forgot to turn around and come in backwards," I lamented, wiping my lenses with the bottom of my shirt, leaving them smeared and worse for the wear.

I settled into my seat opposite of where Sister was working. She had a lineup of greenware in front of her. Several would-be Gussie's Specials, a few tall vases, Nativity figures, and some other odds and ends. To the side, a group of Duncan paint and glaze bottles set with names that seemed better suited to my test kitchen—Butter Toffee, Spiced Cream, Cornmeal, Mocha, Roasted Pepper, Oregano, Curry, Cantaloupe, Lemon Peel, Papaya, Cranberry, Cinnamon, Butterscotch, Caramel, Espresso. My mouth watered.

Blitzen, the ever-faithful hybrid of furry muse and comic relief, supervised from the other table.

"I take it you've been busy these last few weeks," I said, motioning to the counter that ran the length of the wall behind me where the checkout station was. It was filled with Gussie's Specials, plates trimmed with forget-me-nots, statues of the Blessed Mother, Nativities, and other clayware items. All open house orders waiting to be picked up.

I tried to not look too closely at the Gussie's Specials that were already spoken for, or else a few might have gone home with me, adding to Sister's workload. Each one was an aurora of colors—swirling, dripping, running, layered, blended, and even thickly applied in small gobs here and there, creating three-dimensional textures.

"Those bowls are extraordinary! Some of your best ones yet," I gushed.

Sister smiled. "These are more of the open house orders here," she said, redirecting my attention back to the muddy-gray pieces on the table in front of her. "I've been working at these orders just about every day since I last saw you, and I'm still nowhere near finished with them. I've even come in on a few Sundays. Plus, I've gotten several new orders for Gussie's Specials and other pieces from people who have come in since Christmas. This place has been hopping."

I was tempted to call her a "superstar" like I sometimes did playfully, even though it wasn't really a joke anymore and always garnered me a mock scolding. However, I decided to let it slide this time.

The new greenware pieces on the table had been removed from their molds earlier that morning. They were dried, but still fragile, as I had found out the hard way during one of my very first visits with Sister. I kept my curious hands to myself this time.

With an X-ACTO knife and a surgeon's precision, Sister Augustine was carefully trimming off the rough edges denoting the seam where the two halves of the mold had come together, as well as along the lip of the future Gussie's Special she was working on. The clay trimmings were placed on a nearby pile to later be recycled into other pieces, like her tiny cookie-cutter crosses. Sister would then dip a small sponge into a repurposed plastic Cool Whip container filled with water and run the moist sponge over the edges to further smoothen them. Sometimes she used her fingers to placate the rough edges. This was the stage before the pieces were baked in the kiln, becoming the white bisqueware she would then paint or glaze.

"Did you make a New Year's resolution?" I asked.

"I do that every morning," Sister Augustine replied, keeping her eyes focused on the direction of the razor's edge. "Every morning during prayers in the chapel, I pray to become a better person. After all, isn't every day technically the first day of a new year?"

"I never thought of it like that."

"I'm always amused by people who think they have to make some grand resolution or promise to themselves because it's January first."

"Especially since most of those resolutions are forgotten a few weeks later, or sooner," I added with the panache of an expert on the topic. Admittedly not my proudest moments, I had some experience in the area of lax intentions.

"Yes," Sister said, smiling. "All those resolutions people make to be healthier, or happier, or more devoted to their faith or some other endeavor, should be something they promise themselves every day, not just on one day. Otherwise, they're only left disappointed and defeated. Until the next January first, when they make the same promises to themselves and the cycle begins again."

Sister now moved on to a Nativity camel. She dipped her finger in the cloudy water and skimmed the animal's hump, first erasing the seam line running over the middle and then the rough edge around the figurine's base. No beginning or end was left visible.

"But how can people focus on those resolutions every day when their lives are so crazy busy?"

"So many people think that these promises they make to themselves are something that requires lots of time and effort," Sister answered. "That's not true. It really is as easy as repeating the promise to yourself each day, then finding simple ways to set it in motion. Setting a goal like strengthening your faith doesn't necessarily mean rattling off a litany of prayers or going to mass every day; maybe it's just saying hi to God every once in a while. 'Hi, God!' or 'Forget me not, Lord!' That's it. Simple."

"I think everyone makes those promises with good intentions, but then life happens and we forget about them," I commented, thinking, *Guilty as charged.*

"You're right."

"So then what?"

"Make yourself little daily reminders. If you forget the resolutions you make or become discouraged by your lack of discipline, you're not helping anyone, least of all yourself. In fact, you're doing the complete opposite."

"I suspect most people who fail to keep up with their resolutions become so discouraged that it's easier for them to cut their losses and move on," I pointed out. *Guilty again.*

"But they don't move on," Sister countered. "Sweeping dirt under the carpet doesn't make it go away; it eventually just makes for a lumpy carpet that's hard to walk on. Sooner or later, you're knocked off balance. And the next time you make such a promise, those seeds of failure and doubt grow a little more, while your self-confidence shrinks."

"A lot of people do seem to just give up—on their health, their happiness, and their faith these days." I thought of how many times in the last few years I almost gave up on my dreams of being a teacher and writer, and even teetered on the edge of a faith that I had temporarily lost touch with. Each challenge I faced and every rejection letter I received while wandering in the desert that my life had become was like an invitation to quit, written in flashing neon lights.

"You can see the defeat in their eyes and slumped shoulders when people give up," Sister Augustine said. "It's sad to watch. Instead of seeing each day, and each moment really, as a new beginning, suddenly people exist only to run down the clock. They forget that life is precious."

How true, I thought. I once read a book where a young boy, upon seeing a dead bird in the street, asked his father why the living must die. His father told him, Because nothing that's ours forever is ever precious.

"Do you think giving up could have something to do with the fact that we, as a human race, don't exactly like change?" This was a rhetorical question, I suppose, since just saying the word *change* sent a chilly jolt up my spine.

Sister set the camel on the table, and brought another future Gussie's Special to her lap to smooth its jagged edges. "Change is one of the hardest things for us to accept, but it's one of the only things we are guaranteed to encounter in this life, good and bad. We need to embrace change as a gift, even the unpleasant ones, just as we should the sorrows that come our way."

"I'm not a huge fan of change," I confessed.

"Maybe you just found your daily resolution then," Sister Augustine suggested with a wink.

I laughed. "One of them anyway."

"Remember when you first realized that the road to all those yeses you're working toward in life is paved with many nos?"

Affirmative, I nodded. "You helped me to understand that."

"Change is the same way. Each change we encounter is also a stepping-stone, if we let it be. When you think about it, we encounter dozens of changes every day; many are so small we don't even notice them, but they're there. It's the big bad ones that seem to stop us cold in our tracks. But changes that we see as tragic or depressing, or disturbing in some way, are only new beginnings. Just like the good changes, such as realizing at age ninety that you still have a lot of work left to do. That's how change should be embraced."

At age thirty-four, I wondered just how many changes, good and bad, were still ahead of me. I only hoped I would be able to start embracing all of them as the gifts they were meant to be. My new promotional writing class was a big change for me, and it was a blessing for sure.

"Fear is the real enemy, isn't it?" I then asked. "Fear of change and of just about everything else bad that might happen to us."

"Fear is a gift from the Devil," Sister Augustine said.

"Even when something good is happening to us, like my new teaching job at the university, there can still be fears of things like failure and judgment."

"That's because evil thrives on vulnerability and failure. And anything good will always be the target of evil," Sister confirmed. "By the way, I meant to ask you about the class you're teaching," she added, momentarily diverting our conversation. "How's it going?"

"I love it! The students are so great and the subject is right up my alley," I told her. "I have all seniors, who are majoring in public relations. I'm leading them through the different types of promotional writing that are used in the PR field, like press releases, media advisories, proposals, pitch letters, bios, ads, slogans, speeches, newsletters, and things like that. I'm even going to work with them to get their resumes in tip-top shape. After all, a resume is one of the most important pieces of promotional writing they'll ever create for themselves."

"Public relations is certainly a topic you know something about," Sister said, "but I'll take my clay and paintbrushes any day over doing interviews and having my picture taken!"

"I'll eventually be talking about you in class," I teased. "I'm going to tell my students what a natural you are when it comes to doing those interviews and photo ops."

Sister shook her head and rolled her eyes. "Now *that's* what scares me," she bantered.

"I can't imagine anything scares you anymore."

"We're all susceptible to fear and evil, even at my age," Sister Augustine said more seriously. "These walls here aren't immune to those things any more than the walls of your own home or any place else. We always have to remember, though, that like rejection and change, fear can also be used as a tool to make us stronger. When we see fear only as an insurmountable wall, then that's a dead end. There's nowhere to go. That's a hell here on earth."

Fear—an insurmountable wall. My mind turned the image over in my head. I had stood in front of that wall more times than I cared to admit throughout my life, starting early on.

Several red plastic cookie cutters scattered on the table up by Sister's other chair caught my eye. Classic metaphor, the cookie cutter. A Cookie-Cutter Life: born, grow up, go to school, go to work, get married, have kids, work some more, retire, die. All with little deviation, maybe a sidestep of some kind, but more or less the straight and narrow path. Sounds simple and nice. And safe. My life from the beginning was more like the trail left in the black night by a child excitedly waving a sparkler. Especially when it came to fear.

Throughout middle and high school, many of my classmates bullied me. I was a gentle and kind teen, but perhaps as an only child I had been too sheltered, overprotected early on by loving parents. I didn't have brothers and sisters to roughhouse with to toughen me up or to educate me about the world as only siblings can, or to forge a path and protective barrier for me. I preferred spending my weekends doing homework and artwork to going to beer parties and hooking up, like many of my peers. I was a loner for whom my shyness and awkwardness in forming friendships translated to some as weakness. As a result, I was a lamb set out in a field of lions.

Alone, I once walked into a dance in our high school gymnasium—Bon Jovi's "Livin' on a Prayer" blaring from the speakers—to find a gang of older students stomping their feet on the bleachers and chanting my name followed by venomous vitriol. Those bullies changed my life forever. They engendered a fear I still carried in the pit of my chest, which I could forgive but would never forget. That's a hell here on earth.

"Most people stagnate at that dead-end wall, don't they?" I asked.

"Unfortunately, yes. People suffer and the Devil laughs," Sister answered.

"We all hit those walls at times."

"Absolutely. Many, many walls. That, as they say, is life. The difference for some, though, is that they look upward and think, *I can climb right up over this wall.* Or they look to the sides, and think, *I can go around this wall.* Or, if nothing else, they take a step back and carefully examine the wall, thinking, *I can smash right through it!*"

"We always have a choice," I said, as the realization was further solidified in my heart and mind.

"Yes, and it's our choice to go over, around, or straight through our problems and fears, and evil itself, that builds courage and helps fortify us against the next challenge. That is what embracing change, even when it's riddled with fear, is all about."

Sister's perspective lent affirmation to the promise I had made to myself long ago that I wouldn't let other people's opinions stop me from moving forward. Nor would I now give up on my dream of having a renewed life. No matter what. Especially since I was starting to see the first glimmers of that new life. I was dismantling the wall in front of me brick by brick.

Sister set her last, finished piece of greenware on the table with the others, each one now with smooth edges. She then picked up a ballpoint pen, turned every piece over, and using the tip of the pen, etched "Sister M. Augustine, O.S.B.," the year, and "SJC."

Out of the corner of my eye, I saw Blitzen stand and slowly wind his way across the tables and over to the Cool Whip container near Sister for a sip of water.

"Stop drinking that," Sister scolded, momentarily looking up from inscribing the pieces. "You have plenty of fresh water in your own bowl in the corner." She looked over at me. "I don't know why, but Blitzen always drinks this dirty water. When I leave at night, I need to make sure I pour it out or cover it, or else it's empty the next morning, while his bowl of fresh water is still full. I can yell about it until the cows come home, but he doesn't listen. He's not so keen on embracing change. One of these days, I'm going to come in and find a clay cat!"

I laughed. "He's pretty fearless, isn't he?"

"More like spoiled," Sister Augustine said, laughing as well. "He even loves the rain. I have to let him out every time it's raining or he just keeps scratching at the front door. Have you ever heard of a cat who likes to get wet? He's a true original, this one. *Aren't you?*"

Blitzen meowed his response, then darted away.

Before I left, I helped Sister Augustine carry each of the greenware pieces from the table into the kiln room. I was careful now each time to pick them up from below with both hands, firmly supporting them, and then I'd hold my breath until I set them back down. I wanted to avoid personally expediting any sorrows in the ceramic shop.

With each piece I transported, I contemplated how New Year's resolutions—all those promises we make to ourselves—along with change and fear, should all come in the form of fragile greenware. Perhaps then we'd treat them more mindfully, hence more successfully.

I handed Sister the last bowl to place on the shelves near the kiln, sighing in relief afterward. It would remain there with the other greenware until she had enough for a full firing.

"You know, Sister, each time I help you carry this greenware I get to practice patience, slowing down, and letting go of fear," I said with a proud smile. "And, I realize I'm not all thumbs—at least not all the time! I'd say that's a positive change in my life."

"It's well worth the effort then," my friend declared with a chuckle.

12

Amazing Grace

On a cool fall night in 1942, Sister Augustine and Sister Thecla gazed at the starry heavens from a top-floor window during one of their after-curfew chat sessions at St. Joseph Monastery. Sixty-eight miles to the west, in Knox, their brother John's farmhouse burned to the ground with him and his entire family in it—wife, Louise, a set of infant twins, and two other young children.

My friend had known the worst of personal tragedy and loss throughout her life. Her parents and ten siblings had all passed away before her. Sister Augustine and her youngest brother, Ben, a musician whom she once pulled to school every day in an old wooden wagon, were now the last ones left from her immediate family. I knew she would have the understanding and comfort I desperately needed on this particular spring afternoon.

"Sister, Sister!" I called out, rushing past the kiln room, not even noticing she was in there.

I was already to the shrunken doorway leading into the back room when I heard her call back, "In here!" I turned to see her peeking out from the small side room.

I quickly returned to the front of the shop.

"What is it?" she asked, obviously seeing I was distraught. "What's wrong?"

"We were all just called to the nursing home where my Grandma Skok is," I told her. "They say this is it."

Pinecrest Manor was on the same road as St. Joseph Monastery, leading out of town on the western end. My mom's eighty-nine-year-old mother had been there for several weeks, suffering from a cancerous tumor that had only recently been diagnosed. I had been very close to her my entire life. She was one of the first people who taught me that age as a number is meaningless in this life. And that the more important thing is the answer to this question: are you having fun or not? She was always the life of any party, answering that question resoundingly with every breath.

"I'm so sorry to hear that," Sister Augustine said, setting a newly fired dinner plate encircled with forget-me-nots on the shelf behind her. "Is there anything I can do?"

I was in dire need of solace, wisdom, and reassurance, and she was the only person I thought to turn to. "Grandma is the first person in a long time I'm really close to who is going to . . ." I stopped. It was hard to even say the word *die*. Speaking it would make it all too real. Chances were, I'd be there when Grandma Skok actually passed away, which was something I had never experienced before.

"She lived a long life, right?"

"Yes," I answered.

"Did she lead a happy life?"

I nodded. "She turned every minute into a party. In fact, I've never met anyone quite like her and her sisters, and my mom, who can all laugh in any situation, even sad ones."

"Laughter like that is a great blessing, especially during sad times," Sister said. "Does she have a strong faith?"

"One of the strongest! In fact, one time when she was in church alone praying for my cousin, who was very ill at the time, a young boy approached her and asked, 'Ma'am, may I please spend a moment in prayer with you?' He proceeded to kneel beside her for several minutes, then he left. She never saw him again and was always convinced that he was the child Jesus who had come to her in a time of need. Especially after my cousin made a full recovery."

"How wonderful!"

"She always retold that story," I said. "I actually had a similar thing happen to me a few days ago."

Sister's eyes widened. "Really? What was it?"

I settled back against the doorframe to tell my story. The last few days spent at the nursing home had exhausted me mentally and physically. "Once it became apparent that Grandma wasn't going to get any better, I went out for a walk late one afternoon to clear my head and make some sense of it all. Halfway through, I saw two young men in white shirts and black pants coming toward me. My first thought was, *Oh no, Jehovah's Witnesses or Mormons!* I shouldn't have felt that way, but sometimes we become a little territorial over our own faiths and beliefs, and caught up in the stereotypes of others."

"Prideful and egotistical, too," Sister added with a chuckle. "No good has ever come of that yet, but still there are those who insist on persecuting others based on faith and stereotypes."

I nodded in agreement. "You'll be happy to know, I quickly changed my tune as they approached. After they introduced themselves, I smiled and said, 'Please walk with me.' They looked surprised to be greeted so warmly as they quickly turned around and accompanied me. One walked beside me and the other behind me.

"As we walked, I asked them about their thoughts on God, on living and dying, on Heaven, on love. The one next to me did most of the talking while the other young guy behind me kept smiling and blushing, like he could barely keep from burst-

ing with some incredible secret he had to tell me. That's what I
actually thought when I'd look over my shoulder at him every
so often. Something about him made me feel cheerful, and
something about the guy walking next to me and answering my
questions calmed my fears.

"Eventually, we reached the corner by where I live and we
parted ways after I thanked them. I told them that I hoped our
paths would cross again one day. They both smiled at me, and
then they turned around and started to walk back up the hill
that we had just come down, while I headed home in the opposite direction. As soon as I reached my front door, no more than
a minute later, it suddenly struck me—like a humongous flash
of light in my head: The one walking next to me had brown
hair and brown eyes, and the giggly one behind me had blond
hair and blue eyes."

Sister's face lit up. "Your two guardian angels!"

"Had to be!" I confirmed. "I quickly turned back in the
direction I had come from and they were gone. Gone in a flash.
Just like that. Into thin air."

A while back, I had told Sister Augustine how I liked to
think I had two guardian angels. The topic had come up one
afternoon when I noticed two small ceramic cherubs—like de-
scendants of Raphael's famous duo—tucked away behind the
checkout station in her studio. I had never seen them hanging
there before. I believed God had led me to find them there
when I did, as confirmation that we all have guardian angels
around us. The one angelic figurine had brown hair and brown
eyes and the other had blond hair and blue eyes. They gave face
to the two guardian angels in my mind. Sister told me that they
had been left over from the collection of angels she had painted
for each of the nuns as a Christmas gift a few years back before
she and I had even met. I just knew those two little angels had
always been there waiting for me to happen upon them when

the time was right. I took them home and hung them on the wall next to my bed, so I'd see them before falling asleep each night and then again first thing in the morning.

"You were blessed, John. You kept your mind open to such encounters, obviously like your grandmother did all those years ago, and they came to you. God and his messengers come in many shapes and forms, especially when we most need them."

"I felt such a sense of peace about my grandma after talking with them. It was a huge step in this process. Though it still isn't easy."

"Do you think your grandmother is ready to go?"

"No." I was sure of that. "She doesn't even like to go to bed at night and sleep, for fear she'll miss out on something fun."

Sister grinned. "But do you think she's at peace?"

"Yes," I replied. "I've spent a lot of time with her in the last few weeks and I've felt a great serenity around her. Even when I've been anxious about the situation, she's been calm and peaceful. In fact, early on, I even noticed a glow emanating from her face."

"That sounds beautiful," Sister said. "How's your mother? She's such a kind and generous lady."

"Strong. The other night, Grandma called out to my mom in front of everyone in the room. She said, 'Barbara, come tell your mother goodbye.' I just stood there and watched. It was one of those moments in life when you want to run from the room and keep running as fast and as far away as you can."

"But I bet you didn't run. After all, reality and God have a way of catching up with us."

"No, I didn't run. I watched my mom walk over to her mother and say, 'Goodbye, Mom.' It was horrible."

"Not horrible. Extraordinary! How blessed you were to see such an extraordinary example of strength and courage, by both women. It couldn't have been easy for either of them to engage in that moment, but they both did."

"It was really the last thing Grandma has said."

"It's always a blessing to be present when someone is born into this world or passes from it. It's in those amazing moments that God reveals His grace to us. And sometimes, He calls upon us to help in that process by letting someone we dearly love know that they can go."

"I've heard that often a person who is dying waits to see that one special person before they go."

Sister smiled. "We living creatures can be stubborn in that way, and in so many other ways."

I laughed in agreement. "So we basically tell God to hang on?"

"Something like that, though I would guess by now He's already factored that part in. He's not exactly new at this type of thing. He knows every one of the breaths we take. They, too, are manifestations of His grace."

"I'll never forget that moment between my grandma and Mom."

"Good, you shouldn't. You were meant to witness it. Someday, hopefully long from now, you'll be called upon in the same way as your mother was to help a loved one, maybe many loved ones, to know that it's okay to go."

"I don't even want to think about it."

"There's no reason you should dwell on it. This world is for the living. As human beings with human emotions, we naturally become sad when we lose a loved one, but ultimately, we have to choose how to deal with that sadness."

"It can destroy people. I've seen that happen."

"So have I. A husband or wife becomes inconsolable after their spouse dies. Parents lose their own will to live after the death of a child. One friend never recovers from the death of another friend. Even the death of a pet can crack the spirit wide open."

"What's the best way to move through grief?"

"It's certainly not to forget it. So many turn to drugs or other distractions, trying to forget about their loss. Or they run away like you were tempted to. Those things are only cheap cosmetics that soon wash away. The best way to handle grief is to walk through it with the grace that comes at such times."

"So many people are afraid to even cry. They always apologize for breaking down."

"Tears should be welcomed, not feared," Sister Augustine stated, leaning back now against the tower of shelves behind her.

I had brought her work to a standstill. The kiln remained full of forget-me-nots—two complete sets of dinnerware that Patty and Steven had each commissioned. I continued to rest against the door frame while Blitzen snuggled around my ankles, sensing my sadness. From the wall, President Kennedy gazed down upon us, his eyes sympathetic and ever hopeful.

Sister elaborated: "Tears are a tangible sign of grace at times like this. I'll never understand why people feel ashamed or like they need to apologize for one of the most natural outlets we have in this world for moving through grief and other challenges. On the other hand, many people can't cry, because they've bottled up their emotions so much."

"Being ashamed of tears and bottling them up inside aren't very healthy approaches," I said. I didn't have a problem with that. I came from a long line of emotional grandmothers and aunts. Tears came naturally to me; the free flow of that grace was ingrained in my genes.

"No, it's not healthy at all. Those approaches only turn the human body and spirit into a pressure cooker. It would be like me leaving all these forget-me-not plates and bowls and cups in this kiln, and each hour turning the heat up higher and higher."

"KABOOM!"

"Exactly."

"Are you afraid of dying, Sister?"

Sister Augustine smiled at the sharp and direct turn I had taken on the topic. "No. Everyone is entitled to their reward."

"I never thought of dying as a reward."

"Dying is the pathway to the reward that Heaven promises for those who are good and at peace."

I was suddenly reminded of a seventh grader I had met while student teaching a few years earlier in a local public middle school. One morning before school started, the young boy came back to the table where I was arranging materials for that day's lesson and asked if he could help. When I told him that he could, he looked at me with heartfelt eyes and said, "For those who help, the gates of Heaven are opened." His words gave me pause. So young, so profound. A little messenger bearing his own special beatitude. He, too, was speaking of the reward Sister now referred to.

"You better not plan on getting your reward anytime soon," I warned Sister Augustine with a playful grin. "There's too much left for you to do."

"Only God knows that answer," she remarked with a wink. "You know, many in my family have died suddenly. I don't ever want you to be surprised if you come one day and I'm not here."

I couldn't bear the thought, but I understood that she was preparing me for something I would inevitably face. "Do I need to place an order for a million more Gussie's Specials to make sure that doesn't happen for a very long time?"

Sister Augustine chuckled. "Heaven help me!"

"I better get going," I said, checking my watch. The rest of my family would be at Pinecrest Manor with Grandma Skok by now.

"I'll say a special prayer for your grandmother, and for you and your family," Sister said. "Just remember, what you're about to experience is a gift. Embrace it and learn from it."

"Okay," I whispered, bending down to pet Blitzen before turning and walking out the door. A feeling of peace and understanding was beginning to course through me. Like when you see the first glimmer on a chilly, dark horizon and know day has finally arrived after a long restless night.

I gently brushed my fingers across the wind chimes on the porch, relishing every note they sent into the air behind me. Each one, as graceful and fleeting as our own breaths.

13

HOLY THURSDAY

"I TOLD MY PROMOTIONAL WRITING STUDENTS ALL ABOUT you this week," I announced as I settled into my mint-green spindle chair three days before Easter.

"You did?" Sister Augustine sat in her oak chair at the right-hand corner of the horseshoe. Perched on the top shelf over her shoulder, the ceramic eagle stood guard. I made a mental note to buy him at some point, but for now he was where he needed to be. On the other side of the doorway leading to the back room, the pure white statue of the Blessed Mother was also ever watchful from a small corner shelf near the ceiling.

"Yep. I've been telling them about you throughout the semester, but this time I actually took some of your Gussie's Specials from my collection to show them. I told them again all about your shop, the open house, how great you did in the interviews, all the great news stories you got, and how fantastic the turnout was. It was for a lesson I was teaching on promoting special events."

Sister chuckled and shook her head, staring eye to eye with the ceramic rabbit she was dressing with a generous coat of chocolate brown paint. "*Me being talked about in a college class.* Is that what education has come to these days?"

"The students loved hearing about you! I like bringing real-world examples of public relations into the classroom. In fact, I start every class with a discussion about what's happening in the news and then ask the students how they would handle those situations from a PR perspective."

"It's good for students to learn that way," Sister said. "It's more hands-on. Textbooks are only part of what makes a lesson valuable. When I was a teacher, I always believed that sharing personal experiences and real-world examples with students taught them more than they could ever learn from just a book. My students loved hearing stories about my childhood on our farm. Since I taught elementary school, the younger students all thought my father was the real Farmer in the Dell *and* Old MacDonald!"

I glanced down at the ceramic rabbit nestled in Sister's hands. I could see young Anna giggling and chasing real-life rabbits that looked just like that one all over Mockin' Bird Hill.

"Well, I doubt most of my students ever even get to see a nun these days, let alone discuss one in their college courses," I said with a laugh. "So my presentation about you covered several bases."

"Now if we could only get some of those young women interested in joining us here," Sister Augustine commented, glancing up with a wink.

"My students who are also interested in art went especially crazy over your Gussie's Specials." I told her how one of their favorites was the bowl that evoked a southwestern desert—denim sky and cocoa sand with rivers of turquoise and fire that would be at home in an O'Keeffe landscape. Another class favorite was a small dark bowl that looked like the rippling blur of a busy city street at night during a downpour. "I lined the bowls on the table at the front of the room and after class many of the students came up for a closer look. I even showed them your picture and read some of the responses you gave to the interview questions."

Sister chortled. "Did you tell them how much I *love* talking to reporters?"

"I told them you're a dream client and that you handled the reporters like a Hollywood pro."

"Oh, you!" Sister swatted her brush toward me. "I almost had to go to confession after those interviews to repent for what I was really thinking."

I cracked up. "The students' favorite quote of yours was when the reporter asked why you still do this work at age ninety and you told her, 'It keeps me off the streets.' They howled when I told them that."

A grin spread across my friend's face as she continued to focus on giving the rabbit a new coat. Sister Augustine was clearly enjoying the idea that a bunch of college students found her story and artwork so entertaining.

"However, I held my breath the entire time they were picking up your bowls. I kept thinking, *Please don't drop it! Please don't drop it!*"

"I can just see you," Sister said, chuckling.

"Speaking of which, I see you finished some new Gussie's Specials. They look great on the island in the shop." She was now also invoking her technique of cleaning off brushes on vases more often in addition to the bowls she had always used.

"I just took those out of the kiln this morning. All joys and no sorrows this time, thank God. So you think I did an okay job of arranging them? You're the pro at that."

"They look fantastic. I saw a few I'm going to have to add to my collection." Two curvaceous bud vases that looked as though they had rolled across a wet Twombly canvas had caught my eye.

"Haven't you run out of room yet?"

"Nope." I told her how my collection was displayed on

shelves behind my writing desk at home. And there was still plenty of empty space left to fill.

"I finished your eggs, too," Sister Augustine informed me, motioning toward the counter along the wall behind me. "I wasn't sure I'd make it with all the other orders, but I just got them done under the wire."

I turned around to check them out. "Awesome! I love them!" When Sister told me she had molds for large Easter eggs, I asked her to create several and cover them with her forget-me-not motif. One was for my collection and the others were gifts. "I was hoping they'd be ready. I'm planning to give one to my cousin when we go to her house on Sunday."

"This is one of my favorite times of the year," Sister revealed. "Lent, Holy Week, then Easter. It's a time of renewal, hope, and new beginnings. It demonstrates how we can, and should, move from grief and sadness to rejoicing."

"Do you do anything special here at the convent for Holy Thursday?" I asked, focusing on the day at hand.

Sister looked up from the buttercup yellow bow she was painting around her chocolate bunny. "My favorite activity is when we commemorate how Jesus washed the feet of His apostles at the Last Supper."

"Who washes your feet?"

Sister smiled. "I wash the feet of the other sisters."

"*You do?*" At first, I was flabbergasted at how the other nuns could make a ninety-year-old woman get down on her knees to wash their feet.

"It's a great honor for me," Sister Augustine explained.

An honor? The image ping-ponged through my head. Then, I got it: that was the role of Jesus she was re-creating. It spoke to the humility and love Sister had in her heart. And the respect that the other nuns at St. Joseph's had for her.

She continued: "It's also a reminder of the importance of our connections to one another."

"That connection is something the world is starting to lose," I said reflectively.

"When I wash the feet of my fellow sisters, I'm reminded just how powerful the human touch is in this world." Sister Augustine held the ceramic rabbit in the air, examining her brushwork and searching for where she might have missed a spot.

"Yet so many people won't even hug or shake hands, or even look at each other anymore. They're in too much of a hurry," I said.

"It's sad. We can't survive without touch and a connection to each other. From the time we're born, we need to be held and nurtured. We need to feel that we belong to a family and, once we grow older and become more aware, we then understand the need to belong to something greater than ourselves. But today, television, computers, and other gadgets have replaced that hug and handshake, or even simple eye contact. Just as busy schedules have. People isolate themselves from others with these things and they might even be sitting in the same room together. That's what I will never understand. It's a case of so close, yet so far away."

I let her words percolate in my mind for a few moments. I thought about how sometimes my friends and I sat right next to each other but we were either glued to the TV or texting on our phones, instead of interacting. Or we were too busy to even spend any time at all together. When I walked around campus, I saw the same thing among the students and professors. In the rat race we had become as a society, we the rats were the real losers.

"How can we change that and regain that connection?" I wanted to know.

Sister again dipped her brush in the paint bottle aptly labeled

Chocolate Fudge and began dabbing a second coat on the rabbit. "First, by realizing that we are all in this world together. I'm a part of you, you're a part of me. In God's eyes, we are all equal and precious. We must look at one another with those same eyes. Instead, we too often think with a me-versus-you mentality. That only pushes us farther apart. We should think with an 'us' and 'we' mentality. Us and we, all of us are in this moment and this world together."

"That's easier said than done."

Sister plucked a new paintbrush from the bouquet of bristles in the nearby glossy black pedestal cup. She transitioned to working on the rabbit's eyes, choosing a soft blue paint that was cheery and hopeful. "That phrase—*Easier said than done*—has always puzzled me. Somewhere along the line, people got it into their minds that saying something is always easier than actually doing it. I suppose that's true if the words one is speaking are empty. But think of how difficult it is to tell someone, 'I love you' and truly mean it. It's often easier, and just as powerful, to show someone you love them by doing a good deed for them."

"You're right," I said. "My parents and I rarely, if ever, tell each other, 'I love you,' yet we know that we each have great love for one another. We're always there for each other, showing love through our actions."

"That's a great example. It's not always easy to say those three little words, but actions have a voice, too."

I realized I had never told Sister Augustine that I loved her. Not with words anyway. Until that point in my life, those weren't words I spoke very often. Yet, I assumed she knew that I loved her very much, in the same way I knew that she loved me. I hoped I had demonstrated that to her somehow. But still, maybe one day I would be able to actually tell her.

Sister continued: "You exemplify that important connection with your students. You engage them in discussions. You talk with them, not at them. By doing so, you're letting them know that their thoughts, opinions, and actions matter in this world. And that they matter to you."

Very true, I thought. There's nothing like the feeling of closing the classroom door and for an hour and fifteen minutes setting sail on some adventure with students. All for one, one for all—discussing, solving, learning together.

"Unlike the publishers sending me those rejection letters," I said, raising my brow. "The letters are usually form letters addressed 'Dear Author,' and some are like millionth-generation photocopies. I've even gotten a few careless letters where the text was copied crookedly on the page." I scoffed at how ridiculous some were.

Sister chuckled. "I would say that those publishers might need a little work in this area."

"Those kinds of letters are so cold and impersonal."

"That's how society is becoming: cold and impersonal, and distant," Sister lamented. "Yet, think about when you pass someone on the street, especially a stranger, and they say, 'Hello!' or just smile at you. How does that make you feel?"

"Warm and welcome. Like I know them."

"Exactly. That's because you do already know them. In God's realm, you are already attached to them without even knowing their name or anything else about them. When we each start from that place, a place of knowing we are each related to every other living being like brothers and sisters, then we already have a head start on further connecting with them."

I recalled one of my favorite speeches, Saint Francis's Sermon to the Birds: *the bonds are many that unite us . . .*

I thought for a moment. "You know, that reminds me of my dad. While driving, he's always smiling and waving to the people passing by, even if he doesn't know them. One time I asked him why he does that and he told me, 'The quickest way to make a friend is to smile at a stranger.' He once mentioned this to a priest and the following Sunday my dad was surprised to hear the priest use that story in his homily."

"Sounds like your father understands the importance of our connections to one another," Sister said with a smile. "And it sounds like that priest knows a good lesson when he hears one."

By seeing my dad do this every day, essentially igniting a chain reaction of kindness and connection, he taught me how powerful a simple smile can be. His message was clear, and one I would eventually translate into a participatory art piece titled *THE SMILE THAT CHANGED THE WORLD (is yours)*.

"Staying connected really is that simple, isn't it?" I asked.

"Yes—a smile, a wave, a hello. Mother Teresa once said, 'A smile is the beginning of peace.' But staying connected also requires effort. We need to work at it each day or else we can quickly lose it. Think of those people who are shut-in, either because they've removed themselves from society or because various circumstances, such as poverty, or sickness, or old age, have isolated them. We must seek them out as well. If they're suffering, then all of us are suffering.

"Likewise, so often people will ignore others because they don't have as much money, or they don't look a certain way, or they're somehow deemed unworthy. It would be like me declaring to the sisters, 'I'm not washing your feet tonight because I'm one of the oldest here and I have rank!' Me being one of the oldest is exactly the point. Jesus didn't need to wash His apostles' feet, either. He was the Son of God. But He chose to lead by example and show that status in this life is just an illusion at best. It isn't what really matters. We are all equal and here to help guide each other. What matters is reaching out and touching one another in some way."

"I like to think that even after people die, we're still connected to them," I said. "I have what I call my Heavenly Board of Directors . . ."

"Heavenly Board of Directors? That's a new one I never heard of," Sister said. "But I like the sound of it."

I smiled. "My Heavenly Board of Directors consists of family members and friends I was close to, who have passed away. And even people I may have only met in passing but they left some positive impression on me before they died. I like to think I'm still connected to them all, and that they guide me and help answer my prayers." I paused for a beat, then added, "My Heavenly Board is working overtime these days!"

"I love that," Sister said, grinning. "Souls are eternal and powerful, and, yes, our connections to one another are eternal as well."

"It's a big circle," I said.

"With no beginning and no end," Sister added. She then turned toward the mint-green shelves directly behind her. "See the picture of that child?"

I stood and walked over. A thin, dark-skinned boy, maybe eight or nine years old, in a blue and white T-shirt smiled back at me from the small photograph. Over the years, I had often wondered who the boy in the picture was, but I never asked, figuring Sister would one day tell me if she wanted to.

"That's a Brazilian child named Helio, who I sponsor through the Christian Children's Fund," Sister explained. "Every month, I send money to the organization so they can care for him."

During a previous visit, Sister had told me that she and the other nuns at St. Joseph Monastery were given a small stipend every month, the equivalent to a salary the rest of us earn. The difference being, their stipend amounted to only a few dollars, literally. Every cent Sister made in the ceramic shop went directly to the convent, not her. Now Sister Augustine was telling me how she took a portion of that paltry allowance and sent it away to help another human being in another country. A simple act, a sacrifice, a connection.

"That's such a wonderful and generous thing for you to do," I said, returning to my seat.

"It's one more way for me to share and connect," Sister Augustine explained, carefully gliding the Wedgwood Blue–tipped brush around the rabbit's eye with the confident hand of a Good Samaritan. "Even from a world away, I'm connected to that child. In this life and beyond, as your Heavenly Board of Directors shows, each one of us is each other's responsibility."

I thought of Sister's tiny crosses that I had my cousin Father Herald take back with him to Honduras. And all the Gussie's Specials, Nativity sets, forget-me-nots, and other items Sister Augustine had created that were spread throughout our local area, as well as around the country and world. Much like my dad's smiles.

"Each of your ceramic pieces is another way you're connecting with people, many of whom you'll never meet or really get to know," I told my friend. It was like the Greek proverb: "A society grows great when old men plant trees whose shade they know they shall never sit in."

Sister nodded. A swatch of hopefulness was now reflected in each of the rabbit's eyes.

"You may think this is silly," I went on, "but there was once an old apple tree that was very special to me. On the land I've told you about that my family owns called Bear Run, near the old dirt road and field where I like to sometimes go. I was very connected to that tree. I'd hug it, I talked to it, I shared all my joys and sorrows with it. I'd sit under its shade in the summer and I traced the lines of snow balanced on its bare branches in the winter. I always felt like that apple tree was a part of me."

"That's not silly at all. You're right, that apple tree is a part of you, and it always will be. It's a part of God's creation just like you are."

"My Grandma Schlimm always told the story about how when the land there was a lumber camp before my family owned it, one of the lumberjacks spit out an apple seed one day and that's how the tree grew—by accident, really. The tree saw just about every generation of my family pass by."

Sister Augustine smiled. "I can see why you and the tree are so connected then. That affection makes you a modern-day Johnny Appleseed." She laughed. "As you know, I have always loved being outside, from the time I was a little girl on my family's farm. I always had that connection to nature, and still do, even though I don't get outside as much as I'd like to anymore. Just like you with your apple tree, I'm connected to the flowers I've grown in front of my shop here for many, many years. They come and go with the seasons, but every time I see a new bud emerge, it's familiar to me, like seeing an old friend return."

As we talked, another dear friend of Sister's sauntered in. Blitzen debuted from the back room. "There you are, stranger," Sister cooed, as the cat rubbed his cheeks against the bottom of her black robe. "I know what you want."

Sister Augustine placed the finished rabbit on the table and pushed back her chair. "Come on," she beckoned, patting her lap.

Blitzen hopped up and curled himself on top of Sister's bib apron, the midnight blue one with the pack of wolves baying at the moon. She picked up a nearby hairbrush and started combing through his calico fur.

"Animals can teach us a lot about connection," I said. "Ever since my Little Coyote came to live with me, he's often a reminder of the important lessons I tend to forget."

I had told Sister in an earlier discussion about my rescue dog, Little Coyote, who came to live with me shortly after I started visiting the ceramic shop. He had been found abandoned and nearly starved in the woods. After a few months of love and care, and spoiling, he was now a medium-sized, fluffy ball of white fur with a beautiful face and the most penetrating, mysterious brown eyes. Until meeting him when I was in my early thirties, my only pets as a child had been a succession of unlucky goldfish, who never seemed to be long for this world.

Little Coyote's story of survival and the close bond we shared—often lying on the floor and just gazing into each other's eyes or napping side by side—had opened my mind to an entirely new perspective on what connection in this world meant.

"I'd like to meet Little Coyote sometime," Sister said, continuing to brush Blitzen's thick, shiny gold and white coat. "I think animals are some of the best teachers we have in this world, if only we choose to learn from them. When people say animals are dumb, I disagree. They're smart. It's just that their intelligence and instincts are different from ours. Most important, they help remind us just how connected we all are to other living creatures and the planet."

My little sisters, the birds . . . , Saint Francis beckoned in his illuminated sermon, giving loud voice for the ages to this universal kinship.

"All for one, and one for all!" I cheered.

Sister Augustine chuckled. "Blitzen and I second that."

PART FIVE

14

Our Lady of Love

Before heading to Sister's ceramic shop on this sunny summer afternoon, I first stopped at the Trifles and Treasures Gift Shop at the upper end of the convent, by the nuns' pond and cemetery. It was hard for me to believe that three and a half years had already passed since I first met Sister Augustine and discovered that my best friend Steven really did know what he was talking about when he recalled there being a ceramic shop at St. Joseph's in addition to this gift shop.

Sister Margoretta warmly greeted me inside the store and helped me find the crib medal I wanted to give to a friend who had just had a baby. I stayed for about twenty minutes, chatting about some new ideas I had for December's open house, which was months away.

When I left, I strolled down the small paved driveway to the short, canopied walkway that led from the convent's main building to the cement staircase, which descended to the ceramic shop. This was at the opposite end of the porch from where I normally entered when visiting. These were the nineteen steps Sister Augustine traveled daily, to and from work.

When I arrived at the top of the staircase, I paused. Something moving caught my eye in the flower bed that was propped on the giant easel of a steep bank leading away from the Guesthouse.

It was a cat, but not Blitzen. I wondered when this new little black critter had arrived and what Blitzen thought of him. My eyes followed the tomcat as he prowled through the mix of flowers arriving at another, larger figure in black. Only this one was wearing a citrine and orange floral bib apron.

Sister Augustine was lying sideways, the sloping carpet of flowers all around her. At first, I was alarmed. Anytime I'd ever seen someone her age in that position, it ended with a trip to the ER. But something held me back from jumping to conclusions. A little voice inside told me to be still and watch.

I soon realized that Sister was pruning her garden, albeit while practically clinging to the side of a hill. I watched as she would gently cup a flower in her hands, examining it closely, petal by petal. Every once in a while, she would then pinch off a withered leaf, letting it fall the short distance to where it would serve a new purpose. Or she'd straighten a bent stem, allowing a young floret to fully bask in the sunlight.

Like the rolling farmland where she once frolicked with the zeal of a young fawn, Sister Augustine intimately knew the raw earth of this sacred land as well. Her hands had dug and tilled this soil since she first arrived as a postulant at St. Joseph Monastery during the early years of the Great Depression. Back then, she built a greenhouse where she started tomatoes, cucumbers, peas, beans, and other plants from seedlings, then transplanted them in the convent's large kitchen garden. She'd also head up to the blueberry bushes around the pond and pick bucketfuls or help the other nuns can the vegetables picked fresh from the garden. Following her mother's death, Sister's father George moved into a small room at the convent. He assisted the nuns as a groundskeeper, carpenter, and butcher, often working the land once more alongside his youngest daughter. "Sister Thecla was too prissy for such work," Sister Augustine once joked of her real-life sister's preference for cleaner, indoor pursuits.

Now at ninety years old, Sister Augustine cultivated her flower gardens, her hands still finding connection with the cool, familiar earth—her eternal Mockin' Bird Hill.

The new cat strutted around Sister, as if on guard. Meanwhile, at the very top of the slope, a tall white statue of the Blessed Mother also watched. No doubt, my friend was in good hands.

After several minutes, Sister Augustine looked over toward the side of the cement staircase that was her only logical exit from the flower garden, other than climbing upward or rolling to the bottom. She still hadn't seen me. I closely observed, in case she needed me, but I knew how independent she was.

Sister sat up and began to shimmy sideways the fifteen or so feet until she reached the staircase. The tomcat pounced along with her. She obviously had this journey down to a science.

I then wondered how she was ever going to crawl onto the steps without tumbling. Still, I stayed where I was. Saint Christopher had his work cut out for him.

Sister Augustine grabbed hold of the metal railing, first with her right hand and then with her left. In one continuous spry motion, she heaved herself toward the garden and then swung in the opposite direction, coming to rest on a middle step, giggling all the way. Young Anna on the farm, pigtails flapping behind her, flashed through my mind. Her furry companion followed closely.

I covered my mouth to stifle a laugh.

"Who's your new friend?" I finally said a moment later, starting down the steps behind her and pretending I had just arrived.

Sister looked over her shoulder. "This is Tommy. He's come here to live with Blitzen and me. We decided it's too beautiful to be inside today. I was just working on my flowers while Tommy played. Blitzen is inside supervising from the front window. Come have a seat."

Bulbous heads of tall, lanky sunflowers peeked over the banister that ran the length of the porch in front of us. Like they were in line, each awaiting their moment with the resident gardener.

"What does Blitzen think of him?"

"They get along very well, I'm happy to say," Sister answered, the flush of exertion slowly fading from her pink cheeks. "I wasn't sure what was going to happen, since Blitzen was always the lone male here with all us women."

"I was up at the gift shop," I said, sitting down next to her on the step, as Tommy took off running in search of some adventure. "I needed a crib medal for my friend who had a baby. I'm going to send it along with one of the cherubs you made." After discovering the two leftover cherubs resembling my guardian angels, I had asked Sister to glaze a bunch of them for me in Baby Blue and Tearose. They made perfect and unique baby gifts, along with the crib medals.

"That reminds me, I finished the statues of Mary you wanted," Sister informed me. "But I'm afraid we had a sorrow with one of them."

"Why? What happened?" When Sister and I were in the back room a few weeks earlier, I had come across a few new molds for statues of the Blessed Mother. Every time I thought I knew exactly what molds Sister Augustine had, a new treasure—like manna in white plaster—would reveal itself. I had asked her to paint three new statues of Mary for me, to add to the two that I had bought on my very first visit to the shop.

"When I was painting the gold forget-me-nots on the dark blue mantle of the one statue, somehow a few got smeared and I didn't realize it until after I fired it," Sister explained. "You don't have to take that one."

"Oh, but I do want it. That makes it even more special!" I

insisted. "I love when you can see the human hand at work in a piece of art. To me, those imperfections *are* perfection."

"You always have a positive way of looking at things, don't you?"

That's highly debatable, I thought. Though I had come to appreciate how there was something magnificent about the work of a fallible hand when inspired to create—something that was uniquely original and impossible to replicate, which made the result truly precious.

"It's easy when it comes to your works," I said. "For the folk art pieces I create, I purposely chip away at the wooden boards I use as canvases to make them look old and weathered. I even like when my paint seeps outside the borders. You know a human hand did it and not some machine."

"Am I ever going to get to see any of your art?"

"Sometime, I promise." Truth being, I was still a little intimidated to show Sister Augustine my pieces. Still equating it with the brain freeze I feared if I ever tried to recite "Hail Marys" in exchange for her ceramic turtles, frogs, and ladybugs. I knew it was silly, these mind games we inflict upon ourselves. "Did the other two statues turn out okay?" I asked, reverting the subject to her art.

Sister nodded. "Both of those were joys."

"Did you sign them?" That had become a common refrain.

"Yes," she said, rolling her eyes, which had become the common response. "You'll be happy to hear I even went a step further with the one statue."

"How so?"

"Each of the statues comes with a name already, such as *Our Lady of Guadalupe* and the *Kitchen Madonna,* but the third statue you asked me to make didn't have a name when I got the mold years ago. So I named her."

"What did you name her?"

"Our Lady of Love."

"That's beautiful!"

"I thought so. And because I knew you'd probably ask, I wrote that name on the bottom of the statue as a surprise."

"Fantastic! I'm so happy you did that."

"Mary is such a perfect role model for people to follow these days, especially women."

I smiled in agreement. From the time I was a young child, my Grandma Schlimm had always encouraged me to say three "Hail Marys" before bed every night so the Blessed Mother would watch over me. Even our hometown, St. Marys, founded on December 8, 1842—the Feast of the Immaculate Conception— was named after her.

"You have that beautiful statue of her in your studio, the all-white one on the shelf up in the corner by the door to the back room. Did you make her?"

"No . . . I *rescued* her," Sister revealed.

"You *rescued* the Blessed Mother?"

"In a manner of speaking." Sister laughed. "Many years ago, some construction men were working on rooms here at the convent. I happened to pass by one and saw that statue half buried in a pile of garbage to be thrown out."

"Why would anyone throw her out?"

"I'll never know—maybe it was by accident—but I dug her out of the trash and cleaned her up. Then I put her high up where only Blitzen and Tommy can reach her now."

"You *rescued* the Blessed Mother," I repeated now for emphasis, shaking my head in amazement. That feat of heroism had surely earned a few gold stars next to her name in Saint Peter's Big Book.

Sister smiled, framed by the blooming garden behind her

that would have stirred Monet to create. "I think of it more as returning the favor, for all the times she's answered my prayers."

Our attention was momentarily drawn to the road running past the Guesthouse. Sister Jacinta and Sister John Paul both waved as they drove by in the convent's pickup truck, which displayed the words *ora et labora*. A famous Latin phrase meaning "pray and work," it's the nucleus of the Rule of Saint Benedict. Both in their fifties and two of the youngest nuns at St. Joseph Monastery, they handled a large portion of the everyday maintenance, upkeep, and errands—jobs once done by Sister Augustine's father during an era long since past.

Sister Augustine and I waved back.

"Here's something else I bet you didn't know," Sister teased. "The only piece of mine that I've ever kept for myself is a small statue of Mary."

"Really?" How had I never asked her that question before?

"I keep her upstairs in my room, on the dresser. At Christmastime, I have a small crib I've made out of paper and I set that in front of her with a little Baby Jesus in it."

I intentionally avoided asking Sister Augustine about her room. From what I understood, the nuns' bedrooms were basic, with not much more than a bed, a chair, a dresser, a lamp, and a small closet—a testament to the vow of poverty they observed. That area of the convent was strictly cloistered. That's not to say that if someone would have told me, "You have fifteen minutes to explore anywhere you want inside," I wouldn't have been off and running. That was never going to be the case, and so St. Joseph Monastery would always be shrouded in a certain mystery and majesty, including the Benedictine Sisters of Elk County themselves.

Sister Augustine continued: "Mary is very special to me as a nun. That's what the *M* in 'Sister M. Augustine' stands for."

"Sister, if you had been a man, do you think you would have become a priest?" I asked, as the warm air embraced us. Gentle breezes prompted the chimes a few steps below into a soft and ongoing serenade.

Sister gazed out over her flowers. "I suppose if you're meant to get the calling, it doesn't matter if you're a man or a woman, it's going to come. We all have our purposes and missions to fulfill in this life."

"Do you think women should be allowed to be priests?" I had realized a long time ago that one of the best ways to learn in this life and to further develop my own guiding principles was to ask lots of questions. After all, questions lead to answers. Luckily for me, my friend welcomed my ongoing inquiries.

Sister Augustine turned back toward me. "I come from a time when those things weren't even questioned or discussed. I've cherished the vocation I've chosen and the contributions I've been able to make in this role."

"But what about today? Do you think women should be able to be priests if they want?"

"When you look at other faiths that do allow women to fulfill those roles, the women are doing great jobs. Like Mary, they are strong, intelligent, inspiring leaders. At ninety, I'm comfortable with the Catholic Church's stance on this, because it's all I've ever known. But then I was also comfortable with a quiet little ceramic shop no one seemed to remember anymore, until you walked in one day. Now look at the fun we're having. It's been a wonderful thing for me and the convent community."

I nodded with great exuberance. *Yes, yes, yes.* This all was a wonderful thing for everyone involved.

Sister continued: "I do think, though, that women could lead our churches just as well as men. Women are every bit as smart, compassionate, and hardworking as men, sometimes more so. Some of the priests I've met during my life should have found other work long ago. I often questioned who exactly they received their calling from."

I stifled a laugh.

"I've learned some of my greatest lessons from the successful women I've had the honor of working with in my career," I said. "Not a day goes by that I don't reflect back on something I learned while working with women like Tipper Gore at the White House when she was Second Lady or Naomi Judd while I was a publicist in Nashville. They showed a small-town kid a world beyond his wildest imagination."

My mind flipped through a memory book of images: Parties at the Vice President's Mansion on the grounds of the U.S. Naval Observatory, Tipper giving me a tour of the vice president's plane, Air Force Two; traveling in motorcades; being flanked by Secret Service agents everywhere we went; joining Tipper and groups of schoolchildren to take pictures around Washington, D.C., as part of an international photo exchange program she had started; the surprise birthday party for me in Tipper's office; and my quiet conversations with the Second Lady of the United States. In Nashville, Naomi playfully referring to me as her "Duke of Front Page" and me addressing her as "the Queen of Everything"; riding on the Judds' original tour bus, called Dream Chaser; hanging out backstage at concerts; picnics by the pond on Naomi's sprawling farm, called Peaceful Valley; and the voices—*oh, the singing voices*—that were all the proof you needed to know for certain God is a country music fan. There was a lot of hard work involved with these jobs, too, but every moment contained an indelible lesson and a thrill.

"Those ladies taught me so much about what it means to be a professional and to give back to the world, and how to feed my imagination," I further explained. "Then, of course, I've had more personal examples of compassion, hard work, and fun, like my mom, my grandmothers, and my aunts."

"You're so lucky to have had those special women in your life," Sister Augustine said. "Young girls, especially, need those role models and mentors today more than ever, but I think it's just as important for young men like you to also see strong women in action. It instills respect and helps to break down many barriers that only hurt our world."

When I was up at the convent's gift shop thirty minutes earlier, I had seen an old black-and-white postcard photograph depicting several nuns hard at work in a hot, dusty field that would one day be the site of the high school next door. Sister Margoretta told me that one of those nuns was a much younger Sister Augustine—tough, tireless, not afraid to get her hands dirty—toiling alongside her father, George, the convent's groundskeeper in those days.

That image made me think of the young women I had encountered in the classroom. Each one was so talented in her own way, yet not all of them realized their enormous potential or the well of strength they embodied. At the conclusion of my first college course back in April, I had stood alone in my classroom and listened to the fading footsteps outside in the hallway as the seniors I had taught during their final semester walked away. I wondered where their steps would lead them next and in the years to come. I hoped that what they had learned from me would always be a hand at their back. Just as the enthusiasm and hopefulness of youth that they had shared with me would be a driving force as I moved forward in my teaching career.

I knew Sister would be able to give me more direction in my role as a teacher. And in my mission to help the students, especially the young women whom I encountered, to unlock the bounty of potential they had.

"Sister, what would you tell young women and girls today about the world they're entering?" I asked.

Sister Augustine thought for a moment while the wind chimes continued to croon. "I'd tell them to learn how to rely on themselves. I'd want them to know that they have all the potential inside them that young men have. I'd say it's okay to make mistakes, as long you learn from them. I'd hope they would develop a strong faith in God, and learn from examples like Mary and other female saints, who have done as much to build the Church as anyone else. I'd also encourage them to seek out examples of kind, compassionate women in their own lives, like you have, whether it's women they see as professional mentors or their own mothers and grandmothers. Finally, I'd tell them to find some way to serve others, using their talents and interests. By the way, I'd tell young men the same thing!"

"I really think you should write a book," I told my friend, as I did from time to time.

"That's your calling, not mine," Sister said, grinning. "After all, you're the one named after the patron saint of writers. It's your duty to be the messenger with a pen."

"I'm still waiting for my patron saint's help on my cook-book!"

"Who says God and Saint John Evangelist haven't already set a plan in action for you as an author, as we speak? Maybe many plans you're not even aware of yet. Remember, God's time isn't the same as ours."

The promise bestowed in the beloved Ecclesiastes 3:11—"God makes everything beautiful in its time"—settled once more in my mind, for the long haul.

Tommy came dashing down the steps. He hopped in between us as if to quickly say "Hi!" and then jumped in through the front window, which Sister Augustine would leave open during the warmer months for Blitzen and now Tommy to freely come and go.

"Should we see what those two are up to in there?" Sister asked, slowly standing. "I'm sure it's no good," she added with that young farm girl's smile.

"Sure," I replied, standing as well. "Your flowers on the bank are beautiful. And so are these sunflowers in front of the porch. I feel like they're watching us."

"They're really coming along this year," Sister Augustine gushed. "They're a good excuse to get me outside."

There was no mention of what I had seen when I arrived. That would be a special memory I'd keep to myself until someday when it was time to share it.

"Maybe you would have been a gardener if you had never come here to Saint Joseph's," I teased. "Or a farmer!"

Sister turned to me and smiled. "But don't you see, I get to be all those things and more right here: nun, gardener, farmer, businesswoman, animal lover, fisherman; an *artist,* as you like to call me; a schoolteacher long ago. We can be whatever we want, or many things at once if we so choose, in this life, no matter where we are."

"Don't forget statue rescuer!" I added. "I can think of at least one grateful lady who'd insist you add that title to your resume."

Sister Augustine shook her head. "If you say so, John."

"You know, Sister, your name is also on that list of women who inspire me in my life."

My friend replied with a modest nod before leading me down the steps. My own living, breathing Lady of Love was right there beside me as I swiped my hand across the wind chimes and followed her inside.

15

THE NATIVITY DONKEY

AT THE BEGINNING OF NOVEMBER, JUST BEFORE SISTER AUgustine's ninety-first birthday, I ran into the ceramic shop early one afternoon, excited and nearly bursting with the brainstorm I'd just had.

"Sister, wait until you hear the new idea I have for you!"

Rushing through the doorway leading into the studio, I was stopped in my tracks at the worktable. Perched on the edge was a row of five miniature Sister Augustines, as if they were my welcoming party. I got down on my haunches and studied the ceramic figures face-to-face. They were exactly as I had envisioned they would be. Each miniature nun was painted in a full, traditional habit—long black robes and full veil with white coif around the face, praying hands, and a blue denim bib apron, paint smears included.

I heard a familiar chuckle from the other end of the room. I looked up to see the real Sister Augustine framed in the small doorway leading to the back room, wearing her blue denim bib apron, paint smears included. From my vantage point, at eye·level with the table, Sister looked about as tall as the six-inch statues of her in front of me. In fact, she was right in line with them on the table. I couldn't help but laugh.

"Like them?" she asked.

"They're spectacular! Just how I knew they'd be."

"You're easy to please." Sister always told me that, modestly downplaying the talent each of her pieces exhibited.

A week earlier, Sister Augustine had told me that for Christmas that year she was going to surprise each sister at St. Joseph Monastery with a miniature ceramic nun. "You have a mold for a miniature nun?" I exclaimed. "Oh no, I shouldn't have told you," Sister joked. "Here it comes!" My mind was racing. "Do you think you could please paint five little nuns for me, too?" I asked. Sister nodded. "Only thing is," I added, "my little nuns need to be replicas of you." Sister shook her head and laughed. By now, she was accustomed to my off-the-wall requests. "I'm serious! Can you please add little aprons to them, along with the paint smears?" Sister Augustine thought for a moment, then replied, "I suppose I could do that. But only for you!"

I continued studying the ceramic nuns. They were so sweet. I intended to keep two for myself—one as a spare in case the other ever broke—and the other three would be special gifts for Patty, another cousin of ours, and a professor I taught with at the university. These statues were a very limited edition. I knew she'd never do them again. It took a bit of convincing to coax her to do them at all.

"I figured I'd get yours done before starting on the ones I'm doing for everyone here," Sister Augustine informed me. "Theirs will just be regular nuns, not me."

"You realize these are self-portraits, like many great artists do," I told my friend.

"You and your words," Sister said with a soft giggle. "You never run out."

"It always amazes me how perfectly you stay in the lines," I commented, awed by her crisp color blocking. The sign of a confident and contented hand. "I wouldn't have that steady a hand, or the patience."

"Takes practice," Sister quipped. "I wasn't sure how to do my own eyes, so I made them closed. I thought that way I look like I'm praying."

"You look very peaceful and deep in prayer," I observed, studying the fine-tipped crescents Sister had used to portray her own closed eyelids.

"I'll let you guess what I'm praying for," Sister Augustine bantered. "I have to have some secrets after all."

I stood now. "I have a new idea for you for the open house this year," I announced, circling back to the original point of my visit. The annual event was only a month away.

"I better sit down for this," Sister said. For the first and only time I can ever remember, Sister Augustine walked to the mint-green spindle chair I usually sat in along the outside of the one worktable, and that's where she sat. As if it were the most natural thing in the world, I then walked over to her identical mint-green spindle chair inside the horseshoe and sat down.

Looking across the table at my friend, she was backlit by the tall window behind her—the way I must have always appeared to her during our visits. It's interesting what you notice when sitting in someone else's chair. A thin line of white light edged her black veil, her dimples seemed even more pronounced than usual when she smiled, and a happy little cleft I never noticed before graced her chin. An orderly mise-en-place of brushes, a water container, paper towels, small bisqueware trees, and stacks of paint bottles three and four high wound its way between us like a bridge.

"Remember how you did that collection of ornaments for me a while back?"

"How could I forget?"

A few years earlier, I commissioned Sister Augustine to create a collection of Christmas tree ornaments. It started out as just one set, which I had planned to give to Steven as a gift, but then I quickly realized I wanted one, too. *Of course.*

For several hours one afternoon, Sister and I went through her collection of cookie cutters and ornament molds, choosing sixteen to use: tree, church, candy cane, elephant, rabbit, reindeer, rooster, heart, snowman, star, Christmas bulb, bell, butterfly, dove, gingerbread couple. We then chose the colors in which each would be painted: holly berry red, neon orange, cobalt blue, key lime, pine tree green, tomato red, amethyst, cadmium yellow, chocolate, baby blue, Harvard crimson, silver, ivory, butterscotch, hunter green, rosy pink. Finally, we matched special words—*love, hope, peace, grace, joy, awe, faith, fun, laughter, family, imagination, live, be, simplicity, dream*—to each ornament. Sister would then later inscribe one word per ornament during the greenware phase, including "John" on the gingerbread man. It was our own iconography and language. Whimsical, but with a powerful message. A tip of the hat to the work of another favorite artist of mine, Keith Haring.

"That's what gave me the idea," I said. "I think for this year's open house, you should do a limited edition ornament."

"I have lots of ornaments I make already," Sister said. "You had the tree in the shop decorated with them last year. And they all sold. I can make more of those."

"I mean, you should do one special ornament," I clarified. "In a limited edition of however many we think makes sense."

Sister Augustine thought for a moment. "Do you think people would want the same ornament that others have?"

"If *you* make it, yes! They'll fly right out of here. Trust me."

Sister was still unconvinced. "You don't think it's too late to get started on this? The open house is only a few weeks away."

"I have faith in you to get them done in time."

Sister smiled. "I suppose I could do it then, but what would the ornament be?"

"That's the one part of this project I haven't thought of. Maybe we can put our heads together to figure it out."

From the twinkle in her eyes, I could tell the creative wheels were already turning.

"Let's start with what inspires you," I suggested. "This should be an ornament that has meaning for you, which will make it even more appealing to customers. Plus, that will give you something new to talk about during the interviews this year."

"Don't tell me you're bringing the reporters back here," Sister said, wide-eyed with a crooked grin. The sunlight streaming in behind her flickered every time she moved. "I told them everything I know last year."

I laughed, and reminded her, "The stories they wrote about you last year got the open house and the convent a lot of attention, and raised a lot of money."

Sister sighed. "You're right. I guess they weren't too bad."

It was time to focus. "So, what inspires you?"

Sister Augustine thought for a moment. "God, nature, animals, colors."

"That's good. We can work with that." We had some synergy now, artist to artist.

"What is it about Christmas that really inspires you?" I then asked.

"The birth of Jesus, the joy of the season. Love."

"How can we pull that all together into something you already have a mold for?"

"If you want, my cookie cutters are all in a box in the back room on the first table; go get it and we can look through them."

I hopped up, passed by the five miniature Sister Augustines, who were still standing piously at the end of the table, and retrieved the cookie cutters from the back room. When I returned, Sister had rearranged the table, leaving plenty of space for our latest endeavor. Soon the empty surface was a mosaic of scattered tin and red plastic shapes for everything from churches, crosses, and candy canes to hearts, stars, and just about any animal you could name.

"I think maybe it should be an animal ornament, especially since you love animals so much," I suggested, scanning the images of an elephant, lion, giraffe, rabbit, reindeer, rooster, and butterfly. "But how do we tie an animal into Christmas with what you have here?"

"How about this one?" Sister Augustine said, picking up a red cookie cutter I hadn't seen among the menagerie. "A donkey!"

HALLELUJAH!

"*The Nativity Donkey!* That's perfect!"

"I think so, too, but how should I paint it, and how many? I don't have much time, especially with the ceramic nuns I want to do for the sisters and all the Christmas items we want to have available at the open house."

"You can keep it simple. They don't have to be painted realistically with every detail," I explained.

Sister Augustine closely inspected the plastic donkey. "How about if I paint each of them in a gray glaze and maybe add some gold trim?"

"Sounds beautiful and simple. Do you think you could do twenty-five Nativity Donkeys?" A year earlier she had created fifty identical pink bud vases in only a few week's time for a charity event I was helping to organize, so I knew she was no stranger to quickly creating multiples of the same item.

"That sounds reasonable."

"They'll be gone in a flash, but that's the point of a limited edition," I said. "I think we should also add a tag to each one, which I can make on my computer. Naturally, you'll sign and date each ornament. . . ."

Sister Augustine rolled her eyes. She still thought it was

silly that people would want her signature on these pieces. The concept of provenance—the holy grail of art snobs the world over—was as meaningless to her as the names of my favorite artists whom I often referenced in relation to her work.

"And could you come up with a simple one-line statement for the tag?"

"Like what?"

"Just something in your own words about the donkey and how special he is to the Nativity story."

"Why don't you do that? You're the word guy."

"Because it's not my ornament. You're the artist here!"

More rolled eyes were flashed my way, making me chuckle.

❦

A FEW DAYS later, Sister Augustine handed me a Post-it note. "Will this work?"

In her distinctive script, Sister had written the tagline for the ornament: "This humble animal carried Jesus and Mary on their long journey to Bethlehem."

"It's perfect!"

Sister's quote became the focal point on the tag I created for each Nativity Donkey ornament. I used a sheet of blank business cards, which proved to be the ideal size, to print the twenty-five tags. Each was secured to the ornaments with thin satin ribbons that Patty and I added while once again helping Sister decorate and prepare her shop for the open house.

To showcase the special ornaments, while decorating, Patty and I made a few changes from the previous year. We moved the small, artificial tree to the center of the island this time, filling it with the Nativity Donkeys. We then transformed a nearby section of shelves into a tabernacle of Gussie's Specials. The other shelves were filled with freshly painted Santas, snowmen, angels, light-up trees, sleighs, candleholders, poinsettia plates, and candy cane dishes, each punctuated with Sister's neon-orange price stickers.

⁂

IN LATE NOVEMBER, Sister Augustine's second press conference proceeded much like the first one a year earlier. The reporters sat in the chairs I had arranged across the table from their subject, running through many of the same questions about her biography and background, as well as the history of the Gussie's Special. They repeatedly expressed their admiration for a ninety-one-year-old maintaining a full-time, and overtime, work schedule.

"What do you think of the success of the Gussie's Specials?" one of the reporters asked. I smiled, thinking how her most famous piece now had a history and a fan base. By this point, she had created around three hundred of them.

"I'm happy if my customers are happy," Sister replied, preaching to the choir. "I just do as I'm asked."

"They have to be fun to make?" another reporter, an artist herself, asked as a follow-up.

"They're always a mystery. I never know what I'm going to end up with," Sister remarked. "Every time I open the kiln, there's joys and sorrows, but luckily all the Gussie's Specials have been joys so far."

"Are you ready to tell us where you got the name for the bowls?" a reporter from last year asked. Previously, Sister Augustine had toyed with the young man, telling him that the unique title was a secret she was keeping to herself. From the beginning, she had revealed to me that "Gussie" was her nickname among the other nuns.

"Maybe next year," she said coyly. "Next question?"

I laughed.

The reporters then turned their attention to the Nativity

Donkey: "What made you decide to do a limited edition ornament?" "Why a Nativity Donkey?" "Why only twenty-five?"
"Is this the first in a series?"

Sister punted back: "I thought my customers would enjoy
them." "Because I love animals and the story of Jesus's birth."
"Twenty-five seemed like a good number for a limited edition
and that's all I had time to make." "We'll see what people think
of this one, then worry about a series next year."

There was also one new anecdote Sister Augustine told the
reporters that I hadn't even known about, proving once again
that she had a few surprises up her sleeve.

"Earlier this year, my kiln broke down," Sister Augustine
explained during the interview. "They're quite expensive you
know. I began searching for a secondhand one, but kept coming
up with nothing. So, I did what I always do and placed my problem in God's hands. He's boss, after all. I knew He'd find the
solution. Then, one morning when I arrived at the shop, there
was a new kiln setting outside my front door. I never found out
who left it, but I never had a doubt who made sure it got there."

I had a surprised expression on my face when I later asked
Sister about the new kiln after the reporters had left. "Why
didn't you tell me about your problems with the old kiln?"

"I didn't want to worry you," Sister replied.

"I'm so glad you told that story. The readers will love it," I
said. "You're just full of all kinds of surprises *and* miracles."

Sister swatted her hand at me. "Don't go giving me a halo
just yet."

"What made you think to tell the reporters about the kiln?"

Sister chuckled. "I knew you'd get a kick out of it."

I did. And so did the reporters. One of them led into the
story by writing, "There's also miracles, as it turns out, in ceramics." Indeed.

Every article the reporters wrote in the days that followed

also quoted Sister's line from the ornament tag and each emphasized the limited nature of the Nativity Donkeys, which ignited a frenzy, just as I had hoped. Sister's phone began ringing off the hook with people wanting to buy one in advance. "They won't be available until the open house," Sister told each caller. "Hope to see you there!"

I got a kick out of that, too.

❦

ON THE FIRST Saturday in December, the day after my thirty-fifth birthday, customers were lined up in front of the ceramic shop even earlier than the previous year. Almost an hour before the 9 a.m. start time, excited shoppers stretched down the length of the front porch to the right in the direction of the high school, as well as many who were huddled on the steps to the left to keep warm and out of the nearby snow squalls.

My mom, cousin Phyllis, and Steven's mom, Denise, volunteered to help out again. Once Sister Augustine was comfortably seated in the middle of the squared-off horseshoe of worktables, I opened the front door fifteen minutes early.

The shoulder-to-shoulder crowd, double in size from a year earlier, moved through like a fluid piece of performance art that may have been aptly titled *Mob Scene*. Within five minutes, all the Nativity Donkey ornaments were gone. Twenty minutes after that, the shelves where Patty and I had displayed the new Gussie's Specials were bare. And by the end of the day, Sister had an empty shop and a year's worth of new orders to fill.

Before I left at six that evening, I sat down with Sister Augustine to recap the whirlwind of a day.

By then, Blitzen and Tommy had reemerged from their daylong retreat in quieter corners. Sister teased Blitzen with a homemade toy, consisting of an artificial daisy attached to a string. In my mind, I could see a young Anna tempting her kittens with a real daisy in the barn at Mockin' Bird Hill long ago. Slowly, Sister Augustine baited the calico, resting the daisy on the floor and holding the string. As Blitzen approached, Sister tugged the string, causing the daisy to bounce and Blitzen to pounce after it. Making my friend giggle. Meanwhile, Tommy made his way around the studio, batting a tiny stuffed mouse with his paws, causing the Saint Francis medal around his neck to flicker in the light.

"I think next year you should do a hundred ornaments," I told Sister Augustine.

Sister looked up from playing with Blitzen. To my surprise, she agreed. "That might not be such a bad idea," she said.

"We'll just have to think carefully about what the next ornament in your series should be."

"Well, we have a little time to think about that."

I couldn't contain my excitement. "It's never too early, *or* too late, to get started!"

Sister Augustine nodded. "You're making a believer out of me," she said, turning her attention back to Tommy and Blitzen, who were now both resting at her feet, completing a perfect picture of peace and harmony.

16

THE BOOK OF REVELATION

NOT LONG AFTER SISTER AUGUSTINE CAME INTO MY LIFE, IN A nearby town a few kids found a puppy, completely bald and nearly starved to death. They saw something stir under an old abandoned car and didn't even know what "it" was. Had they not found him when they did, the helpless animal wouldn't have survived another day. Thanks to those kids and our local Elk County Humane Society shelter, the dog was rescued and eventually he came to live with me. I named him Little Coyote.

Even though I had spent a considerable amount of time with Sister Augustine, I had never introduced her in person to my four-legged best friend, though she often heard me talk about him. She was particularly amused when I told her how every day for lunch while I was making a salad for myself, I had to also make one for Little Coyote. His favorite meal was a plateful of mushrooms and red bell peppers. He would excitedly dash into the kitchen and run in circles at the sound of me chopping up the vegetables for him.

One of the many things I learned from my conversations with Sister Augustine was how it is a gift to share your life and stories with others. So just before we went our separate ways before Christmas, I decided to surprise her with two important pieces of my life.

When I got to the ceramic shop, I swiped my hand across the

wind chimes on the porch, letting her know I was there. Walking in, I couldn't see her from the front door, but I heard her.

"Hello, John," she called out. "That has to be you."

With a backpack holding one surprise slung over my shoulders and another furry surprise on a leash next to me, I peeked through the doorway leading into the studio. For one of the only times I can remember, Sister Augustine, in her blue-and-white-checkered bib apron, was seated on the outside left of the squared-off horseshoe of worktables. With a moist sponge, she was smoothing the rough edges on Nativity figures that had been left by the seams of the molds. I knew several orders had been placed at the open house for new Nativity sets for the following year since this Christmas was only a few days away. She was getting a major jump-start. The table was covered with dozens of muddy-gray Marys, Josephs, Wise Men, shepherd boys, cows, donkeys, camels, sheep, and Baby Jesuses.

"I brought two surprises for you!" I told her, as I leaned through the doorway.

"*You did?*" Sister exclaimed with a girlish lilt. It was easy to forget that we were separated in age by fifty-six years. "Come in, come in. What have you brought?"

I laughed. "One is a what and the other is a who."

A curious expression grew on Sister's face. She set down the sheep that she had been working on and leaned forward for a closer look.

I decided not to keep her in suspense any longer. My dog and I strolled into the studio and over to where Sister Augustine was sitting.

My friend beamed. "This has to be Little Coyote!" She reached out to him, and he hurried toward her basking in the warm attention she offered.

"Yes, I figured it was time you two finally met."

Sister looked down, eye to eye, with my fluffy white dog.

"You are so handsome, just like John said you were." Little Coyote licked Sister's hand. "And you have the most beautiful eyes," she cooed, as he ate up every ounce of affection.

Sister turned and motioned for me to have a seat in the chair next to hers. "How long did you say he's been with you?"

Setting my backpack on the floor, I recounted Little Coyote's rescue from the beginning, even though she had heard it before. The story always took on a more heartfelt meaning when my little pal was right there in front of me, adding a living, breathing face to the details.

"Oh my," Sister Augustine said, continuing to stroke the top of Little Coyote's head as he gazed adoringly at her, when I was finished. "Thank God those kids found you," she told him.

I often thought how I would love to find those kids and thank them in person. They would likely never know how much their actions on that day impacted my life for the better. Little Coyote was a precious reminder of how interconnected we all are and how everything we do has the potential to help or hurt others in ways great and small.

"God makes sure we all end up where we belong," Sister reminded me.

I nodded. "Little Coyote's story of survival has inspired me so much. When I think of him out there in the cold woods all alone and so scared, it breaks my heart. But he held on. He knew that somewhere in this world, someone was waiting to love him. Anytime I'm having a bad day, I lie on the floor next to him and just stare into those big eyes. They express so much, which always makes me feel better. If he could survive what he did, I know I can handle whatever comes my way. We understand each other in a way that words could never begin to express."

"That's the power of true love. No words are necessary, it's just there," Sister Augustine said.

I nodded again. "He's taught me a lot."

Sister glanced over to the doorway leading into the back room. "Look who's joining us." Blitzen and Tommy sauntered in, surely to checkout the newest ball of fur to arrive on their block.

I wasn't sure how this introduction would go. The image of a *Looney Tunes* episode suddenly ran through my mind, ending with a ransacked ceramic shop and three animals with mischievous grins.

"Blitzen, Tommy, come meet Little Coyote," Sister Augustine said.

Turns out, I didn't have to worry. The two cats walked up to Little Coyote and all three nuzzled their noses together between our chairs. Sister Augustine and I laughed. "Who says cats and dogs don't get along?" Sister said with a chortle.

"I guess opposites really do attract," I added.

We watched the three of them for a few minutes. Little Coyote gave Blitzen and Tommy kisses by lapping his tongue up the front of their faces. They returned the gesture with a gentle swat of their paws, causing Little Coyote to hop back, bumping into my chair. It was one of the countless snapshots from the ceramic shop that I filed away in my mind.

"I also brought a second surprise for you," I then announced.

"This is my lucky day!" Sister's eyes were lit with anticipation.

I reached down and hoisted the heavy backpack onto my lap. "It's in here," I said, unzipping the bag and pulling out an overstuffed navy blue binder.

"What is it?"

"It's a portfolio of all my artwork."

Sister clapped her hands together. "I'm *finally* going to get to see it! It took you long enough. After all, you've seen just about every inch of this place, so it's only fair that I get to see what you do, too."

Sister Augustine cleared a space on the table, creating a fanned-out amphitheater of Nativity figures in front of us. They became our instant, packed-house audience.

I set the thick binder in front of her. "It's all in there. I photograph each of my pieces after I finish them."

Little Coyote and his two new friends were now curled up on the floor between our chairs. They faced one another as if they were challenging each other to be the first to blink.

Sister opened the binder and proceeded to study each photograph of my primitive Americana folk art. "How long have you been doing this?"

"Several years. I really started creating a lot of pieces after I finished my master's at Harvard."

"And you call me an artist. *You're* the artist! These are beautiful, and so unique."

"We're two different types of artists," I reminded her. She wasn't getting off the hook that easily. Unlike most, including me, she was a self-taught artist who could do everything from realism to abstract. Even after all the attention she had received for her clayware pieces, particularly the Gussie's Specials, Sister Augustine still modestly viewed herself as an ordinary person simply doing something she enjoyed.

"What inspired you to do primitive folk art?" It was now her turn to play interviewer.

"I like how you can see the human hand at work in it, which is why I like your artwork so much. For most of my pieces, I start with new wood, then chip away at it with a hammer and use sandpaper to make it appear old and weathered. Also, I've come to appreciate that any mistakes I think I've made only lead the piece in a fantastic new direction I never imagined. I studied art in high school and college, but have spent the many years since then *un*learning all of that, so my pieces can have an authentic and primitive look."

"Do you sell your art?"

"Not really. Maybe a piece here and there, but I mostly give it away as gifts," I answered. "The first paintings of mine ever to be sold in any way were some of the first folk art pieces I did while at Harvard. I had just started my fall semester there when Nine/Eleven happened. . . ."

Sister looked over at me with widened eyes.

"I donated two American flag paintings and a checkerboard painting to an auction event called Art Heals in New York City, which benefited the Twin Towers Orphan Fund. I'll always be grateful that my first works to ever be sold helped children."

"That's such a great honor and a perfect way to thank God for the gifts He's given to you," Sister commented. "Did you know that your Saint John Evangelist is also the patron saint of painters, in addition to writers?"

"He is?"

"Looks like you really lucked out with that one!"

"That means he's watching over your work here, too," I said. A symbol of Saint John Evangelist, the valiant ceramic eagle overlooking the studio from the top shelf at the back of the room now made perfect sense for many reasons.

Sister Augustine smiled and proceeded to page through the hundreds of photos of my paintings, sculptures, and other pieces—checkerboards, American flags, maps, angels, Uncle Sams, Santas, snowmen, star ornaments, crosses, birdhouses, landscapes, and my *Little Country Church of the Stars* series. Meanwhile, the greenware audience in front of us watched quietly, as if riveted by every moment of the performance before them.

"I had no idea you did all of this artwork," Sister gushed. "Along with your writing and teaching, too. You're prolific."

"Now who's giving who an ego?" I said with a laugh. "It's all just what I enjoy doing, like you always say about your artwork."

"And these angels . . ."

"I knew you'd like those. I draw an angel on the back or bottom of each of my folk art pieces. They're like little secret guardian angels. I figure everyone can use an extra angel."

"That's for sure."

Sister Augustine continued to study each photograph.

"I like how you write on a lot of your pieces," she said, squinting to read my own homespun gospel, rendered in wood, nails, wire, and acrylics.

"It's a nice way of merging my writing and art. The writing is mostly inspirational thoughts I have while creating each piece. These works, like yours, are all about making people feel good and reminding them how wonderful life can be. That's also why I use stars on them. To me, stars are so symbolic and just happy."

Creating those pieces also made me feel better and provided traces of hope during otherwise challenging times. I could lose myself in the quiet and brightness of the paint and other materials while working with my hands to create. Comfort and inspiration also surrounded me in the settings I had repurposed for my studios. I completed most of my pieces either on a hill above the pond at my beloved Bear Run where generations of family have laughed and embraced nature, or in the space that my father, a former butcher, had previously used for his meat-processing business. Where once the tables and floors of this latter studio were laden with death, blood, and the grinding roar of meat saws during my youth, now the birth of new creations, a galaxy of paint splatters, and the humming of my imagination illuminated the space. This all also helped me to better understand and appreciate Sister Augustine's contentedness while working alone in the stillness of her studio all these years.

"What's this last picture of?" Sister pointed to a photograph of a multipaneled painting.

I leaned in closer. "That's one of my larger works. It's my portrayal of the story of Creation."

"So unique! I've never seen Genesis depicted like this before."

I then pulled a slim binder from my bag. "I also brought this to show you. It's a manuscript for a children's book I hope to have published someday. It's called *The Star Jumped Over the Moon*."

"Great title! It already piques my interest," Sister Augustine said, smiling. "What is it about?"

"It's about a little star who wakes up one morning in a bird's nest in an old apple tree . . ."

Sister giggled.

"He doesn't know how he got there and he quickly realizes how different he is from everything else around him. Then the little star becomes friends with the old apple tree, who teaches him just how special he really is and that he can do amazing things."

"That's a great message, especially for children," Sister said with a wink. "I loved climbing the apple trees in the orchard on our farm as a child."

"Remember when I told you about the old apple tree in Bear Run that I loved so much?"

Sister nodded. "The one your grandmother told you grew from a seed that a lumberjack spit out, right?" She chuckled once again at the image.

"Yes. Well, I never told you what happened to it. Some of my cousins cut it down."

"That's awful!"

"One day, my dad came home and told me the tree was gone. Just like that. No warning. My cousins claimed it was old and no longer served a purpose, and so it had to go, which never made sense to me. It served a great purpose to me! I raced to Bear Run and to the field where the apple tree had been, only to find a scattering of blossoms on the ground. Even the stump had been removed. It was in the spring, and I'll always be grateful that the last time I saw my apple tree it was engulfed in the most stunning pink and white buds. Eventually, my cousins built a small pavilion with a cement slab and two picnic tables where the tree stood, which is the real reason I think they cut it down. That old apple tree taught me so many lessons about life, and still does. I wrote *The Star Jumped Over the Moon* with the tree and those lessons in mind. It was like a very dear friend I'll never forget."

"That's very special. You certainly had an incredible connection with that wonderful old apple tree."

I smiled. "That's all I'm going to tell you. I don't want to give the story away. I also created paintings to illustrate the book. Pictures of them are in the binder, too, at the back behind the manuscript pages."

Sister opened the binder and slowly read through each stanza of the story. When she was finished, she looked over and smiled at me, then started flipping through the photographs of my illustrations.

When she got to the end, Sister Augustine turned to me and said, "God has so greatly blessed you, with so many talents—as an artist, a writer, a teacher . . ."

She then glanced down at the three animals sound asleep between us, and continued, ". . . and as a friend to animals. You are so blessed, John."

I felt so comfortable in that simple and divine space with her, where the rest of the world was kept at bay. How blessed, indeed, I had been to go there almost every week for nearly four years now.

I looked over at Sister Augustine. "I want you to know how grateful I am every day to have you in my life," I told her. A hundred blessed eyes watched from the table as I spoke. As did the unflinching eagle—the symbol of a kindred spirit and namesake—who gazed down approvingly from his top shelf. My words were a simple affirmation, yet not easy to express, even to someone I dearly loved.

Sister smiled. "And I'm grateful that a talented and compassionate young man like you walked into this shop one day and became my friend."

I couldn't speak. My eyes filled with tears.

Sister Augustine reached over and placed her hand on top of mine.

All I could do was smile back. Those tender words between two friends embodied one of the most beautiful moments I will ever experience in this lifetime.

My friend then turned her attention back to the two binders. She began to once more go through each of the photographs, closely studying my artwork with a huge smile still on her face. She also reread *The Star Jumped Over the Moon*, while Little Coyote, Blitzen, and Tommy rested at our feet.

No more words were necessary.

That's the power of true love, I thought, looking at her. *It's just there.*

PART SIX

17

FOOD FOR THOUGHT

THE POPEMOBILE ROLLED SLOWLY ACROSS THE SCREEN OF Sister Augustine's old twenty-four-inch television set. Such a funny little vehicle—like a museum display case, hauling precious cargo, loaded into the back of my dad's pickup. We sat and watched archival footage from World Youth Day in Toronto years earlier. Thousands of young people greeted the pontiff like a rock star, chanting, "John Paul Two, we love you!" His face was warm and beatific, his cupped wave welcoming the next generation into the fold.

I was amused by how charmed Sister was by him. Her eyes dewy, cheeks flushed. I half expected her to exclaim, "He's the bee's knees!"

As a teacher, I had been especially touched by the fervor that the late Holy Father elicited from young people during his lifetime. Although leader to the world's one billion Catholics, during his papacy he often inspired beyond boundaries of religion, age, gender, politics, and so much more. He set a high bar for the contemporary Church and for his immediate successors, Popes Benedict XVI and Francis, to progress upon in the years following his death and canonization. There was clearly still a lot of work for the Church, just past the threshold of a new century. Its rules, issues, and ensuing controversies were often the crux of the struggles and questions I had, leading me like so many others to explore the varied palette of other faiths and philosophies in search of a deep understanding of who we are and what we can become.

While watching the pope's historic procession, Sister Augustine and I tailgated, snacking on a picnic basket full of sample dishes—dips, veggie chili, and double chocolate cake, all made with beer—from my cookbook manuscript. Since I had now shown her my artwork and for a long time before that she had heard me talk and complain about the challenges of trying to get the book published, I thought she might enjoy an actual taste of what all the fuss was about.

"Sister, do you think it's wrong for people to explore other faiths?" I asked. She was huddled over a bowl of my veggie chili. We had already polished off the crackers and dips.

Sister Augustine lowered the television's volume with her remote. "No, exploring other religions isn't wrong, especially if done out of a desire to learn. It's important for people to understand other faiths and their teachings. What you discover is just how alike we all are. This helps us to respect and accept each other."

"Tomato, *tomahto* then when it comes to the nuances of other religions?" I challenged playfully, while curious what her answer would be.

"Not exactly," she said, grinning. "But I think we're all closer together in our beliefs rather than farther away from each other. Love is the core for the majority of faiths. As is forgiveness, prayer, service, salvation. Just the terminology and practices are different; the underlying sentiments are virtually the same. Understanding what makes each religion tick is one of the best ways I know to bring this world together, not to tear it apart with hatred, judgment, ignorance, and war. Unfortunately, many powerful people and whole armies don't get that. But we everyday folks can."

"Once when I was younger, I had a cousin who was going to be baptized a Lutheran," I told her, "and my Grandma Schlimm, who was a devout Catholic, actually pleaded with me to not go to the Lutheran church for the service, telling me it would be a sin. She practically cried when I still went anyway. Yet, remarkably, I wasn't turned into a pillar of salt or anything."

Sister smiled, savoring her last spoonful of chili. "You can't blame your grandmother for feeling that way; it's what she was taught to believe in her day. *The God's honest truth,* but according to whom exactly? That's why it's so important for your generation and those even younger to continue building upon the global perception of different faiths and religions, and to open more hearts and minds."

The gleaming faces of the young people on the television screen gave me pause. They vividly illustrated Sister's words. They were the newest builders of the Church. Just arrived, with shiny new tools in hand and heart. Their talents and perspectives and unbridled enthusiasm, all fresh blocks being set upon the solid foundation that generations going all the way back to Peter had created. Looking deeply into their eyes, I knew the future was staring back at me.

"What do you think of the buffet approach to religion where people pick and choose what works for them?" I enjoyed my last spoonful of chili while I awaited an answer.

"What *works* for people is one thing; what is *convenient* for them is another."

I suddenly wondered which category I fell into. I thought I knew, but did I? I often felt like the canon law I was taught my whole life was sometimes more like another kind of cannon, one with a lit fuse that shot me flailing into parts unknown. Mostly, by my own admission, this was because I hadn't taken more time to better understand it. Until now.

Sister continued: "Often, people choose a piece of this religion, a chunk of that one, and snippets of a few others, but only because the combination justifies their lack of any real foundation. In their mind, it condones a lifestyle that is absent of any real purpose or morals."

"What if someone already has a strong foundation of faith—a core belief system—and is just looking for new ways of seeing and understanding God? I think that's where I'm at right now."

"Knowledge is power, especially when it comes to faith. From a strong foundation of knowledge and belief all else flows: daily decisions, morals, actions, emotions, relationships. Becoming a more informed person of faith doesn't mean you're a fanatic or looking for an easy way out. It means you know there's something greater than yourself and that you want to be the best person you can be by better understanding that greater something, which is God."

"I've spent time studying different religions so I could be better informed and I found many similarities among them," I said, while unwrapping two pieces of double chocolate cake and handing the larger one to my friend.

Sister Augustine nodded her thanks and commented, "Similarities are the glue that binds us together. That exploration shows you're engaged with the world and with God on a deeper level. I think we all need to keep a more open mind to this approach. That doesn't mean people can run wild with what's convenient for them, carelessly jumping from one religion to another, but we need to give people the room to become comfortable with their faith, whatever it is, and to let them grow into their faith. That is what serves the world and God the best."

Now I thought of my students at the university. I saw the future reflected in their eyes as well. The new spring semester was just getting into full swing. While I never specifically asked them about their religious backgrounds or preferences, I assumed they represented a melting pot of different beliefs and practices. All barriers were lowered in my classroom. It was a sea, welcoming to all. There, we learned and grew from one another each time we gathered. Minds opened, differences faded, and lanes merged.

"Right or wrong, 'open mind' isn't a term you hear associated with religion too often," I said.

"Well, a closed mind is like giving the Devil a handful of grenades," Sister said, raising an eyebrow and suspending a forkful of chocolate cake in midair so she could make her point. "Unfortunately, he's got a pretty good pitching arm."

I cracked up. My friend had mastered her own brand of wisdom and humor. She once again simplified the complex into something more vernacular, which was an art form unto itself. I remembered my high school theology teacher, Sister Kathleen, giving us Bibles and then spending the year telling us what to underline and highlight, all in order to make a very large and daunting volume more relatable. That dog-eared Bible still set on the nightstand next to my bed.

While we missed the rest of the pope's procession, I felt like I had taken a few more steps forward in my own journey. My conversations with Sister Augustine were like having a gentle hand at my back, nudging me ever forward, which was the same role I hoped I was fulfilling for my students.

When we finished eating the cake, Sister invited me to follow her into the back room. She had some work there that she wanted to get done before the end of the day. In addition to a picnic basket, I had also arrived that afternoon with an agenda of my own, which I was hoping Sister would be open to considering.

"I have a very special request for you," I said.

Sister Augustine and I were now standing at a long table filled with molds. Using an old metal pitcher covered in patches of dry clay, Sister began to slowly pour the thick gray liquid into a small plaster block.

"I thought you already used up all your *very special requests* for the year," Sister bantered. She kept a constant eye on the stream of muddy soup disappearing into the small round opening at the top of the mold.

I laughed. I knew the mold she was currently pouring was for an early Christmas order I had placed, even though we weren't even officially into spring yet. I had asked her to use a bird mold she had in her collection to create what I would call the Christmas Partridge. Each plump little bird would be painted with holly berry red on top and white for the underbelly, then trimmed in silver. I planned to give the Christmas Partridges as gifts. I had learned to get my Christmas gift orders in early, so the majority of the year could then be focused on her other orders and creating pieces for the open house in December.

"Well, this idea will be a one-of-a-kind piece just for me, and you can take as long as you need to do it," I informed my friend.

"I like the sound of that last part," Sister quipped.

"Remember when we were looking at my folk art pieces and you liked all the writing I put on them?"

"Yes, I never saw words on paintings like that before."

"I'd like you to take one of your bowls and paint it all white. Then, with a black paint pen, I'd like you to please add your favorite quotes to the bowl."

Sister glanced up with a certain look in her eyes. I knew that expression well, and chuckled.

I further explained, "I got the idea after seeing something called a singing bowl on TV."

"You're not going to ask me to sing, are you?!"

I laughed so hard that tears pooled in my eyes. "No, singing bowls are like special upside-down bells that make a pretty sound. For my bowl, I want you to write your favorite quotes all around it." Her words would be a silent song of inspiration encircling the bowl.

Sister Augustine finished filling the partridge mold and set the pitcher on the table. She looked at me and pondered the idea. By now, Blitzen had hopped onto the table and was also vying for her attention. Tommy was apparently keeping busy elsewhere, perhaps sunning himself on the outside walkway, which was one of his favorite places to lounge. We were only now starting to see the sun again after a very long winter.

"My handwriting isn't very good," Sister said, running her hand along the calico's back.

"I like your writing, and that's an important part of the piece. It has to be in your handwriting." I loved how some of my favorite folk artists, such as Howard Finster and Sister Gertrude Morgan, wrote on their pieces.

"I don't think I can come up with sayings like you do on your paintings. You're the writer, not me."

"You don't have to make them up," I clarified. "Just write all of your favorite quotes that mean something to you around the bowl."

Sister paused to think for a moment.

"And when you're finished," I added, "I would like you to please write your favorite word inside the bowl on the bottom."

Sister thought about it some more. "I *suppose* since you brought me that delicious meal today, it's the least I can do. After all, your chocolate cake was one of the best I've ever had."

My smile pinged from ear to ear.

Sister Augustine pointed to the next table over. "Will that bowl work?"

I turned to look. It was a large, rippled bisqueware bowl, usually the kind Sister used for her Gussie's Specials, only there was no curved lip around the edge. "That one will be perfect."

"It was originally meant to be a Gussie's Special, but part of the rim got ruined, so I trimmed it off and fired it as is. I thought perhaps it was a sorrow, but apparently not."

Imperfection is perfection, I thought. "Then it definitely is a one of a kind! You always have exactly what I'm looking for."

Sister shook her head and laughed. "You better wait until you see it finished first before you get too excited." She then scooped Blitzen into her arms and nuzzled her nose to his.

"I can already see it in my head, and it's spectacular!"

AFTER PAINTING THE bowl white in her studio a few days later, Sister Augustine took it to her bedroom, where, for the next month, she told me she was working on compiling her favorite sayings and quotes every night after dinner. Meanwhile, I was nearly bursting with excitement while waiting to see the finished piece.

I could picture Sister in her sparsely furnished room somewhere on the cloistered floors of the convent's main building. Sitting in her comfortable chair, she'd carefully choose and inscribe each quote—a personal creed—because it touched her in some way.

Then, one afternoon, I walked into the studio, and there the finished black and white bowl was on the table, waiting for me. Sister Augustine's distinctive script looped around it like garland.

"Hope it's what you wanted," Sister said. "I told you not to expect much."

I picked up the bowl and turned it slowly in my hands. I could tell she had put a lot of time and thought into this very special request of mine. Then came the big reveal of her all-time favorite word, which as I requested, she had written on the bottom of the inside. Unlike the lines in cursive on the outside, she had rendered her favorite word in large printed letters: "Peace."

"It's even more extraordinary than I imagined," I said. *The bee's knees.*

Sister Augustine smiled.

I raced home and settled into a comfortable chair of my own. I read each line as one might sing a hymn—in a flowing harmony that rises and falls. This was as close to a written manifesto as I would ever get from her. Within these favorite quotes were reflections of her own thoughts, humor, and inspirations.

I knew that any time in the future when I needed a spark to keep me going or wanted to hear Sister's voice, I could now simply pick up this bowl and choose a random point from which to start reading . . .

"It is more blessed to give
than to receive. God loves a cheerful
giver. Give a man a fish and you feed him for a
day, teach him to fish and you feed him for a lifetime.
A negative attitude is like a flat tire, you're not going far
until you change it. U. I. O. G. D. Lord to whom shall we go
you have the words of eternal life. You never get dizzy doing too
many good turns. Hope never abandons you, you abandon it. God
bless you. Too soon old, too late smart. This is the day the Lord has
made let us be glad and rejoice and be glad in it. A man is as big as the
things that make him mad. O Lord, unwearied is your love for us. A
smile is an inexpensive way to improve your looks. You can never
do an act of kindness too soon, for you never know how soon it
will be too late. Laughter is carbonated holiness. There is plenty
of time if you don't hurry. Anyone who would not work
should not eat. Friends are forever. People may forget what
you say, people may forget what you do, but people
will never forget how you made them feel.
The heart that loves is always young.
Decide whom you will serve.
Peace."

18

ILLUMINATUS

LATE ONE AFTERNOON AFTER I HAD JUST GOTTEN HOME FROM teaching at the university, Patty called to relay a message she had received from Sister Margoretta. "Blitzen passed away today," she told me. "He became suddenly ill and had to be put to sleep."

"Oh," was all I could utter, the wind knocked out of me. I knew how very much Sister Augustine adored her calico. They had been together since well before I knew her. I, too, had grown fond of playing with him and Tommy when I visited the shop. "I'll go see her," I said.

I drove onto the grounds of the convent as the sun was starting to sink toward the horizon far to the left beyond the high school in the distance. As I drove past the chapel on my right and then the western expanse of the convent's main building, the light reflected off the tan bricks in such a way that made the building appear gilded. Each of the dozens of windows was ablaze with its own setting sun shining back at me.

The Guesthouse was ahead of me to the right. As I approached, I saw Sister locking the front door to her shop. I had just caught her. I stopped my car on the road and jumped out.

Hurrying down the steps leading to the long porch, I yelled, "Sister, Sister!"

She had already started up the cement staircase at the opposite end. By now, she was using a cane when going anywhere outside the shop and studio. I had to keep reminding myself that she was in her nineties, and, therefore, a cane was to be expected.

Sister Augustine turned, just as I reached the bottom of the staircase. She stood on the third step, using her cane for support.

"I heard about Blitzen. I'm so sorry," I said, out of breath. "I know how special you were to each other."

Sister smiled, but with sad, tired eyes I had never seen before. "Thank you. He's at peace now."

Running onto the porch, I had noticed the sharp line created by the sun. Golden light was inching its way across the porch in Sister's direction.

"Do you think animals go to Heaven?" I grinned. "I like to think they do."

I could imagine myself and an eight-year-old Anna conducting a memorial service for Blitzen on Mockin' Bird Hill, like she once did for the other animals there. A tiny mound of rocks, two crossed sticks with his name carved into them, a bouquet of buttercups and forget-me-nots, and the two of us blowing white dandelion seeds into the air, watching them rise and float away.

Sister chuckled softly. "I'm sure God takes care of them. They're His creatures, after all. They deserve their reward, too, for all the joy they bring to the world and to each of us."

"I also feel bad for Tommy. He'll miss his friend."

The vitreous light had reached the step on which Sister Augustine stood. "We're always being reminded how precious this life is and how very fast it goes," she said.

"Every moment counts, doesn't it?"

"They certainly do," Sister agreed. "We never know what moment may be our last. Or the last for a loved one. There's a beautiful, sacred design to that, though, encouraging each of us to live in the moment and be grateful for what we have right now. I wish more people would understand that."

We stood for a moment longer, quietly. The lambent tide was gradually encompassing us both. I then said, "There really are no words at a time like this, are there? Even as a writer, I'm always at a loss when something like this happens."

Sister Augustine looked at me, still with somber eyes. "One of the most important things in this life is just showing up. I appreciate you being here, John. That speaks for itself, where words never could. Just like a smile does."

"I should let you go," I said, smiling. "I'll see you later."

"See you later," Sister said just above a whisper, then she turned to continue up the staircase with the help of her cane.

I swiped my hand across the wind chimes like I had done countless times before. It was ingrained in me by now to do so. I got about midway across the porch, face-to-face with the sun in the distance, when I heard a happy chuckle join the chiming behind me. I turned around.

Sister Augustine was once more facing my direction. Amused by how I never forgot to set the wind chimes in motion, she was laughing. The twinkle had even returned to her tearful eyes. She was on the sixth step leading up to the convent's main building and now fully bathed in the golden light as the sun lingered on its horizon shelf. My friend appeared how I had always imagined a vision of the Blessed Mother would be.

I memorized the way she looked in that moment—transfigured—and hold that image close to my heart even today.

I laughed back and gave her a little wave, which she returned. Then we and the sun all went our separate ways until another day.

19

Talk of the Town

Our planning for the annual Christmas Open House on the first weekend in December had started the minute the previous one ended. The year before, the crowd had doubled, the Gussie's Specials and other pieces were once again gone in a flash, and Sister Augustine had debuted her first limited edition ornament, the Nativity Donkey, all twenty-five of which vanished within minutes. "For a slow animal, they sure moved fast today!" Sister had said, laughing in amazement.

Over the next several months, we discussed what her follow-up ornament should be, without coming to any conclusion. The one certainty was that this time she'd create one hundred in the limited edition. "Fifty can be made available before the open house and fifty can then be reserved for the day of the open house," I had suggested to her. "Sounds like a good plan," she concurred. That was sometime around February or March.

Flash forward to July. "Sister, I know what your new ornament should be!" I exclaimed as I raced into her studio. She was sitting in her oak chair at the right-hand corner of the horseshoe.

She looked up with excited eyes. "I knew you'd think of something!"

"Well you're the one who actually gave me the idea," I said. "The Peace Dove."

"The Peace Dove," she repeated. "I like the sound of that."

"You wrote 'peace' inside my bowl, because it's your favorite word, so I think a Peace Dove ornament would be fantastic."

"So do I. Plus, it's a nice way to get the Holy Spirit in on the act."

"Yes," I said with a smile. We were covering a lot of territory. "I also think you should paint it in a light blue, because I read somewhere how that's the international color for healing. Or at least it will be once we're done with it."

"I can do that. Sounds easy enough."

"Plus, the word *peace* can be inscribed on the front of each dove. Just like you did with all the words for the ornament collections you made for me and Steven."

"I can do that, too."

Our creative rhythm was flowing.

"Also like last time, I'll create a special tag we can tie to each ornament. Which means I'll need another quote from you for the tag. Something about peace, of course."

"I have the perfect quote, but it's not something I came up with," Sister Augustine said with that twinkle in her eyes. "It's something Elie Wiesel said a while ago that I recently read again."

I knew Wiesel was a Holocaust survivor and the Noble Peace Prize–winning author of the groundbreaking book *Night*, and many other impactful works. The fact that Sister had chosen a quote by a Jewish man was not lost on me. It spoke volumes about my friend—a Catholic nun—that she would never say about herself for fear it might sound like boasting.

"What's the quote?"

Sister smiled, then spoke from memory, paraphrasing the line Mr. Wiesel had used to conclude his 1986 Nobel Lecture. "Peace is not only God's gift to us; it is our gift to each other."

"It's perfect."

❦

By October, all one hundred of the baby blue Peace Doves were ready to take flight. I did my part by drafting both a formal press release to help spread word of the open house as well as a promotional "About the Artist" bio of Sister M. Augustine, O.S.B.

The one-page bio led off with a testimonial blurb from our local newspaper, the *Daily Press:* "Sister Augustine is St. Marys' Best-Kept Secret. . . . [She] is a cross between Berta Hummel and Grandma Moses." The bio was also added to the back of a photo I had taken of Sister Augustine with her beloved cat Blitzen. The photo/bio—my homemade avowal of each piece's divine provenance—was then affixed to the several dozen new Gussie's Specials and other pieces Sister Augustine had created for the open house during the year.

I also shared both pieces of promotional writing with my students in the courses I was teaching at Pitt-Bradford that fall. I often invoked this backpack to briefcase approach, showing how what they were learning in class translated to the real world, whether you were promoting a Nashville superstar, a White House principal, a Fortune 500 company, or a nun and artist who ran a small-town ceramic shop. The same foundation of tools and techniques, and sheer excitement, applied.

Which got me thinking. Amid the swift pace we were now caught up in, heading toward the final stretch of open house prep and planning, I decided to take my own advice on a more personal matter. One of the lessons I taught in both Promotional Writing and Writing for Management was how to craft an effective proposal to pitch a personality or a product. Yet, all this time, when pitching my beer cookbook to publishers, I was sending the entire four-hundred-page manuscript. It only now occurred to me how that was surely a daunting package for any editor, already buried under a pile of paper, to get dumped on them. Especially since I didn't yet have a literary agent to fight the good fight on my behalf and stay on top of editors for an answer. Plus, the postage for what was the equivalent of sending a pile of logs through the mail every week was draining my bank account. So, I translated the behemoth of a manuscript into a clear and concise fifteen-page book proposal: synopsis, chapter outline, a dozen sample recipes, and a brief bio. Simple and to the point.

By the beginning of November, I sent out a batch of the proposals to new publishers with renewed vigor. Like Sister said, the act of creating and producing is a process with its own learning curve. All in God's time.

I had the highest hopes yet that this new approach would eventually pay off.

⚜

ONE THING THAT did pay off almost immediately was the press kit about Sister and the open house that I widely distributed to local and regional media outlets.

When the interview requests started to come in, I visited Sister Augustine one afternoon to make a deal with her. Weeks earlier, she had declared, "I'm not doing any more interviews. Period. I have nothing left to say." I knew at least the second half of that statement wasn't true. However, the first part had me coasting in on a wing and a prayer, hoping she'd change her mind.

I entered the shop as one would enter a diplomatic summit. A compromise was in order. I hoped my already-overworked guardian angels and Heavenly Board of Directors would have my back on this. Especially considering the Heavenly reinforcements Sister could call in if she wanted.

Sister Augustine sat on one side of the table and I on the

other. Duncan paint bottles—Plum Blush, Cornsilk, Winter Fog, Iced Mint, Miami Pink, Fire Thorn, Bluebonnet, and Banana Cream—were stacked across the table like a wall between us. She was currently working on a series of poinsettia plates for the open house.

"I have a deal for you," I offered.

"Shoot," she said, holding firm and maintaining a razor-sharp focus on the plate and brush in her hands.

"A very popular radio show called *Talk of the Town* wants to do an interview with you."

"I've never done radio before."

"I know, but this is a really big station for our area. They have thousands of listeners across something like sixteen counties."

"That *is* big," she said.

I felt confident the negotiations were starting to swing in my favor.

"Yes. So here's my proposal: If you will please do this one big radio interview, which you can do with Sister Margoretta so you're not alone and which will get a lot of attention for the convent and open house, then I will make sure the print interviews with the newspapers are kept to a bare minimum."

"How will you do that?" She was a tough cookie.

"I'll give the newspaper reporters most of the information they want. I'll even take a photo of you and we can submit that for the reporters to use. That way, all they'll need is maybe a quote or two from you. Does that work?"

Sister thought for a moment, continuing to sweep her wide brush in broad strokes across the bisqueware petals of the poinsettia plate.

"Deal," she finally said, glancing up with a wink.

TWO WEEKS BEFORE the open house, I invited the local print reporters to the ceramic shop for Sister Augustine's third official press conference. As promised, I made sure it was short and sweet.

I supplied the reporters with so much background, including a photo of Sister glazing a large snowman, they really only had one question for her. And it was the most important question: "Why did you create the Peace Dove this year?"

Without missing a beat, Sister Augustine replied, "Peace is such a rarity these days, it's almost as though we could help out a little by having a Peace Dove. We're at a time when we need a lot of peace in the world, so I'm trying to help spread the peace."

The fact that Sister was now ninety-two years old combined with her exquisite statement about peace became the cornerstone of all the media coverage that year.

⚜

IN LATE NOVEMBER, Sister Augustine held up her side of our deal. The two hosts of the popular radio show *Talk of the Town* arrived at the ceramic shop early one afternoon. Sister Margoretta joined Sister Augustine along the outside of the table where she and I always sat in the studio. Patty and another gift shop volunteer named Pam had accompanied Sister Margoretta and stood off to the side to watch. Inside the horseshoe across from their guests, the hosts, Denny and Joe, set up their equipment on the table to record the interview, which would air the following Sunday.

I had prepared two pages of talking points to help the hosts craft their questions and to help Sister Augustine and Sister Margoretta answer them. I knew that once the interview started rolling live to tape it would be out of my control.

I stood three feet away from Sister Augustine, in case she needed me.

From the start, Denny and Joe were enamored by Sister Augustine. While Sister Margoretta, who had been introduced on air as "Sister *Margarita*," eliciting a muffled laugh from me, provided the logistics about the upcoming open house at various intervals throughout the hour-long interview, it was Sister Augustine who provided the spunk and color.

"Would you mind sharing your age with us?" Denny asked Sister Augustine, handing her a microphone of her own to use. She had never used one before, but still wrapped her hand around it like a pro, bringing it to her lips and jumping right in.

"I'm ninety-two."

"Did you say *ninety-two*?"

"Ninety-two," my friend repeated as if it were the most obvious fact in the world.

"You look like a young chick yet. You get around here pretty good," the host, a friendly man in his sixties, gushed. I covered my mouth to stifle another laugh, as did Patty and Pam. This live taping was going to be a real trip. I was pretty sure Sister had never been called a "chick" before, even though Denny had meant it as a lighthearted show of respect and admiration.

To my surprise, Sister let out a girlish giggle and rolled with it. "Not nearly like I used to do," she responded.

Denny shifted gears, focusing on her art.

Sister explained the full process of making her ceramic pieces, from mixing the wet clay and pouring the molds to firing the greenware and glazed bisqueware, and her special ritual: "I sprinkle the Holy Water in the kiln so the poor souls in Purgatory will help to take care of what's inside."

"Sister, do you work in the shop five days a week?" Denny asked.

"*Six* days a week," she corrected.

"Wow!"

The host's gleeful reaction earned a chuckle from his guest.

He now glanced in my direction. "Would you say John Schlimm pushes you a little bit?"

Hey, wait a minute, the little voice inside me chirped.

Sister looked over and laughed at the surprised expression on my face. Her mischievous grin told me it was payback time. I was about to become part of the story. "He has so many ideas," she said. "And I've learned to follow them because they turn out so well."

"Here, all along, we thought you were the brains behind this," Denny teased.

Sister chortled. "John is a really good guy."

My heart skipped a beat.

Denny moved on to the Peace Doves, which were a prominent bullet I had bolded and underlined in the talking points.

Sister Augustine explained, "We made a hundred of them. We did donkeys last year—the Nativity Donkey—we only did twenty-five, and they sold out. So this year, we did a hundred of the dove."

"We're trying to sell those out, too, before the door opens, aren't we?" Denny, a successful businessman himself, commented.

Like any publicist would, I wanted to jump in. No, only fifty were available before the open house, and the other fifty on the day of. That, too, was in the talking points. I bit my lip.

"This year I have enough I know," Sister Augustine remarked.

"They're not gonna get ahead of you sisters, are they?"

"We're trying not to let you!"

"Could you tell me a little bit about the Gussie's Specials? Are you Gussie?"

Sister giggled. The first hint of a blush rose in her cheeks. "Yes, that's my nickname," she revealed publicly for the first time. Naturally, I had been whispering that gem of an anecdote to customers for years. "We're not supposed to have nicknames here, but I got one anyhow."

She then gave a CliffsNotes version of how the Gussie's Special came about by accident: cleaning her brushes on bisqueware so as not to waste any paint . . .

"So at your big open house, if people want to meet Gussie, they can come up here and meet Gussie, too?"

Sister let out another round of laughter. If I wasn't mistaken, she was really enjoying herself. The full rosy glow in her cheeks now gave her away as much as the melody in her voice. "I hope to be here. God willing. I'll be happy to see a lot of people."

Periodically throughout the interview, a patient Sister Margoretta, whom the hosts still referred to as "Sister Margarita," was asked to provide the who, what, where, when, why, and how details of the open house as well as talk a little bit about her Trifles and Treasures Gift Shop. The conversation then inevitably circled back to Sister Augustine.

"Sister, you mentioned that you're ninety-two years old. What do you attribute your longevity to?" Denny asked.

"Just living, I guess," Sister Augustine deadpanned, practical and to the point. Everyone in the room laughed.

"What's your favorite meal?" Denny asked next.

OMG! I smiled. The interview had suddenly gone tabloid.

"My favorite meal?" Sister asked. That wasn't in the talking points. I knew her well enough to know what she was likely thinking. When she glanced over at me, my assumption was confirmed. The tape was rolling, so all I could do was shrug my shoulders and grin. Translation: *The show must go on!*

"Yeah, what's your favorite meal?" Denny repeated, smiling broadly and anxious for her answer.

"That's hard to say." A chuckle. "Depends on what it is. I don't really have a favorite."

Denny pressed on. From there, the interview turned into *Lifestyles of the Holy and Famous*. I was loving every minute of it.

"Living to ninety-two years old, do you have a favorite drive you like to take on a Sunday, a ride around the countryside?"

Another offbeat question. Sister glanced in my direction again. "I haven't done that for some time. I would like to do that again, though," she answered.

That gave me an idea, which I filed away for another day. I couldn't believe I hadn't thought of it before. I was always looking for guest speakers for the PR classes I taught at the university. *And* my hour-long commute to campus was all through the countryside.

Denny next moved on to her family—her childhood growing up on a Pennsylvania farm—and then he swapped fishing stories with her.

"What kind of fish do you catch?"

"Whatever takes the hook!" Sister Augustine lobbed back.

"What's the biggest one you ever caught?" Fisherman-to-fisherman now.

"A northern pike. It was twenty-nine inches."

"I know a little something about northern pike. That's what I fish for up in Canada."

"That's where I got mine," Sister said. "In Canada."

Patty slipped over to the back corner by the sink, where there was a picture of Sister at Pymatuning Lake holding her catch of the day. She handed the photo to Denny. "That's pretty impressive!" he said.

"Those are bluegills," Sister Augustine clarified. "We got a hundred and fifteen that day."

Denny's eyes popped. "*A hundred and fifteen!*"

Sister grinned ear to ear. Game, set, match.

"I'm trying to figure out your secret to live to ninety-two

years old!" Denny trailed off in a giddy laugh. "I'll tell you, Sister, it's amazing what you've done here."

"It keeps me off the streets!" she quipped, reviving a surefire sound bite from her first press conference two years earlier.

I guess that sounded like a closing line to her. Thinking the interview was over, Sister set her mike on the table, rose from her chair, and started to walk back to her seat in the corner. An open bottle of Candy Apple red paint and a bisqueware Santa Claus, who looked like he was covered in a fresh snowfall except for his coal-black boots, were waiting for her. My instinct was to reach out and grab her by the arm, but I was too far away and she was fast. All I could do was glance over at Patty and Pam, and shrug.

The host chased after her. "We just can't let Sister Augustine get away here. She just can't wait to get back to making these ceramics," Denny bantered, rounding the table, with his microphone extended toward her like a determined paparazzo. I was busting up on the other end of the room. "She's running from this mike and I can't even keep up with her! I'm trying to catch her!"

He finally snagged her at the back of the studio for an encore. "Sister, is there anything else you'd like to say about your history here or your upcoming open house?" He held the mike toward her.

I saw a mischievous glint in her eye as she leaned in. I held my breath.

"I think everything's been pretty well said," Sister Augustine replied.

I exhaled in relief.

But Denny wasn't giving up. He dove right back in with a marathon of new questions about everything from her favorite pieces to how many molds she had to her favorite time of day to work.

"This is a lot of work for someone who's ninety-two years old."

"Yes, it is. It's about time I quit!" Sister chortled.

From the other side of the room, I got caught up in the moment, yelling, "You're not allowed to quit!"

My friend laughed.

"I don't think there's any quit in you, Sister," Denny said, finally winding down.

"Well, somebody's going to stop me someday!"

Then just as Denny finished, Joe, the younger of the two hosts, chimed in, taking his long-awaited turn with their star guest. Sister sat down now, eye to eye with Santa Claus.

"After ninety-two years, tell us what Christmas means to you," Joe said, lowering the mike to record her answer.

"Well, right now it's just a relief all this stuff is done!" Sister replied, her head bent toward jolly old Saint Nicholas, who was still in need of a red coat and pants.

I was pretty sure what she meant was: *this interview is done.*

Denny and Joe dissolved into fits of laughter like two smitten schoolboys.

Her head still bent, Sister Augustine looked up at me with a subtle grin, and winked.

Twenty feet away, I shook my head, smiling, and winked back.

❧

ALL FIFTY PEACE Doves that were available before the open house sold out once the newspaper articles and *Talk of the Town* interview were released. "They all flew the coop!" Sister exclaimed when the last one was purchased. She had called me at home to tell me. It was the first and only time she ever called me. "What should I do?" she asked, almost in a panic. "People keep coming in for them!" I laughed and told her, "Just tell them to come back to the open house to buy one, and keep the other fifty hidden till then."

The day before the open house, I restocked the small artificial tree on the gold-sheathed island in the middle of the shop with the remaining conclave of fifty Peace Doves.

Nearby shelves were filled with three dozen new Gussie's Specials that Patty and I had arranged during our now-annual housecleaning and holiday decorating day. Sister had finally agreed to raise the prices on them, but only because the cost of the glazes and paints had gone up. The small neon orange price stickers on the bottom of each noted that the large bowls were now ten dollars and the small bowls were eight dollars—still the bargain of the century. I had only insisted on absolutely having to buy one of them beforehand.

It was a smaller bowl—lightly brushed in sky blue, grass green, sandalwood, pink, purple, periwinkle, red, and ivory. An Impressionist's Garden of Eden, or Mockin' Bird Hill. Or my favorite field in Bear Run. "I can see the sky and tulips, columbines, poppies, foxgloves, Queen Anne's lace, lilies of the valley, spongy moss, high grasses, even a cardinal," I told Sister excitedly upon seeing it for the first time weeks earlier. "It's my favorite of all your Gussie's Specials. I feel like I'm meant to have it." Sister Augustine smiled and said, "It's my favorite, too." There was also one other image in the landscape of that exceptional bowl, something I would only discover many years later when the time was right and keep mostly to myself. Next to the stroke of red that resembled a cardinal—a traditional symbol of keeping the faith in seemingly hopeless situations—in the confluence of paint was the visage of a man. A striking, familiar face. Maybe my eyes were the only ones meant to see Him, and I would be content if that were the case. I didn't even bother to ask, *Could it be?* I just knew and felt blessed.

By this time, Sister Augustine had created more than four

hundred of her magnum opus in just over four and a half years. A few dozen were in my personal collection, displayed mostly on the shelves behind my writing desk. That way, she was always with me.

⚜

ON THE DAY of the open house, my mom, Phyllis, and Denise resumed their stations at the checkout counter and snack table for a third year in a row. Sister Augustine was again seated in the middle of the horseshoe where she could easily greet and chat with the customers. I resumed my role as salesman.

I opened the doors at quarter to nine, fifteen minutes early, just as I had done for the past two years. Thanks to the press coverage, Sister Augustine and her work were *the* talk of the town. Customers streamed in like a flash mob.

Amid the rapture, the remaining fifty Peace Doves also flew the coop within minutes. As did the Gussie's Specials and, over the course of the day, the other items that Sister Augustine had spent a year creating and stockpiling.

And my eagle on the top shelf. Rushing by midafternoon, I glanced up, and he was gone.

A continuous line of fans relished their few moments with Sister. Including a courageous young girl who recited four "Hail Marys" to score both a small ceramic frog and a ladybug. Plus a hug from Sister Augustine. I had never even hugged her yet.

This particular open house happened to fall on my birthday, December 1. I downplayed that to Sister, not wanting her to think she needed to do anything special. What *was* special was getting to spend my thirty-sixth birthday exactly as I was. The plan worked well for most of the morning, until a cousin came in just after lunchtime and exclaimed, "Happy Birthday, John!" Sister looked at me with a surprised expression when she remembered the date, as if I had pulled a gotcha moment on her.

I shrugged my shoulders, smiled, and raced on to help the next customer find the piece in Sister Augustine's shop that I was convinced was waiting there just for them to buy it.

As in years past, after everyone had finally left, I locked the front door and turned off the strings of little, multicolored lights that meandered across the bare shelves like a festive constellation. I then sat with Sister and tabulated the nearly one hundred new orders customers had placed for everything from Nativity sets and Gussie's Specials to forget-me-not plates and decanters.

Tommy and a new addition to the shop, a calico named Heidi, joined us. Some of the sisters had recently surprised Sister Augustine with this new rescue cat from the local Elk County Humane Society shelter, where my Little Coyote had also come from. The frisky little feline had earned her name because of her penchant for rounds of hide-and-seek with Sister that often lasted all day long.

"What would you think of us doing two ornaments next year?" Sister Augustine asked, while she held Heidi on her lap and Tommy raced happily around the empty shop.

Amen to that, I nodded.

"Now you're speaking my language," I said.

"It's never too early to get started, you know," she teased with a chuckle, knowing full well she was quoting a line I had once used on her.

"My thoughts exactly!" Both of our imaginations were racing ahead.

"By the way," my friend said, "Happy birthday!"

20

THE GIFT

TWO DAYS BEFORE CHRISTMAS, I ARRIVED AT SISTER AUGUStine's ceramic shop with a present for her. My friend was wearing her midnight blue bib apron with the pack of baying wolves on front and sitting in her usual mint-green spindle chair inside the horseshoe. The paint bottles and bisqueware cleared away for the open house a few weeks earlier had returned in force to the tabletops. It was back to business.

"Did you give all your students A's this semester?" Sister asked with a smile. A large, white rippled bowl sat in front of her on the table.

I laughed. "Not quite, but I just turned in my grades and most of them should be very happy. I had a lot of really talented students this semester," I answered, assuming my usual seat across from her. "I always end up learning as much, if not more, from them as they do from me."

Heidi popped in for a second and then darted back out of the room. Tommy was AWOL.

"What are you working on?" I asked, surveying the crowded tablescape.

"I'm getting started on all the new orders for Gussie's Specials," Sister answered. "Several dozen more were ordered at the open house, as you know." Ten open bottles of glaze formed an arc around Sister and the bowl.

"With these new orders, I figured out that you will have created close to five hundred Gussie's Specials so far."

Sister Augustine shook her head in amazement, dipping her brush into one of the Duncan bottles labeled Ultramarine. "To think at one time I cleaned my brushes on these bowls to make them. Now I have to order in paint especially for them, just to keep up." She pulled the brush from the bottle, studied the blank bisqueware bowl for a moment, then slid the bristles across, up, and down its rippled surface, never breaking stride.

"Think how many people you've made happy with them. As well as with your forget-me-not pieces, the ornaments, Nativities, and everything else."

"I should have run when I saw you walk in that first day," Sister joked, keeping her eyes on the bowl. A new brush was now plunged into Sun Yellow. The loaded bristles were swatted across the bowl like a playful cat paw. The bowl was turned and swatted lighter this time. Turned again, swatted again.

I laughed. "You wouldn't have gotten very far. I bet I could outrun you," I teased back.

"I'm sure you could," Sister agreed with a chuckle. Another brush, another color—Rain Tree Green. This time, the tip of the brush stippled and flicked as the bowl was spun around. The seasoned hands of a creator giving soul to her creation. "If my bowls and other pieces have made people happy, then that makes it all worth it. You know, I could be retired by now."

Once when Sister Augustine had invited Patty and me to join her for lunch in the convent's dining room, afterward she took us to a long porch on the western side of the building. It was a quiet, warm, secluded place, enclosed with windows. "When I retire, this is where I plan to spend my days," she confided. From the porch, you could look out over the convent's manicured lawns toward the high school in the distance, and the setting sun. Looking to the immediate right, you could see the Guesthouse and the front door to the ceramic shop. Squint, and there were our wind chimes. The chapel was to the left. "There's only one problem with your plan," I told my friend. "I don't *plan* on letting you retire!" We all laughed. Sister quipped, "That's what I was afraid of!"

"You'll be happy to know that I've been giving a lot of thought to the ornaments for next year," Sister informed me, as a fresh brush was dipped into another glaze—Creole Spice—and then zigged and zagged over the bowl's small furrows. Only the artist knew the brush's destination, like a master cook who instinctually knows where a pinch of this and a dash of that can lead.

"I can't wait to hear what you have in mind." Usually it was me going to her with ideas and brainstorms. This was a great surprise.

"For one of the ornaments, I was thinking I could do another dove, so the doves become a series of their own."

"Fantastic idea!" As unassuming as Sister Augustine was when I first met her, I was quickly learning that she was a latent genius when it came to public relations and marketing. Both jargon she'd never use herself. She simply proceeded ahead on her own terms and on her own time frame, no matter the lexicon and labels I tossed her way.

"I thought this new dove could be pink, a light pink like the Tearose I use for your cherubs. And I'll inscribe the word *love* on each one, just like I inscribed *peace* on the first series."

"The Love Dove!"

Sister flashed me a huge smile. By now, the bowl she was working on was awash with dull grays, teals, browns, and pinks—a marinade of colors that the kiln would forge into whatever the bottle labels promised and the mind's eye was open to seeing. I had come to appreciate the benevolence of glaze. How it allowed light to permeate and echo back, converting or igniting whatever lay beneath it. Finished, Sister set the bowl aside to focus on our chat.

"Yes. And for the other ornament, I think it would be nice to continue the Nativity theme that I started with the donkey."

"I like where this is going."

"I have a cookie cutter for an angel."

Hark! the little voice in my mind rang out. "The Nativity Angel!" I then declared aloud.

Another huge grin was sent my way across the table. "Yes."

"Both are going to be incredible. You realize that you'll have to do a hundred of each, right?"

"Of course."

We both sat silently for a moment, letting this all sink in. I was so excited and inspired at the moment that I could have gone home then and there to start working on the press materials for the next open house. Which was a year away.

"I can see it all in my head," I told Sister. "We'll probably need a larger artificial tree to display all the ornaments since there will be twice as many as last time."

"Your mind never stops, does it?"

"Nope. Now this is the part you may not be thrilled by," I said, "but I plan to go after even larger media outlets next year before the open house, especially now that your Gussie's Specials have become so popular and this ornament series just keeps getting better and better. I think the national media will go crazy over you."

Sister rolled her eyes. "I should have kept my mouth shut."

I laughed. "I told you I was going to make you a superstar." Locally, that was a done deal.

"Heaven help me!" Sister Augustine smiled and looked upward. "I can barely keep up with the new orders as is, and I've never seen so much traffic through here before."

"I brought you a gift," I then announced, switching gears

as the rush of adrenaline flooded every cell in my body. I slid a small package across the table through the maze of paint bottles, brushes, and bisqueware. It was wrapped in glossy red-and-green-striped paper with a shimmery gold bow.

"You didn't have to do that."

"I know I didn't."

Sister picked up the package, mindfully examining it. It was one of those wonderful times when, no matter a person's age, you can see the spark and excitement of youth in their eyes—a young heart—as they behold a wrapped mystery.

Sister Augustine set the gift on her lap and slowly started to unravel the shiny paper.

"It's beautiful," she gushed, seeing the special ornament inside. "This is my star on top."

"And my heart," I told her.

It was a small yellow star she had originally created as part of the two ornament collections for me and Steven a few years earlier. The word *be* was inscribed on the front of it. I had found a simple clay kit at Wal-Mart from which I sculpted a four-inch-long heart, baked it in the oven, and painted it holly berry red. With a white paint pen, I wrote the word *grace* in cursive on the front of it. Using a thin moss-green ribbon, I strung together the two pieces, with the tiny star resting on top of the heart. Together, the star and heart read: "be grace."

"I like to think of the piece as a collaboration between us," I told my friend.

Sister Augustine studied the ornament closely, turning it over in her hands. She ran her fingers over the smooth, uneven surface of the heart that my own fingers had fashioned. On the back, I had drawn an angel and inscribed, "To Sister M. Augustine, from your #1 Fan, JES2."

She brought the ornament to her chest and looked across the table at me. "I'll cherish this forever."

"I'm so glad you like it."

"I love it! But I don't have anything for you."

"Sister, don't be silly. You've already given me the greatest gift you ever could, for almost five years now."

"You're easy to please. Besides, God will know how to reward you better than I for every footstep you've taken here."

"Well, we have many more steps ahead of us, my friend. This is only the beginning!"

Sister Augustine smiled. "God willing. He's boss after all."

I could only nod in agreement.

There was no arguing with that.

PART SEVEN

21

BORROWED TIME

THREE WEEKS INTO FEBRUARY, I ARRIVED AT THE CONVENT with an invitation and some good news. Hurrying through the shop, I noticed that Sister Augustine had completely restocked the shelves and center island, which were all left practically bare after the successful Christmas Open House almost three months earlier. A lot of new pieces had appeared just during the previous two weeks when I had been busy at the university and hadn't gotten to stop in. Including a lone Gussie's Special—a tall vase that looked as though it had been spray-painted in cobalt blue, lime, evergreen, brown, white, and flickers of red—which was the focal point in the middle of the island.

My friend was seated at the back corner of the horseshoe. Tommy and Heidi were racing around the studio headed for a finish line only they knew about.

Before I could deliver my news, Sister Augustine said, "I'm glad you're here, I have a surprise for you!"

That was always music to my ears. "What is it?"

She stood and motioned for me to follow her into the back room. I noted for the first time that she was now using her cane, once reserved only for outside travel, inside as well. I tried not to dwell too much on the simple wooden stick. Yet I became aware of how sometimes we purposely choose not to see what is right there in front of us.

"You've been really busy," I said. "The front room is completely full again."

Sister looked over her shoulder and smiled. "Yes, I've been making the most of every moment. I even finished all the special orders from the open house."

"There were almost a hundred orders!"

"No time to waste," she declared with a hint of urgency that was never there before.

"That Gussie's Special vase out front, is it new? I don't remember it."

"I only fired it this week," Sister replied. "Which is why you haven't seen it before."

"It looks like a piece of street art or graffiti," I commented. "Some of the brushstrokes appear like you used a can of spray paint to apply them. It's cool and edgy."

Sister shook her head and chuckled. "I wish I had an imagination like yours, and all those words you have!"

I was pretty sure no one had ever compared Sister's work to graffiti, but the piece definitely had that vibe. No doubt Banksy would have been in love.

"You may have to start creating more Gussie's Specials in that style," I suggested.

Sister Augustine swatted her hand toward me with a playful grin and then led me to one of the long tables that divided the back room in half widthwise. A crisp white sheet covered whatever was on the table, creating the illusion of an ancient marble bas-relief. It was a thin layer of something. Rows of subtle peaks and ridges sent my imagination soaring.

Sister turned to me with a smile. "I was hoping you wouldn't come in when I was working on these all last week, because I wanted to surprise you with them."

I could hardly contain my excitement.

Sister leaned her cane against the table and with both hands pulled back the sheet. "*Ta-da!*"

It only took me a split second to register the two hundred small, muddy-gray forms in front of me. "The Love Doves and the Nativity Angels!"

Sister was pleased by my reaction. "They're only in greenware, and I didn't get to write 'love' on the doves yet, but I thought you'd be excited to see that I got a jump-start on the ornaments for this year, especially since the open house is still nine months away."

"I can't believe you did all this already, plus finished all your open house orders and made the new stuff for the shop." I reached down and gently ran my hand over the cool, moist doves and angels. Per our previous discussion about the ornaments, I knew the Love Doves would be glazed in Tearose and the Nativity Angels would be coated with a clear glaze to keep them as white as Christmas snow. "You're on a roll!" I said. "These are fantastic."

"You can never take tomorrow for granted," my friend said.

With every ounce of self-restraint, I diverted my eyes from the nearby wooden cane.

"This is great!" I exclaimed. "Once these are done, I can get an early start on promoting them, *and* you." We had also previously discussed that, as with the Peace Dove, half of each of the two new limited edition ornaments would be made available before the open house to help create a buzz. The other fifty of each would then be sold on the actual day of the event in early December to ensure a joyous frenzy in-house.

I had big plans for pitching the story of Sister Augustine to national media later in the year. Now that she and her work were well established locally, it was time to introduce her to a larger audience. After all, her work was already in every state in the United States and in other countries, which had happened organically and mostly during her earlier years in business. Back then, visitors—often former St. Marys residents—from across the country would stop by the shop and take her pieces as mementos to their new hometowns or ship them to friends overseas. Now that was happening on a grander scale, because people were being exposed to her in a new way. People were learning to appreciate Sister Augustine as the gifted artist she was, along with all the added trimmings of the convent to sweeten the pot.

Thanks to the public's renewed interest in her work, I figured that by the end of the year Sister would surpass the five-hundred mark when it came to her Gussie's Specials. I had done my part by giving many of the bowls as gifts, including to some of my more notable pals, which always amused Sister. She was speechless one afternoon when I brought in a handwritten note I had received from former second lady Tipper Gore. I read aloud the part pertaining to her: "Thank you so much for Sister's beautiful Gussie's Special—it goes right into my home office which has pale green walls. I love it!" I told Sister how Tipper's office in the larger suite comprising the Office of the Vice President at the White House during the 1990s was painted green, the Second Lady's favorite color. For that reason, I had asked Sister Augustine to paint one of her larger bowls in a green palette for me to send to Tipper, who continued to be a special friend of mine, for her birthday. I had also given Gussie's Specials to my pals Ethan Zohn and Jenna Morasca, both early winners of the CBS hit reality show *Survivor*. Politics to pop culture, I had Sister covered.

Looking now at the two hundred doves and angels in front of me and listening to Sister tell how she had worked overtime during the previous week to get them this far just to surprise me, I could hear a joyous choir singing in my mind. *Amazing grace, how sweet the sound . . .*

"When do you think you'll finish them?" I asked.

"I'll try my best to have them done in the next few weeks, but I have a few new Nativity orders to finish first, and I want to get your Easter eggs done, too."

"I can't wait to see how those eggs turn out!" It was so exciting to have multiple projects in progress with her at one time. I had asked Sister Augustine to create a dozen small ceramic Easter eggs for me, just as she had done the two collections of Christmas ornaments for Steven and me a few years earlier. Each egg would have a word, such as *love, hope, peace, grace, joy, awe,* or *laughter,* inscribed into it and each would then be painted in a solid color. We had spent an entire afternoon at the beginning of January deciding which glazes and words she'd use.

We later decided that there would also be an extra-special, thirteenth egg in my collection. It would be a red egg that held a very special meaning for my friend. Every Easter morning on the farm when she was a young girl, Sister's parents would hide eggs that they had painted for the kids to find. Her father always painted one egg bright red and whoever found it received a prize of chocolate. We had decided that she would inscribe my red egg with the word "Knox."

"The greenware eggs are out on the table," Sister informed me. "I'm planning to get those done early, too. When you walked in today, I was just about to start writing the words on them. This year, Easter is the earliest it has been in almost a hundred years, so the clock's ticking."

I helped Sister to cover the Love Doves and the Nativity Angels again with the sheet. I knew the next time I'd see them, they'd be glazed and shiny, just as she and I had planned. Then I would create the tags that we would tie onto each one.

We headed back into the studio to our usual mint-green spindle chairs across from each other. On the way past her station at the back corner, I saw my baker's dozen of Easter eggs, currently muddy gray and fragile, awaiting the inscriptions and their first firing before the rainbow of glazes would be applied. The slip of paper on which I had written the words she'd inscribe on each egg was setting nearby.

Whatever race Tommy and Heidi had been running earlier, it was apparently over and with no clear winner. Both were lounging now on the floor without a care in the world.

"You don't mind if I continue painting these Nativity figures while we chat, do you?" Sister Augustine asked, settling into her chair in the middle of the horseshoe. She propped her cane against the table behind her, where luckily I couldn't see it.

"No, go right ahead." I settled into my chair as well.

"I can get more done this way," Sister told me. "I have to make the most of each moment these days with so much to do."

"Speaking of making the most of each moment, I have an invitation for you *and* some really great news. Which do you want first?"

My friend looked up from the Baby Jesus figurine she was painting. "The really great news first," she answered with a glimmer in her eyes.

"One of the publishers I approached about my beer cookbook asked to see the manuscript and they seemed excited about it."

"That's wonderful!"

"It's not exactly a yes just yet, but it's definitely a step closer, and it's a lot better than a no right off the bat." Sending the brief book proposal as opposed to the full manuscript seemed to do the trick. *Live and learn,* I told myself. My confidence in all things was definitely on a refreshing rise these days.

"All in God's time. I have a good feeling about this," Sister said. "I have you on our prayer list here, so sooner or later God's going to have to give in or else He's going to have to keep hearing from all of us women about getting your book published."

I laughed. "I can't think of a better endorsement than all of your prayers."

"If only He could have a bite of that chocolate cake you brought me, I think God would probably hand-deliver your manuscript to publishers Himself." Sister smiled at me and then returned her attention to Baby Jesus. His eyes were peacefully closed like crescent moons and rendered in the same Sandalwood paint she was now applying to his hair.

"Now for the invitation," I announced. "I was talking about you in the PR course I'm teaching this semester at Pitt-Bradford and the students asked me to invite you to visit our class to talk to them."

I paused, letting the invitation sink in while carefully watching Sister Augustine for her reaction. I knew she rarely left the convent, let alone traveled to a college campus. Though not long ago, during her *Talk of the Town* interview, she did say that she wouldn't mind a drive through the countryside. My one-hour commute to the campus was just that.

Baby Jesus was once more put on hold as she rested him on her lap and looked up. "They want *me* to visit their class?"

"Yes, I told them all about your work, the Gussie's Specials, the open houses, the interviews and articles. I even handed out copies of the press materials I've created for you as samples of promotional writing. They thought it would be fun to meet you and to hear about what's happening here from you directly."

"What would they want me to say?"

"Well, don't worry, they won't be expecting the Sermon on the Mount," I said, cracking up. "Just a little bit about your life, your work, the shop here. They're an easy audience. Most of them have probably never even met a real-life nun."

Sister's face lit up and she blushed. "When would you want me to go? I'm pretty busy right now."

I bit my lip with excitement. That certainly wasn't the no I expected I'd get, and which I certainly would have gotten just a few years earlier. I smiled. "I could take you to my class in April, after Easter and once you get most of the work you're doing here now finished."

Sister Augustine thought for a moment while Baby Jesus and I patiently waited. Finally, she said, "That could be fun!"

"So that's a yes?"

"Yes, I'll go," she confirmed, adding, "God willing. He's boss, and I never know what He has planned for me from one day to the next."

"I think God would be happy to get you on a college campus to talk with young people," I said. "They're already inspired by your story. I can't wait for them to actually meet you. There's a lot you can teach them. Having you visit my class will take your making the most of every moment to a whole new level. It can be the start of your lecture tour!"

"If you say so, John." Sister giggled and finished painting the powdery blue blanket in Baby Jesus's manger.

In silence, I watched my friend work from about four feet away across the table, just as I had done for five years. Her aged hand gently held a thin-tipped paintbrush as she now gracefully added a soft pink blush to the infant's lips and His chubby little cheeks.

I grew even more excited about the plans I had for Sister Augustine, plans that were now starting to become a reality, just as my own dreams of a writing career and new life as a teacher were as well. I knew in my heart that this would be the year that would change both of our lives forever.

I had big plans.

22

DARKNESS

DRIVING TO THE CONVENT ONE AFTERNOON IN EARLY MARCH, I wondered how many times my car had made this mile-and-a-half journey across town to visit Sister Augustine. Hundreds for sure. I could have probably done it blindfolded by now. This would be our last visit before I went to New York for a little vacation and some meetings during my version of spring break, while my students headed off to beaches and on other adventures. It was a gray, cloudy day—the kind where an icy breeze announces winter's reluctance to let go.

I thought perhaps Sister would be finished with my Easter eggs, and I intended to buy the graffiti vase I had seen on a previous visit. I was also looking forward to seeing if she had made any further progress on the Love Doves and the Nativity Angels. I was already formulating the press release for the Christmas Open House in my head, as well as the list of national media who would be introduced to her in a few months. And I couldn't wait to tell her again how excited my students were that she'd be visiting our class in April. They had brought it up in every class since I told them she accepted their invitation.

As usual, I swiped my hand across the wind chimes, sending their music into the chilly air, letting Sister Augustine know I was there.

I then turned to open the door. I first noticed that the shop and studio were dark. Only the dull ecru light from outside was pouring into the rooms like giant tears.

The door was locked. I saw a note taped to the inside of a glass pane. It was rendered in printed letters, which I knew wasn't my friend's handwriting.

I read the note, then reread it:

"Due to sickness, the ceramic shop will be closed until further notice."

Now looking from the outside in, my mind raced back to an afternoon chat years earlier:

"Are you afraid of dying, Sister?" I asked my friend.

"No. Everyone is entitled to their reward."

"You better not plan on getting your reward anytime soon. There's too much left for you to do."

"Only God knows that answer," she said with a twinkle in her eyes. "You know, many in my family have died suddenly. I don't ever want you to be surprised if you come one day and I'm not here."

I took a deep breath.

That one day had come.

The wind chimes had grown silent by then. I stood for several minutes in front of the locked door, staring into the shop and studio. The thick, gestural lines of the lone Gussie's Special vase on the island moved me. So close, yet so far away. Just looking at it brought me some comfort, as if Sister Augustine were communicating with me through it and calming me.

My eyes then shifted to the far back corner of the studio, where I wondered if my Easter eggs still set, waiting for their inscriptions and glaze. Above was the empty space where my eagle once stood guard. Beyond that in the back room, I could envision the two hundred greenware doves and angels resting peacefully under a white sheet. Unaware, waiting.

Unfinished work, still left to do.

I rarely ever ventured beyond Sister's shop and studio on

the convent grounds. Now she was bedridden inside the main building, somewhere within those cloistered halls, out of reach. I turned away from the door. I softly swiped my hand across the wind chimes, looking up at the rows of windows on the convent, each black with no sun to enliven it.

I paused and thought for a moment. I then swiped my hand across the wind chimes again, much harder this time.

Maybe Sister Augustine would hear the chimes wherever she was inside and she'd know that I was there if she needed me.

She had once told me, "One of the most important things in this life is just showing up."

I wanted my friend to know that I had been there. And that I'd be back soon.

23

INTO THE LIGHT

ON THE SEVENTH DAY, GOD COMPLETED HIS WORK, AND HE rested.

The call came around 3 p.m. on Holy Saturday, the day before Easter. I had just gotten home from my trip to New York on Good Friday. While my time in the Big Apple was filled with meetings and a little R&R with friends, Sister Augustine was never far from my mind. Since my cousin Patty volunteered at the Trifles and Treasures Gift Shop and had become friends with many of the nuns, she had kept me updated on our friend's condition almost daily while I was away. Sister's congestive heart failure, coupled with her age, had finally taken its toll.

On the other end of line, Patty told me that I should go to the convent to see Sister Augustine. The heavy tone in her voice communicated what her words didn't specifically say. I hadn't seen Sister since our last visit a few weeks earlier, before she had become ill. Still, I knew my Heavenly Board of Directors was about to get a new superstar.

I quickly changed my clothes and left my house, heading to the west side of town. Just as I had done for five years.

Minutes later, I was standing with Sister Margoretta and Sister Dolores in a long hallway where all the doors were closed, except one. Midway down the hall, sunlight poured out of the open bedroom door, flooding the corridor with white and gold.

"She's in there," Sister Margoretta said, smiling and nodding toward the pool of light.

My eyes widened and I hesitated, just as anyone would before doing something they sensed would change their life forever.

Then I heard her voice, so familiar. "I've been waiting for you," Sister Augustine called out from the room. "I want to hear all about your trip!"

I flashed a huge grin at Sister Margoretta and Sister Dolores. "Business as usual," I said.

"We'll wait for you out here," Sister Margoretta told me, smiling back.

"Okay," I whispered, as if sharing a secret. I was grateful to these women, who, like two guardian angels, had led me to one of those pivotal moments that makes life so special.

I then turned and walked toward the light.

As I neared the open door, I became determined that this visit would be like any other of the hundreds Sister Augustine and I had had over the years.

"Hello!" I called out from the doorway. Sister was in a bed against the wall on the far side of the room. She wasn't wearing her traditional habit. Instead, she wore a light-colored hospital gown and a small white covering over the top of her head. I could see wisps of gray hair peeking out. Next to her, a triptych of windows looked out over the convent's front yard toward Church Street. The sun's golden light poured in over her and engulfed the entire room in warmth and peace.

"I wondered when you were going to get here," Sister Augustine said, smiling.

"I just got home yesterday," I told my friend. "And I wasn't sure . . ." I let the sentence drop off into the air from there.

I sat in the chair next to her bed. It just happened to be a mint-green spindle chair.

"How was your trip?"

I beamed. "I have incredible news to tell you!"

"What is it?" Sister's eyes widened in anticipation.

"The publisher who asked to see the manuscript for my beer cookbook . . . said *yes*."

"Oh, you're finally going to get your big cookbook published!" Sister exclaimed. Now she was beaming right along with me.

"Can you believe it? After all these years," I said, "it's finally happening."

"Yes, I can believe it. God's time," Sister Augustine said. "Your road of nos finally paid off."

"You'll love this," I then added. "The first thing I did when I got to New York was go to St. Patrick's Cathedral. There's a statue of Saint John Evangelist there that I like to visit when I'm in town. Though usually, there are tourists taking pictures of him, so I have to stand back until they're done. He's such a ham. . . ."

Sister chuckled.

"And this time was no different. I waited until a few people had taken their pictures with him and then I lit a few candles in front of the statue, thanking him for the role he surely played in getting this book to where it belonged. Prayers and not giving up are what did it."

"You're lucky to be named after him," Sister said. "But I don't think that was by accident. You two are a good fit for one another. He'll help guide your career as a writer, a teacher, an artist, and anything else you do in your life."

"I sure hope so."

"You have amazing work ahead of you, John," Sister Augustine said. "You'll do so many wonderful things in your life, things you haven't even dreamed of yet. The world will be a better place because of your work and because of the compassion you have in your heart. I know it will."

"Just like you," I chimed in.

Sister softly chortled. "Never would I have guessed at age eighty-seven that I would start a whole new chapter in my life and still be at it all these years later. I never would have started that new chapter had you not walked into my shop that day. It just goes to show how life never stops surprising you, or teaching you new lessons."

"You have unfinished work left to do," I said, thinking of the greenware Love Doves and Nativity Angels, and everything else waiting in her studio and shop. Plus all the plans I had for her: the visit to my class, more interviews, and more projects—like the statue of Saint John Evangelist I wanted her to create from scratch but never got around to discussing with her. We were just hitting our stride.

Sister smiled. "That's what life is meant to be: an unfinished piece of work that others carry on in some way after you've gone," she told me. "That way there truly is no beginning and no end."

Not long after I had walked into the room, I became aware of the sharp line dividing night and day against the wall to my left, forming an exalted headboard behind Sister's bed. When it first caught my eye a few minutes into our chat, the line was near the ceiling, but as the sun set outside, the line inside also slid the curtain of dusk down the wall.

The river of warm light from outside reached a few inches above Sister's bed now, enough to cover us both for only a few minutes more.

I knew I only had time for one final question.

"Sister, how do I get to Heaven?"

Sister Augustine looked me in the eye. "We've already had that discussion," she answered. "Many times."

"We have?"

My friend nodded. "Every discussion we've had since we first met has been about living a life that is full and points toward Heaven."

It all then finally clicked in my mind.

Embracing the joys *and* the sorrows of life with gratitude; forgiving those who have hurt us and seeing them as teachers; connecting with our fellow living beings through love and patience; opening our hearts and minds to tap into our true potential and gifts, then using those gifts to help others and the world; accepting one another for who we are and as God has made us; realizing that change is a good thing, fear is something we can walk right through, and simplicity is powerful; seeing God and His blessings through the many different eyes He has given us; remembering that life is precious; understanding that every moment is a new beginning—those are all pathways of compassion and humility that anyone can use to get to Heaven.

With the help of my friend, the past five years had transformed me. From confused and frightened to luminous and hopeful. From someone desperate and clinging to an uncertain future into someone confident that moving home in search of a simpler, more genuine pathway and embracing the passions within my heart had been the right decision. Where once I was lost, now I had a foundation of guiding principles to follow and build upon. Where once I stood frozen at a crossroads, now I had the strength to put one foot in front of the other, come what may. Darkness, light.

Jesus's own words from John 3:3 flickered through my mind: "Except a man be born again, he cannot see the kingdom of God."

I breathed fully and deeply. Renewed.

"You've guided me so much on my journey," I told Sister Augustine. "You've been a beacon for me."

"And you have guided me, too," Sister said. "You have also

been a beacon for me, in more ways than you could ever possibly know."

"I have?"

Sister Augustine winked at me.

The horizon line on the wall was now gently touching the top of her head.

"I guess I should be going," I said reluctantly. "Is there anything I can get for you before I leave?"

"Could you prop up my pillows a little, please?"

"Sure." I stood and Sister leaned forward just enough that I placed my one hand on her upper back to support her while I fluffed up the two pillows with my other hand. "There you go," I said, helping her to comfortably rest her head back against the pillows.

"Thank you," she replied with that twinkle in her eyes, which I knew I'd never forget. I understood that she was referring to more than my pillow-fluffing talents.

Sister looked up at me from the bed now, bathed in the golden sunlight that was quickly leaving the room.

"I love you. You know that, right?" I said.

Sister Augustine smiled. "Yes, I know that. I love you, too."

I smiled back and paused a moment longer, looking into her bright eyes.

I then turned and walked out of the room.

Sister Margoretta and Sister Dolores were waiting for me in the hallway. Quietly, they led me back through the many corridors we had traveled earlier and up the staircase to the door by the gift shop.

"Thank you," I whispered.

Without hesitation, I opened the door and headed back into the world that was waiting for me on the other side.

24

REWARD

EASTER SUNDAY.

I spent the holiday with my family at a cousin's house. It was a sunny, warm day with the most brilliant blue sky. Unusual for March in my neck of the woods. The kind of day where you want to just lie in the grass and gaze Heavenward while the rest of the world passes by. When your heart and mind are somewhere else.

I returned home early in the evening. There was a single message on my answering machine.

On the small box with the blinking red number one, I pressed PLAY.

Sister Margoretta's voice said, "John, I wanted to let you know that Sister Augustine passed away this morning."

I stared at the answering machine, and at the number one, which was now stilled, letting the words slowly seep in and become real.

I then glanced out the window toward the west, where the sky was brightly streaked like a Gussie's Special, hearing my friend's own words echo from years earlier: "Everyone is entitled to their reward."

And I smiled.

Acknowledgments

Sister Augustine once said to me, "Every story has its time to be told, John."

Indeed.

This book would never have been written if not for the persistence of my agent and friend, Steven Troha, who by some divine intervention led me to Sister Augustine's shop and studio for the first time on a dark, late winter's afternoon. Following Sister's passing five years later, Steven encouraged me to write this memoir, but I was doubtful if I ever could—the story being so personal and close to my heart, no topic was ever off-limits during Sister's and my discussions.

But Steven continued to gently nudge me, so a few years ago I asked Sister Augustine to send me a very specific sign—one that only she and I would ever know. If I received the sign, I would feel confident of her blessing to share our friendship and her lessons with the world. If I never received the sign, I would be at peace with that, knowing how the universal lessons I learned from her are threaded throughout my daily life and all the work I currently do.

Years then passed during which I taught at the university, wrote more cookbooks, completed more artwork, and travelled the country to meet my neighbors from all walks of life. Then one random afternoon, not unlike those of years earlier when I would have been sitting in my mint-green spindle chair across from my friend, the sign came. Just like that. *In God's time*, my mind whispered. I called Steven and told him I would be sitting down the next morning to begin writing, which I did. Without any hesitation, the book you have before you poured forth.

❦

To Steven Troha at Folio Literary Management . . .

Thank you for the illuminated role you have played in this process—as a champion and guardian of this story, leading it to its rightful home at Image and into the hands of readers; as a cherished friend; and as another one of my greatest teachers in this life.

To my editor Gary Jansen . . .

You are a brilliant light in this world. It's by no accident that our paths crossed on these pages. I have no doubt that Sister Augustine is smiling upon you just as I am for gently and enthusiastically shepherding our story into print so that it may now inspire generations across the ages, long after you and I have both passed this way ourselves.

To the media who covered Sister Augustine during these five years . . .

Namely, Andy Swasta, Amy Cherry, Katie Weidenboerner, Sandy Rhodes, JoAnn Seltzer, Denny Heindl, Joe Disque, JJ Michaels, and John Salter; and *The Daily Press, The Bradford Era, Tri-County Sunday, FaithLife,* WKBI 93.9-FM, WQKY 98.9-FM The River, and WDDH 97.5-FM The Hound's *Talk of the Town*—thank you for the roles you each played in helping me to introduce Sister Augustine and her work to the world, and for helping Sister to realize that her life still had one very important last chapter left to go.

To Patty Burden . . .

Thank you for sharing so many of the footsteps with me

in Sister Augustine's shop and studio, and for more than words could ever begin to express in gratitude.

To the Benedictine Sisters of Elk County . . .

Thank you for sharing your Gussie with me. May God bless each one of you for the gifts and legacy you bestowed upon our community for more than 160 years.

To the team at Image . . .

Namely, Amanda O'Connor, Tom Pitoniak, Lauren Dong, Jessie Bright, Heather Williamson, Katie Moore, Carie Fremuth, Beverly Rykerd, and Johanna Inwood—because of your efforts, Sister Augustine's and my story will ripple out into the world where countless others will find their own meaning in the answers revealed within these pages. Thank you for helping me to be a messenger with a pen.

To Gilda Squire and Simone Cooper . . .

Publicists whose hearts and spirits are as kind and gentle as their talent is great. Thank you for your role in making this book beautiful in its time by helping spread its message far and wide.

To Dado Derviskadic at Folio Literary Management . . .

Thank you for your support and expertise from the very beginning of this literary journey. And for sharing your own appreciation of art and artists with me. May your pathway through life be filled with light and adventure.

To the many others with whom I crossed paths during these five years and who contributed to the journey chronicled within these pages in ways great and small . . .

Know that Sister Augustine and I hold the kindness and generosity you showed to both of us in our hearts, always. Your rewards will be great. Thank you.

And, finally, to Sister M. Augustine, O.S.B. . . .

I'm looking Heavenward with a huge smile on my face just for you! Until we meet again, my dear friend . . .

A READER'S GUIDE

INTRODUCTION

EVERY CHAPTER IN *Five Years in Heaven* PRESENTS SEVERAL launching points for discussion about the numerous questions and topics we all confront in our lives every day. From forgiveness, death, and even the existence of God to love, success, creativity, sin, relationships, and numerous other daily challenges, this reading group guide will allow you to further explore and maximize the inspiration and lessons in the book.

Five Years in Heaven is meant to be a personal journey, upon which you—the reader—join in and actively engage with the wisdom, humor, and lessons shared throughout the book. This companion guide will direct you toward discovering your own Heaven on earth, and your own meanings to the universal questions and topics that Sister Augustine and John discuss.

PRELUDE
On the Seventh Day

1. John writes of his surroundings at the convent and the feelings they evoked, "It was like a gift you can only hold on to for a few moments before it must be let go." Can you think of a similar moment in your life when you realized you were

experiencing something rare? How do you think this line sets the stage for the story that follows?

2. John writes, "Time as we know it doesn't have much use in a place where the aim is eternity." What is the greater meaning here? How can this statement be applied to your life?

3. What are some examples from your life that have been pivotal experiences, demonstrating how special life truly is? Did you feel a divine intervention at any time throughout those experiences?

PART ONE

CHAPTER 1
In the Beginning

1. At the beginning of the memoir, John finds himself at a crucial crossroads in life. When in your life have you found yourself at a crossroads like John did? How did you feel at the time? In what way can you relate your experience to John's description of how he felt at the time?

2. While Steven and John are driving to the ceramic shop for the first time, John describes the many roads he had traveled, literally and figuratively, to get to that point. How have the literal and figurative roads you have traveled in life gotten you to where you are right now?

3. John writes of the ceramic shop, "Though I had passed the place a thousand times, I never knew our local convent had a ceramic shop." Why do you think we sometimes fail to see what is right in front of us? Can you think of an example of this from your life? How does this reflect our universal habit of taking life for granted?

CHAPTER 2
Joys and Sorrows

1. Upon his second visit to Sister Augustine's ceramic shop, John writes, "Something much deeper was leading me back to Sister's studio." When have you been led somewhere because of a deep feeling or calling you've had? Explain what happened.

2. John initially questions how sorrow can be a "gift," as Sister Augustine calls it, which should be greeted with gratitude. What are some examples of joys and sorrows in your life? How did you choose to handle each one? How is your perception of sorrow similar or different from John's reaction here? Have you ever found sorrow to be a gift in your life? Explain.

3. Just as John experienced, when have you realized that a great teacher entered your life? What lessons did you learn from that teacher?

CHAPTER 3
Patience

1. In what ways is the art of creating clayware pieces from scratch a metaphor for your life and/or your goals?

2. While helping Sister Augustine to pour the mold for the Wise Men, John writes, "It was literally an epiphany in the making." What is the greater, symbolic meaning that he is expressing here? When in your life have you experienced an epiphany? What lessons did you learn from that experience? How can the practice of patience be an epiphany?

3. Sister Augustine says of creating ceramic pieces, "This process is a slow one that tests each piece along the way over time. More often than not, they're tougher than you'd think by just looking at them." How can you relate this sentiment to your life? Are you tougher than you look to others? Explain.

PART TWO

CHAPTER 4
Forget-Me-Not

1. Are you surrounded by meaningless stuff? If so, explain.

2. Sister Augustine says, "So much in nature tends to have a calming effect on us. Is there anything simpler than a tree, a rainfall, a full moon, or a field of flowers? That's why nature is a perfect retreat." What effect does nature, even something as simple as a potted flower, have on you? Like the old dirt road and field in Bear Run that John writes about, is there a special place in nature where you like to go to feel closer to God? Describe why you feel closer to God in that space.

3. Sister explains how "simplicity begins with each person." In what ways does simplicity begin with you? In what ways do you embrace and spread simplicity, and in what ways do you hinder simplicity in your day-to-day life with layers of complications and stuff? How did Sister Augustine and her ceramic shop embody simplicity? How can those traits be applied to your life?

CHAPTER 5
Lost and Found

1. Sister Augustine says, "That's when gratitude counts the most. It's in those challenging moments when we get a little closer to our true purpose in this life. We need to be thankful for those challenges." Think of a disappointment or challenge in your life. How can being grateful for that situation help you to move through it into a better place?

2. John writes, "It's so hard to have faith in a greater purpose that you can't see or easily explain. Or to find belief in a world that no longer seems to believe in you." Have you ever felt this way? Explain. What did you learn from the experi-

ence? What do you believe you are called to do in this life? Has that calling taken unexpected turns and encountered challenges?

3. Sister tells John, "God has His ways. His reasoning may not seem obvious to us at the time, but someday you'll look back and say, 'That's exactly how my life had to happen, good *and* bad, right down to the second, to get me where I am.'" How does your life journey so far support this sentiment? How can this sentiment be connected to the imagery of Joseph (and his life) that is used in the chapter?

Chapter 6
Tiny Crosses

1. Sister tells John, "Forgiveness is an act of love and compassion. Yes, it is a gift we give to the person who hurt us, which is often the hardest part for people to understand. In our minds, that often means we're letting that person off the hook for whatever they did to us. But ultimately, when we forgive someone, that act is also a gift of love and compassion, *and* freedom, that only we can give to ourselves." How did this statement support or change how you view the act of forgiveness? Do you have a hurt that you have harbored for a long time? How can forgiveness help you to finally let go of that hurt? When has forgiveness been a turning point in your life? When has the lack of forgiveness brought your life to a standstill?

2. The image of the cross is used throughout the chapter. In what ways was the image and symbolism of the cross used? How is the image of the cross used throughout the chapter to convey the importance of and the journey to forgiveness?

3. John comes to the realization that "from whom much is taken, much is also expected." What does this sentiment mean to you? How can this be applied to your life?

PART THREE

CHAPTER 7
Joyful Mysteries

1. John writes, "The topic of God had been weighing heavily on my mind lately. I started to have major doubts as I continued to face personal and professional challenges. I prayed, and pleaded even, for God to help me with so many things, but I feared either He was hard of hearing, since I was still not seeing the results I was hoping and asking for every day, or that no one was on the other end of my long-distance call for help." Have you ever felt this way? Explain. Do you ever doubt God? Do you think it's okay to doubt God or wonder if He even exists? Explain. Is there a benefit in doubting God? Explain.

2. Sister Augustine comments, "I always know God will lead me in the right direction, whether I want to go or not at the time." Do you agree with her? Why or why not? How does this relate to John's realization that "The road to yes is paved with many nos"? What meaning does this have for you in your life's journey so far?

3. In discussing our pursuit to know God, Sister Augustine says, "We have to see, with our entire bodies and souls, before we can truly understand." What do you think she means by this? Can you relate this sentiment to an example from your life? Besides your eyes, how else can/do you "see" God at work in your life?

CHAPTER 8
God's Time

1. John invokes Marshall McLuhan's famous line "the medium is the message" to describe Sister Augustine's forget-me-not pattern. What is the general correlation between this descrip-

tion and Sister's art pieces? How can that be applied to daily life?

2. Of the people who had treated him unfairly at the high school, John writes, "It was clear how God had used those people at the high school and their ulterior motives as navigational instruments, sending me on the right pathway." When have others been used as a positive navigational instrument in your life to move you in the direction you were truly meant to go?

3. Sister Augustine says, "It can take a long time, and a lot of rejections and disappointments along the way, to get from one point to the next, each a new starting line. But eventually you'll come to appreciate the journey itself." What is an example from your life when you realized that God's time is not the same as our time when it comes to seeing results? What did you learn from the experience? How can this sentiment be compared to Ecclesiastes 3:11: "God makes everything beautiful in its time"?

CHAPTER 9
Footsteps

1. Upon seeing the decorated and rearranged shop for the first time, John writes, "Sister Augustine's mouth fell open as she scanned the room, experiencing her oeuvre through new eyes." How is this a turning point in Sister's life, especially as an artist? When have you had a similar experience, seeing something you created or completed through fresh, new eyes or from a new perspective? How did that experience change your life?

2. Sister Augustine tells John and Patty, "God knows exactly how many footsteps you both took today in this shop for me, and He'll reward you for every one of them." John then explains, "Sister's words reminded me of the familiar saying,

Do unto others as you would have them do unto you." When have you used your "footsteps" to help someone else? When has someone used their "footsteps" to help you?

3. John describes Sister Augustine as ". . . there was more to her than meets the eye." In what ways does the press conference demonstrate how Sister Augustine is an example of this description? Who is someone in your life about whom you could say the same thing? Explain. In what ways might someone say this about you?

CHAPTER 10
The First Noël

1. This chapter conveys the point that second acts are always possible in life. In what ways does this chapter demonstrate how second acts are always possible in life? Have you had a second act in life? Explain. Have you witnessed someone else experiencing a second act in life? Explain.

2. When shown each glowing review that was written about her and her work, Sister Augustine would say, "If this is what God wants, so be it." What does this statement say about her faith? Are there experiences in your life, good or bad, when you could have responded with the same words? Explain.

3. John writes, "In midafternoon, I paused. I once more backed up against the kiln room door in the shop. Just for a moment, to absorb what was happening right in front of me, which Sister Augustine often encouraged me to do." What is the significance of this moment for John? What is the message he is trying to convey to you, the reader? When was the last time you paused and absorbed what was happening right in front of you? Describe the experience.

PART FOUR

CHAPTER 11
New Year's Resolutions

1. Sister Augustine says, "Sweeping dirt under the carpet doesn't make it go away; it eventually just makes for a lumpy carpet that's hard to walk on. Sooner or later, you're knocked off balance." Can you relate this to any experiences in your life? Explain. Have you gotten caught up in the cycle of disappointment and defeat that comes from failing to maintain resolutions? Explain.

2. Sister says, "Change is one of the hardest things for us to accept, but it's one of the only things we are guaranteed to encounter in this life, good and bad. We need to embrace change as a gift, even the unpleasant ones, just as we should the sorrows that come our way." What is your general reaction to changes in life? In what ways can you relate to this statement? Did this viewpoint alter your perspective on changes in your life? Explain.

3. While at one time or another we all stand before a wall of fear and challenges, Sister says, "The difference for some, though, is that they look upward and think, *I can climb right up over this wall.* Or they look to the sides, and think, *I can go around this wall.* Or, if nothing else, they take a step back and carefully examine the wall, thinking, *I can smash right through it!*" When in your life have you taken this proactive approach to overcoming fear, change, or some other challenge?

CHAPTER 12
Amazing Grace

1. When his grandmother was on her deathbed, John writes, "I was in dire need of solace, wisdom, and reassurance, and [Sister Augustine] was the only person I thought to turn

to." Who is someone in your life to whom you turn during challenging moments? Why is that person the one to whom you turn for guidance? Have you ever served in that role for someone else who was facing a challenge? Explain.

2. After telling Sister Augustine about his encounter with his two guardian angels, Sister says, "God and his messengers come in many shapes and forms, especially when we most need them." Have you had an experience with your guardian angel(s)? If so, describe it.

3. Sister Augustine says, "It's always a blessing to be present when someone is born into this world or passes from it. It's in those amazing moments that God reveals His grace to us." Have you ever been present when someone passed away? If so, describe the experience? What did you learn about life and death in that moment? What did you learn about God in that moment? What did you learn about yourself in that moment?

CHAPTER 13
Holy Thursday

1. Sister Augustine reveals to John that her Holy Thursday duty at the convent is to wash the feet of the other nuns in homage to Jesus doing the same for his apostles at the Last Supper. What does this act reveal about Sister? What lesson(s) can you take away from this?

2. Sister Augustine says, "When we each start from that place, a place of knowing we are each related to every other living being like brothers and sisters, then we already have a head start on further connecting with them." Throughout the chapter, how did Sister's views on the importance and innate existence of our connections to one another influence your own thoughts on the subject?

3. Sister says, "Actions have a voice, too." Do you believe this,

especially when it comes to expressing your love to someone? Explain. What are some examples of your actions that expressed love to someone, or vice versa? How did John demonstrate his love for Sister Augustine?

PART FIVE

CHAPTER 14
Our Lady of Love

1. At the beginning of the chapter, John describes how he observed Sister Augustine pruning her flower garden. What do you think John learned from watching his ninety-year-old friend doing something she loved so much? Have you ever had the experience of watching someone engaging in an activity they enjoyed? What did you learn from that experience?

2. In reference to a clayware statue of the Blessed Mother where the gold forget-me-nots had accidentally gotten smeared, rendering it as a "sorrow" in Sister's mind, John instead says how "those imperfections *are* perfection." How can an imperfection be a perfection? Can you think of examples from your life when an imperfection was actually a perfection?

3. Sister talks about the importance for both young women and men to "see strong women in action" in their lives. Who are some strong women who have inspired you throughout your life? Explain how they impacted your life journey. In what ways has Sister Augustine shown herself to be a strong woman in action, and a role model for others?

CHAPTER 15
The Nativity Donkey

1. Just as John and Sister found inspiration in the Nativity Don-

key, which character from the Nativity story most inspires you? Explain.

2. How can the Nativity story inspire our everyday lives?

3. At the end of the chapter, when talking about a possible second limited edition ornament for the following year, John tells Sister, "It's never too early, *or* too late, to get started!" What is the significance of this quote, not only within the context of the passage where it appears, but throughout the book? What is the significance of this statement in your life?

CHAPTER 16
The Book of Revelation

1. John writes, "One of the many things I learned from my conversations with Sister Augustine was how it is a gift to share your life and stories with others." Who do you often share your life and stories with? In what ways do you see that time and those exchanges as a gift?

2. In reference to John's close connection to Little Coyote, Sister Augustine says, "That's the power of true love. No words are necessary, it's just there." John later uses this same sentiment at the end of the chapter to describe his connection to Sister. When in your life have you experienced this same sentiment? Explain. How does this statement reflect God's love for each one of us?

3. At various points throughout the book, John's namesake Saint John Evangelist is mentioned. In addition to being the patron saint of writers, in this chapter, John learns that Saint John is also the patron saint of painters. A perfect fit for him. Were you named after a saint? If so, who is he or she? What is your saint the patron of? In what ways do you feel connected to your patron saint? Or, is there another saint with whom you feel connected? If so, describe your relationship with that saint.

PART SIX

CHAPTER 17
Food for Thought

1. Sister Augustine says, "Understanding what makes each religion tick is one of the best ways I know to bring this world together, not to tear it apart with hatred, judgment, ignorance, and war." Do you agree with her? Explain. Have you ever explored faiths other than your own? If so, why? What did you learn from your studies? How did those studies inform your own faith and beliefs? What are some similarities between different faiths that serve as the glue that ultimately binds us all together? What do you think of the buffet approach to religion where people pick and choose what works for them?

2. Sister says, "Knowledge is power, especially when it comes to faith." In what ways do you agree with this statement? Has this sentiment played a role in your life? Explain. If you could pull just one lesson or tenet from your faith to share with others, what would it be? Why did you choose that particular lesson or tenet?

3. John writes of his classroom at the university, "Minds opened, differences faded, and lanes merged." In what ways is this a powerful message for people of faith and the world at large? How are you facilitating this message in your life? Or, in what ways could you better facilitate this message within your life?

CHAPTER 18
Illuminatus

1. On his way to see Sister Augustine after learning Blitzen passed away, John describes the setting, "As I drove past the chapel on my right and then the western expanse of the con-

vent's main building, the light reflected off the tan bricks in such a way that made the building appear gilded. Each of the dozens of windows was ablaze with its own setting sun shining back at me." How did this description make you feel? Have you ever encountered a similar setting? Explain.

2. Sister Augustine says, "We're always being reminded how precious this life is and how very fast it goes. . . . We never know what moment may be our last. Or the last for a loved one. There's a beautiful, sacred design to that, though, encouraging each of us to live in the moment and be grateful for what we have right now. I wish more people would understand that." In what ways can you relate to this sentiment? What do you think she means by "sacred design"?

3. Sister says, "One of the most important things in this life is just showing up. . . . That speaks for itself, where words never could. Just like a smile does." What is an example from your life when "just showing up" made an important difference?

CHAPTER 19
Talk of the Town

1. In deciding that Sister Augustine's second limited edition ornament would be the Peace Dove, John writes, "We were covering a lot of territory." What did he mean by this? What does the concept of a Peace Dove mean to you? When looking at art, do you see the divine? Explain.

2. Sister Augustine's interview with the radio show *Talk of the Town* provides more insight into her character. What did you learn about Sister's character from the interview? How does this interview establish and celebrate this new phase of Sister's life? How can you help someone to recognize and celebrate a new phase in their life?

3. During the interview, the host keeps returning to the fact that Sister is ninety-two-years-old. How does the host's fasci-

nation with Sister Augustine's age emphasize and explore the stereotypes we attach to certain ages, especially the elderly? How does the interview demonstrate a break from these stereotypes, especially regarding the elderly? What is your perception of age, especially of someone in her/his nineties? How did this interview and the overall book so far impact your perception of age?

CHAPTER 20
The Gift

1. The word "gift" in the chapter title takes on several connotations throughout the chapter. In which ways did you interpret "gift" throughout the chapter? How did this chapter and those connotations impact how you think of the concept of a "gift" in your everyday life?

2. In talking about his students, John says, "I always end up learning as much, if not more, from them as they do from me." In what ways does this describe a genuine teacher/student relationship? How does this relate to John and Sister Augustine's relationship throughout the book?

3. John writes, "I had come to appreciate the benevolence of glaze. How it allowed light to permeate and echo back, converting or igniting whatever lay beneath it." How is this statement a metaphor for John and Sister Augustine's friendship? How is this statement a metaphor for the friendships in your life? In what other ways might "glaze" be interpreted as a metaphor here?

PART SEVEN

CHAPTER 21
Borrowed Time

1. The theme of making plans runs throughout this chapter.

Where in the chapter do you see this theme illustrated? What are the takeaway messages from these various illustrations of the theme? How can these messages be applied to your life and your own practice of making plans?

2. The passing of time is portrayed throughout this chapter. How is the passing of time specifically emphasized in this chapter? How do you see the passage of time represented in your life?

3. Near the end of the chapter, John writes, "In silence, I watched my friend work from about four feet away across the table, just as I had done for five years." What do you think is going through John's mind during this reflective moment?

CHAPTER 22
Darkness

1. How is the theme of darkness used throughout this chapter?

2. Have you ever had a moment in your life when darkness or some other event stopped you in your tracks? Explain.

3. Can you describe "darkness" as a feeling(s)?

CHAPTER 23
Into the Light

1. Sister Augustine says, "That's what life is meant to be: an unfinished piece of work that others carry on in some way after you've gone. That way there truly is no beginning and no end." Did this statement influence your own views on living and dying? Explain. Can you think of examples from your life that support this statement?

2. John writes of the lessons and pathways to Heaven that Sister had taught him, "Embracing the joys *and* the sorrows of life with gratitude; forgiving those who have hurt us and seeing them as teachers; connecting with our fellow living beings through love and patience; opening our hearts and minds to

tap into our true potential and gifts, then using those gifts to help others and the world; accepting one another for who we are and as God has made us; realizing that change is a good thing, fear is something we can walk right through, and simplicity is powerful; seeing God and His blessings through the many different eyes He has given us; remembering that life is precious; understanding that every moment is a new beginning—those are all pathways of compassion and humility that anyone can use to get to Heaven." Which of these lessons impacted you the most? Explain.

3. John writes about how his friendship with Sister Augustine had transformed him. Think of a close friendship you have or had. In what ways did that friendship transform you for the better? In what ways did that friendship help guide you along life's journey?

CHAPTER 24
Reward

1. There is a powerful symbolism to Sister Augustine passing away and receiving her "reward" on Easter Sunday. Discuss your thoughts on that symbolism.

2. This story from the beginning has explored the topic of Heaven on earth. In what ways has this story been the portrayal of Heaven on earth? When in your life have you had an experience that you would describe as Heaven on earth?

3. John ends the book by writing, "And I smiled." What do you think was going through his mind at that moment? Why in that moment do you think his reaction was to smile? How does this seemingly simple smile reflect his growth in the five-year journey he just completed?